Burden or Legacy

The editor would like to thank the following organizations for their support during the development of the research.

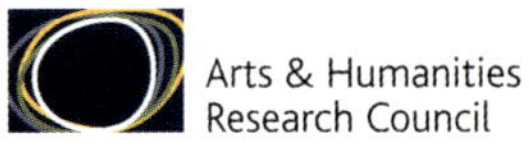 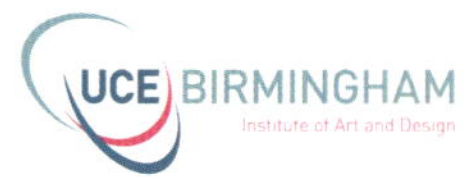 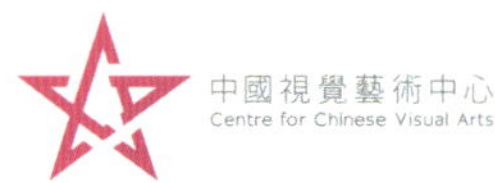

Burden or Legacy

From the Chinese Cultural Revolution to Contemporary Art

Edited by **Jiang Jiehong**

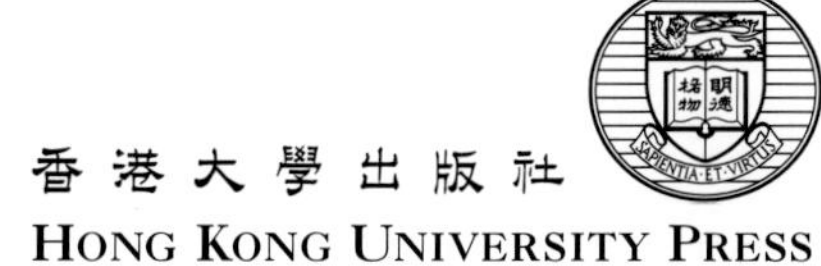

香港大學出版社

HONG KONG UNIVERSITY PRESS

Hong Kong University Press
14/F Hing Wai Centre
7 Tin Wan Praya Road
Aberdeen
Hong Kong

Hardback   ISBN 978-962-209-869-5
Paperback   ISBN 978-962-209-870-1

British Library Cataloguing-in-Publication Data
A catalogue record for this book is available from the British Library.

Secure On-line Ordering
http://www.hkupress.org

Printed and bound by Paramount Printing Co. Ltd., Hong Kong, China.

Contents

Preface

The drama of Chinese history is always reflected in the arts. During the social, ideological, political and cultural conflicts of the twentieth century, Chinese art changed more rapidly than in any other period. It did continue the tradition of literati art, including artists such as Wu Changshuo, Huang Binhong and Qi Baishi, and also began a modernization movement, that may be read as 'Westernization', with the influence of such styles as impressionism, fauvism, primitivism and cubism, as shown in the works of Lin Fengmian and Pang Xunqin. At a more official level, Western realism, which filtered through Soviet art, was reshaped to suit the particular needs of the Chinese revolution and dominated Chinese art institutionally for over half of the century. With this background of literati tradition, modernization and realism, inherited from the past or imported from the West, how do we understand the rise of 'contemporary' 'Chinese' art after the Chinese Cultural Revolution (1966–1976)? This book will explore neither the institutional development of Chinese art, nor the disruption of political turbulence; instead, it will provide a new perspective to look at both the prosperity of contemporary Chinese art and the influence of the Cultural Revolution.

In May 2004, I convened an international symposium, *The Visual Legacy of the Chinese Cultural Revolution in Contemporary Art*, hosted at Birmingham Institute of Art and Design, University of Central England in Birmingham. Six scholars and artists were invited to present papers, which now contribute to this book, reflecting upon the impact of the Cultural Revolution to Chinese art with various perspectives.

Wang Mingxian and Yan Shanchun are two of the most important scholars conducting research on art of the Cultural Revolution. Their co-authored book, *Xin Zhongguo Meishu Tushi (The Art History of the People's Republic of China), 1966–1976* (2000), has been the only work so far published in mainland China that looks specifically at the art products of the Cultural Revolution, including works in the Red Guard exhibitions, posters and pictorial leaflets. Yan Shanchun has developed his own study, particularly concentrated on the image of Mao, while his paper in this book focuses on the pictorial representations of Mao and its re-appropriation in contemporary art. Wang Mingxian began collecting the visual products of the Cultural Revolution in 1986 and became involved in art critique and curatorial practice with the 85 Art New Wave Movement. A pioneer observer of the potential links between the Cultural Revolution and Chinese avant-garde art, he provides a detailed background of the Red Guard art movement that showed the strength and importance of art and, in so doing, during the decade, completes a 'lost chapter' in Chinese art history. Envisaging the significance of written words in Chinese visual culture, especially during the Cultural Revolution, Chang Tsong-zung discusses how the power of Chinese written words and figurative icons could be transformed in the revolutionary era and become Mao's visual legacies that would be re-invented in contemporary art. Katie Hill invites us to revisit the hysteria of the political movements in a different way. The trauma of the Cultural Revolution can be revealed behind the manic grin — an expression of apparent vacillation between pain and laughter — in contemporary paintings and, indeed, by live art, which promotes the hysterical bodies. From a more personal perspective as an independent artist couple based in Beijing, Shao Yinong and Mu Chen present an autobiographical narrative of their visual memories and reflections. The majority of their visual works have been derived from reshaping the past, while the Cultural Revolution is the core event stimulating the central concerns for their visual practices.

I am deeply grateful to all the Chinese artists involved in the research; to Tina Pang at the Museum and Art Gallery of the University of Hong Kong, and Darren Newbury and Nick Stanley at Birmingham Institute of Art and Design for their inspiration, generosity and friendship throughout the development of this book; and to Colin Day for his enthusiasm in making the publication possible.

Fory years ago today, from the balcony of Tiananmen Mao inspected his millions of Red Guards in the square for the first time. It marked the climax of the revolutionary fervour of the generation. Along with this book, my recent curatorial projects — including the 2007 touring exhibition *Collective Identity* at both the Chinese Arts Centre in Manchester and Hong Kong University Museum and Art Gallery — are dedicated to the dead and the alive, who experienced the decade-long Cultural Revolution. If the past enthusiasm of the Red Guards has been re-contextualized in China's economical development after Mao's era, then the rebellious spirit becomes the key legacy in contemporary Chinese art. *The Revolution continues ...* in art, which frames another curatorial topic.

Jiang Jiehong
18 August 2006
Birmingham, England

Burden or Legacy:

From the Chinese Cultural Revolution to Contemporary Art

Jiang Jiehong

The end of the Chinese Cultural Revolution opened an entirely new chapter for modern Chinese history, and indeed, for Chinese art too. In the last decade of the twentieth century, Chinese art has attracted the world's attention by frequent participation in important international events such as the Venice Biennale. There are various definitions of Chinese new art in the post-Cultural Revolution era. From a political point of view, on the one hand, the art has been categorized into 'official' and 'unofficial art', 'non-official art'[1] or 'underground art' in a totalitarian society; on the other hand, in terms of artistic radicalism, the idea of the avant-garde became popular as a means of labelling those artistic experiments outside the domains of institutional and academic art from the 1980s on. Moreover, "to 'decentralize' ideologic-centricism", the term 'un-unofficial art' is fabricated to "encourage real freedom of creation in an open, multi-orientational

---

1 Yang, Alice, *Why Asia? Contemporary Asian and Asian American Art.* London: New York University Press, 1998, p. 107.

space ...";[2] or even far away from political classifications, 'experimental art (*shiyan yishu*)', increasingly has been employed as a looser and broader definition.[3]

This research offers neither a chronological review of contemporary Chinese art, nor does it invent new terminology; instead, it focuses on the relationship between the Chinese Cultural Revolution and contemporary art, aiming to explore the significance of the former to the prosperity of the latter. Without the Cultural Revolution, contemporary art would continue to exist in China, but very differently. The influence of the Chinese Cultural Revolution is complex and exists at various levels. I argue that it is the foundation of the development of contemporary art in China and a crucial source of identity for Chinese art in the global art world today.

This chapter is divided into six sections. First, I will outline the historical background of the Chinese Cultural Revolution, echoes of which will be heard throughout the text. Second, my analysis of artists' works will show how the Cultural Revolution has been read and reflected upon by artists with their different attitudes, sitting somewhat contradictorily between critique and nostalgia. Third, I will demonstrate how the image of Mao Zedong has been appropriated and reshaped in contemporary art practice — the deification and de-deification of Mao in modern China. Fourth, following Mao's appearance as a dominant motif of the visual environment of the Cultural Revolution, I will turn the lens on Mao's people themselves in the Cultural Revolution to explore and analyse their collective identities. Reflected in art, there is a pair of contrasting approaches of visual representation, between revolutionary conformity and hysterical carnival. Fifth, I will demonstrate that Chinese characters are another significant visual source drawn upon by contemporary artists. Finally, I will discuss the ways of artistic reflections on the Cultural Revolution in visual experimentation. Should the Cultural Revolution be seen as a burden for Chinese artists or its opposite — a legacy to re-identify Chinese art on an international platform?

Ruination or Revolution

The Chinese Great Proletarian Cultural Revolution (*Zhongguo Wuchan Jieji Wenhua Dageming*) is almost a mysterious happening to many of us, sometimes referred to as "one of the most bizarre events in history".[4] It is generally accepted that the Cultural

---

2   Hou Hanru, 'Towards an "Un-Unofficial Art": De-ideologicalization of China's Contemporary Art in the 1990s', *Third Text*, 34, Spring 1996, p. 41.

3   Wu Hung, *Exhibiting Experimental Art in China*. Chicago: The David and Alfred Smart Museum of Art and The University of Chicago, 2000, pp. 10–11.

4   Fairbank, John King, *The Great Chinese Revolution 1800–1985*. London: Harper Perennial, 1987, p. 316.

Revolution began with the so-called *Wuyiliu Tongzhi (May the Sixteenth Circular)* from the Central Session of Chinese Communist Party on 16 May 1966, which provided the guiding principles, and lasted until the death of Mao Zedong and the fall of the Gang of Four in 1976.[5] *The Resolution of the Party's Several Historical Issues since the Establishment of the State* in 1981 officially described the Cultural Revolution as a 'ten-year turbulence (*shinian dongluan*)'.

The editorial of the *People's Daily* clarified the anti-revolutionary 'Four Olds' as targets of the Cultural Revolution: "The Proletarian Cultural Revolution is going to thoroughly eliminate all the old ideas, old culture, old customs and old habits of the exploiting classes, which have corrupted the people for thousands of years, and to create and construct the proletarian new idea, new culture, new customs and new habits among the masses."[6] The Red Guard, as the executor of the instruction, pioneered this mass movement. The organization of the Red Guard was established spontaneously by a group of teenage students from the Middle School attached to Tsinghua University on 29 May 1966, followed by other school students nationwide. The Red Guards at the Second Middle School of Beijing put up their big-character poster, *Xiang Jiu Shijie Xuanzhan (To Declare A War against the Old World)*. It read: "We are critics of the old world. We want to criticize, to smash all old ideas, old culture, old customs and old habits. All the barbershops, tailors, photo studios, and old bookshops, etc., that served to the bourgeoisie … None of them can be excluded. What we do is to overthrow this whole old world!"[7]

Mao's full support and encouragement to the Red Guards became noticeable during the inspection on 18 August 1966 in Tiananmen Square (Fig. 1). The next morning, the Red Guards in Beijing went onto the streets, starting the movement of '*Po Sijiu* (Smashing the Four Olds)'. They distributed their fliers, slogans and big-character posters; delivered speeches; and began to devastate all the 'Olds' across the city. During the summer, the

---

5   The duration of the Cultural Revolution has been defined in various ways. For example, in Mao's view, the Cultural Revolution was launched by Yao Wenyuan's *Ping Xinbian Lishiju 'Hai Rui Baguan' (The Criticism on the New Version of the Historical Play 'Hai Rui Dismissed from Office')*, which was published in the Wenhui Daily on 10 November 1965. Most early scholars, such as Fairbank (1987, p. 317), claimed that the Cultural Revolution proper lasted three and a half years, from late 1965 to April 1969, when the Ninth Session of the Chinese Communist Party announced its successful completion. Again, in the Party's Eleventh Session in 1977, Mao's successor, the new Chairman Hua Guofeng, declared that the first Cultural Revolution that had lasted for eleven years was successfully finished by smashing the Gang of Four (*Siren Bang*).

6   '*Hengsao Yiqie Niugui Sheshen* (Sweep Away All the Ox-demons and Snake-spirits)', *Renmin Ribao (People's Daily)*, 1 June 1966, p. 1.

7   Cited in Yan Jiaqi and Gao Gao, *Wenhua Da Geming Shinian Shi (The Ten-Year History of the Cultural Revolution)*. Hong Kong: Chaoliu Publisher, Vol. 1, 1989, p. 90.

Red Guards searched over ten million homes across the country and confiscated or destroyed 'old' property, including dynastic calligraphy and paintings, ancient books and archives, gold, silver or jade ware and jewellery. In the city of Ningbo alone, more than eighty tons of books from the Ming and Qing dynasties were pulped.[8] All the idols — including statues of Buddha, folk gods, even Confucius — religious architecture, frescos and books failed to escape from this cultural disaster. Records indicate that there were 6,843 cultural relics registered in Beijing in 1958, but only 1,921 remained in the 1980s. Most of them were destroyed during the Cultural Revolution.[9] These radical actions of Red Guards soon turned into the 'red terror' across the country. In forty days, from the middle of August to the end of September 1966, more than 1,700 people were killed, and 33,600 houses of residences were searched and confiscated. In one of the most tragic examples, in Daxing, a small county located to the south of Beijing, 325 people were killed within a week (from 27 August to 1 September) — the oldest was eighty and the youngest was only thirty-eight days old — and twenty-two families were entirely exterminated.[10] However, it is impossible to know the full extent of the terror.

Undoubtedly, the Chinese Cultural Revolution was a tragedy for the whole nation: millions of people suffered and died during the political campaigns, normal school education ceased and innumerable cultural legacies were ruined for the purpose of a revolutionary reconstruction. If we can imagine what the Cultural Revolution did to the dead, what does it mean to the living? The Chinese Cultural Revolution was identified as "a great revolution that touches people to their very souls".[11] It proposed metaphorically the depth and significance of its influence. People who experienced the Cultural Revolution in their adulthood, youth or childhood, and living in various places in China, would have different understandings of the Cultural Revolution and their lives influenced in different ways. Artists are among those who have been reflecting upon the phenomenon through different perspectives and at different depths of perception.

The period of the Cultural Revolution is often referred to by many as the 'ten lost years' or, metaphorically, as a 'cultural desert'; most of the cultural outcomes of the Cultural

---

8 Ding Shu, *Jiduo Wenwu Fuzhi Yiju — Yijiu Liuliu Nian 'Po Sijiu' Jianji (How Many Cultural Treasures Were Burned Off — A Brief Record of 'Smashing the Four Olds' in 1966)*, 2000, available at http://ww1.cnd.org/BIG5/HXWZ/ZK00/zk237.b5.html [Accessed on 11 May 2005].

9 Wang Mingxian and Yan Shanchun, *Xin Zhongguo Meishu Shi (The Art History of the People's Republic of China): 1966–1976*. Beijing: China Youth Press, 2000, p. 4.

10 Yan Jiaqi and Gao Gao, *Wenhua Da Geming Shinian Shi (The Ten-Year History of the Cultural Revolution)*. Hong Kong: Chaoliu Publisher, Vol. 1, 1989, p. 110.

11 '*Shiliu Tiao* (Sixteen Points, the initial name for *Zhonggong Zhongyang Guanyu Wuchan Jieji Wenhua Da Geming de Jueding* The Resolution of Proletarian Cultural Revolution by the Central Authority of Chinese Communist Party)', *Renmin Ribao (People's Daily)*, 9 August 1966, p. 1.

Revolution are seen as valueless. However, if the Cultural Revolution offers nothing of cultural value, why has its visual legacy continually been appropriated by Chinese artists and, in a sense, somehow contributed to the prosperity of contemporary Chinese art?

Critique or Nostalgia

Following the end of the Cultural Revolution, a new generation of Chinese leaders made a dramatic turn to develop a capitalist market economy under the name of 'socialism with Chinese characteristics'. Although the party has never given up its control over artistic affairs, its cultural policies have oscillated between extremely strict and relatively relaxed, depending on the political situation. Although stylistic changes did not appear immediately in post-Mao China,[12] Chinese artists began to breathe and have more space to resume their self-consciousness in art practice.

Artists started to think more independently and keep away from the Maoist ideology after the Cultural Revolution. At the end of the 1970s and the beginning of the 1980s, a movement that has been labelled 'critical realism (*pipan xianshi zhuyi*)' or 'new realism'[13] emerged to rethink and narrate realistically the decade of the Cultural Revolution. In literature, Lu Xinhua's novel *Shangheng (Scar)* was published in the *Wenhui Bao (Daily)* on 11 August 1978. The novel per se told something unfamiliar but truthful about people's life, while *Shanghen* (Scar) became a more accessible and direct depiction for the immediate response of the Red Guard generation after the Cultural Revolution. With a similar approach, a thirty-two-piece set of illustration and an adaptation of the story *Maple (Feng)* that appeared in *Lianhuan Huabao (Serial Pictures Gazette)* a year later, describing the tragic death of the young lovers as a result of battles between contending Red Guard factions, marked the beginning of '*Shanghen Yishu (Scar Art)*'.[14] As the authors recall, "We sincerely believed that we were destroying the 'old world'. With our selflessness and faithfulness, the Red Guard Movement destroyed the original orders, from schools to the whole society … and we were unavoidably driven by the great spiritual power … Until years later, we realized that our future and own nation had also been badly destroyed too, by ourselves."[15]

---

12 In the first National Fine Art Exhibition after the Cultural Revolution in February 1977, one-sixth of 695 works were images of Mao, Mao's successor Hua Guofeng or the other communist leaders.

13 Andrews, Julia, *Painters and Politics in the People's Republic of China: 1949–1979*. London: University of California Press, 1994, p. 393.

14 Li Xianting, *Zhongyao de Bushi Yishu (What Is Important Is Not Art)*. Nanjing: Jiangsu Art Press, 2000, p. 196.

15 Cheng Yiming, et al., '*Guanyu chuangzuo Lianhuanhua "Feng" de Yixie Xiangfa* (Some Thoughts on the Illustration *Maple*)', *Meishu (Fine Art)*, 1980, Vol. 1, pp. 34–35.

Cheng Conglin's *Snow on X Month X Day, 1968 (Yijiu Liuba Nian Mouyue Mouri Xue)* (Fig. 2) and Gao Xiaohua's *Why (Weisheme)* marked the peak of Scar Art, picturing the artists' personal experiences in political battles. Both Cheng and Gao were trained in realistic techniques at Sichuan Academy of Art. Like all artists of their generation, they had seen their childhood revolutionary ideals smashed by the political turbulence of their adolescence. As Gao Xiaohua states, "I am also the witness, the participant, and the sufferer of the tragedy, and we have got the scars engraved on our hearts as the evidence. We have the right and responsibility to record and tell true history."[16] The exhaustion and doubt can be clearly read through those 'truth' defenders and Mao's loyal soldiers, while the realistic work offered a space for viewers to reflect on the past and ask 'why'. Pursuing the truth, political dogma was rejected, while Scar artists envisaged the human cost rather than the glories of the Cultural Revolution. However, because of their young age and the close proximity of their response to the Cultural Revolution, their perception of it could not be comprehensive. The paintings could be read as the "expression of a sentimental humanism"[17] rather than rational critiques. In comparison with the Red Guard generation, Zhao Yannian, the 'direct target' of the Revolution, was unable to reflect on his sufferings for many years. As the head of the Printmaking Department in Zhejiang Academy of Fine Art in Hangzhou,[18] Zhao was accused of being one of those '*niugui sheshen* (ox-demons and snake-spirits)' and 'counterrevolutionary academic experts'. During the public criticisms, a heavy banner was hung around his neck as a sign of humiliation — astonishingly by his own students. If he were not so aware of his responsibility for the family, he would have given up, and the beautiful West Lake would have been his doom.[19] Because of the ways in which they were implicated in the political campaign, these older artists cannot confidently re-envisage the Cultural Revolution. Even the date of Yan Han's *Book Collecting Stamp (Cangshu Piao)* (Fig. 3), in which the artist portrays himself suffering criticism, still remains unknown.[20] Zhao Yannian did not start his woodcut series *Nightmare (Emeng)* (Figs. 4 and 5) until 1989. This work was included in the jubilee exhibition of his professional life, the first time it was shown to the public. To depict the trauma of the experience, *Nightmare* focuses on the detailed expressions of individuals. As a victim himself, Zhao Yannian believes that "only real experience with real feeling will produce real art."[21]

---

16 Gao Xiaohua, '*Weishenme Hua Weishenme* (Why Painted Why)', *Meishu (Fine Art)*, 1979, Vol. 7, p. 7.

17 Gao Minglu, *Zhongguo qianwei yishu (China Avant-garde)*. Nanjing: Jiangsu Art Press, 1997, p. 57.

18 Zhejiang Academy of Fine Art *(Zhejiang Meishu Xueyuan)* is the former name of China Academy of Arts *(Zhongguo Meishu Xueyuan)*.

19 Interview with Zhao Yannian, 10 November 2003, Hangzhou. All interviews in this paper were conducted by the author.

20 Interview with Yan Han, 29 October 2003, Beijing. The artist was reluctant to provide further details of this woodcut or show any another relevant works, which were expected to be published only after the artist's death.

21 Interview with Zhao Yannian, 10 November 2003, Hangzhou.

However, to some, the Cultural Revolution was not just a disaster, but something to which they had dedicated their youth and, hence, so complex that it simply could not be negated or criticized. In the summer of 1967, the Red Guard factionalism reached its peak. After one year, Mao dispatched the People's Liberation Army and worker's organization to control the schools and dispersed more than fourteen million students to the countryside and border areas. [22] Rather than attempting to learn from the masses, the true aim of this so-called movement of *shangshan xiaxiang* (going to mountains and countryside) was to mitigate the turbulence across the cities. To many artists, their experience in the rural area is unforgettable. As his final work at Sichuan Academy of Fine Art, Zhou Chunya's more than thirty-piece woodcut series *Half of the Life (Rensheng de Yiban)* 1980 (Fig. 6), influenced by the style of Belgian artist Frans Masereel (1889–1972), is a narrative illustration about the story of this generation. The artist claims it to be an artistic statement of the ideal of his youth. [23] Graduating from Sichuan academy in the same year, He Duoling produced his final work, *Spring Wind Revivified (Chunfeng Yijing Suxing)* (Fig. 7), which was clearly inspired by Andrew Wyeth and which has been labelled '*xiangtu xieshi* (rustic realism)'. [24] In this work, cruelty and indignation are replaced by a kind of loneliness and sentimental expression that one may also see in Wyeth. The title of the work literarily metaphorizes the end of the Maoist era, while the visual itself implicates a nostalgic representation. More explicitly, in the work *A Song We Used to Sing (Woman Ceng Changguo Zheshou Ge)* (Fig. 8), the artist poetically presents the youths singing after their hard work on the farm. However, instead of sorrow and tears there is expectation and optimism, highlighting their rustic life. The 1984 work *Youth (Qingchun)* (Fig. 9) is a conclusion of the artist's personal retrospection and reflection on the Cultural Revolution. In *Youth*, a girl student, dressed in Red Guard uniform, is monumentalized in a wasteland, with a fragment of a farm implement at her side. "To me", says the artist, "the Cultural Revolution was an idealistic era, no matter whether it was real or illusory. The eagle in my paintings symbolizes the ideal of our generation, while the pale sunshine attempts to lacerate and destroy the beautiful youth. However, the strength of life still enables the youth to envisage all the tribulation taking place." [25]

If the youths had a sense of nostalgia for the Maoist utopia, the children, could imagine the Cultural Revolution as romantic and heroic. Liu Ye was one of these children. "I

---

22 Liu Xiaomeng, '*Xiaxiang Nu Zhishi Qingnian Hunyin Poxi* (An Analysis on the Marriages of Young Female Intellectuals in the Going-to-Countryside Movement)', in Liu Qingfeng (ed.), *Wenhua Da Geming: Shishi yu Yanjiu (The Cultural Revolution: Facts and Analysis)*. Hong Kong: The Chinese University Press, 1996, p. 149.

23 Interview with Zhou Chunya, 2 November 2003, Chengdu.

24 Gao Minglu, et al., *Zhongguo Dangdai Meishushi (A History of Chinese Contemporary Art): 1985–1986*. Shanghai: Shanghai People's Press, 1991, p. 47.

25 Interview with He Duoling, 3 November 2003, Chengdu.

remember the first lesson of drawing in my kindergarten", Liu recalls; "I was taught how to draw a red sun and a ship on big waves, an illustration of Lin Biao's famous slogan, 'sailing on the sea relies on the Helmsman'. I did not have any other choice, and the red sun [a symbol of Mao] was the only motif. All these memories are rooted deeply in my unconscious mind. Although now I am not attempting to focus on the Cultural Revolution, my understanding of contemporary issues, such as love and sex, were addressed on the canvas somehow as revolutionarily red"[26] (Fig. 10). In Liu Ye's work, those children dressed in navy represent the next generation of the revolution with their loyalty towards Mao, the Great Helmsman, confident in their success (Fig. 11). A ship carrying the revolutionary ideal could sometimes appear dramatically either behind theatre curtains or even as a mirage (Fig. 12). The romantic and fairy tale-like imagination of the utopian redness has been interwoven between childhood memory and the intellectual inheritance from his father, a writer of children's stories; the artist continues the story in a surrealistic space. Similar to Liu Ye, born two years later in 1966, Yu Hong's understanding of the Cultural Revolution is also received from the interpretation of her parents' generation. The artist's recent work *Witness to Growth (Muji Chengzhang)* is an ongoing series started in 1999. It has been a private space for Yu Hong to reflect on her own experiences since 1966 — the year of her birth, and the year of the start of the Cultural Revolution (Fig. 13) — compared with the life of her daughter, Liu Wa, born in 1994. As Przerwa suggests, in *Witness to Growth*, Yu Hong studies "the balance between collective meaning and individual irrelevance and depicts its various nuances, and this idea lends itself exceedingly well to an investigation of China's tumultuous recent history and the effects it has had on the individual".[27] Each painting imitated from a photograph of the time is paired with another photograph collected from a wide variety of official publications, such as *China Pictorial (Renmin Huabao)*. For Yu Hong, who trained as a painter at the Central Academy of Fine Arts for more than ten years, photography itself is a meaningless medium and only given significance when photographs are chosen and reinterpreted within her native language, painting. "It seemed that painting the old photographs enables me to physically touch the past", explains the artist: "during the practice, I could experience every single detail of my past. My favourite dress and even a button become tangible in the strokes and I could almost recall their original smell."[28] For example, the photograph of the celebration of the poster *Chairman Mao Goes to Anyuan (Mao Zhuxi Qu Anyuan)* in 1968 is juxtaposed with two-year-old Yu Hong with a *Chairman Mao Goes to Anyuan* badge proudly on her chest (Fig. 14). In another combination, one could almost hear the soldiers' voices in support

---

26 Interview with Liu Ye, 29 October 2003, Beijing.

27 Przerwa, Xenia Tetmajer Von, 'Yu Hong's *Witness to Growth*: Historic Determination and Individual Contingency', *YiShu: Journal of Contemporary Chinese Art*, Vol. 2, No. 3, September 2003, pp. 34–42.

28 Interview with Yu Hong, 30 October 2003, Beijing.

of "*Mao zhuxi wansui* (long live Chairman Mao)" immediately from the photograph, but the girl's purpose in the picture is more ambiguous (Fig. 15). Comparatively, child Yu Hong would not have the same agenda as today's children, like Liu Wa's generation, but indeed, heroic ambitions for the communist success (Fig. 16).

Critique or nostalgia, the distinction between them gets more ambiguous in the artist couple Shao Yinong and Mu Chen's photograph series *Da Litang (Assembly Hall)*. From the dynasties to the People's Republic, China's tradition of change is always revolutionary — to demolish and to re-establish — while the speed of change increases dramatically towards the post-industrial twenty-first century. As has been introduced previously, many dynastic relics disappeared during the Red Guard movement of 'Smashing the Four Olds'. Tragically, even today, to recuperate the legacy of the Cultural Revolution can also be difficult because of the government's efforts to remove the Cultural Revolution from people's memory and reshape history. For example, one of the few remaining representative buildings from the Cultural Revolution — the Exhibition Hall of Sichuan Province at Tianfu Square in Chengdu — is to be pulled down to build a new one in the Qing dynasty style.[29] In other words, ironically, an original tradition is to be replaced by an artificial reproduction. Britta Erickson describes, "There is a sense of loss, resulting in nostalgia for what is gone", and continues, "Shao Yinong and Mu Chen bring the urgency of nostalgia into sharp focus … the images are a poignant reminder of the Cultural Revolution political fanaticism that necessitated regular meetings in these halls. Empty of people, the photographs invite the projection of personal memories."[30]

With a background as a photojournalist, Mu Chen questions the 'realness' of photojournalism. She discussed, "the camera could be considered as a relatively honest and reliable tool, but the moment when the shutter clicks would bring a subjective choice or decision."[31] The boundary between photo-documentation and art, therefore, is meant to be vague in the *Assembly Hall* series, where we could only see the simplest execution of photography and the least artistic intervention involved. More like anthropological research, the artists' itinerary is based on their substantial literature review of the historical background. Departing from Yan'an, the artists travelled for over two years to locate hundreds of revolutionary shrines and assembly halls built since China's revolution. These first-hand materials then were documented as specimens to be considered suitable for inclusion in the series.

---

29 Interview with Liu Jiakun, 3 November 2003, Chengdu.

30 Erickson, Britta, *Memory Devolved and Evolved: Photographic Works by Shao Yinong and Muchen*, 2003, unpublished manuscript provided by Shao Yinong and Mu Chen.

31 Interview with Mu Chen, 28 October 2003, Beijing.

Assembly halls, the most communal space where masses gathered for events of either celebration or criticism, played an important role in the Cultural Revolution. "It was a stage where one could have played the role of hero with dignity and then suddenly become a guilty counter-revolutionary", said Shao Yinong; "it was once filled with glory and humiliation, happiness and agony, passion and violence, resounding with enthusiastic and hysteric voices, but all passed today."[32] Some assembly halls have fallen into ruin (Fig. 17); some have survived, even with Mao's portrait on display; others have been converted to warehouses (Fig. 18), factories (Fig. 19) restaurants (Fig. 20) and, even more ironically, Buddhist temples.

Similarly, in the photographic series *Wenge Yijing (Vestiges of the Cultural Revolution)*, that began in 1994, Wang Tong uses his camera to search and rescue the disappearing vestiges, including Mao's images and big-character slogans (Figs. 21 and 22) on the wall, and points out the decay of the era. Interestingly, some local residents did not even notice the existence of the legacy — even a big image of Mao (Fig. 23) right in their view — which the artist had travelled extensively to find.[33] The image of the Chairman — once the central focus of every man, woman and child — now is an indifferent mark on the wall.

Envisaging these factual documents that mirror the experiences of people, artists' are less explicit about the Cultural Revolution and mainly serve to provide a reminder for those who have had the experience.

Words or Images

From a visual perspective, the beginning of the Cultural Revolution can be linked to the appearance of the first big-character poster *(dazi bao)* at Peking University on 25 May 1966. This poster was written by Nie Yuanzi and the other six members of staff from the Department of Philosophy. It criticized Song Shuo, the vice minister of Higher Education Beijing Municipal Committee, Lu Ping and Peng Peiyun, the secretaries of Communist Party Committee of Peking University. On the same day, suddenly more than a thousand big-character posters covered the whole campus to join the criticisms and discussions.[34] Soon afterwards, this bottom-up 'mass voice' was supported by Mao, and the content of the poster was broadcast to the whole nation through the Central People's Broadcast

---

32 Interview with Shao Yinong, 28 October 2003, Beijing.

33 Interview with Wang Tong, 17 June 2004, Beijing.

34 Yin Hongbiao, '*Wenge de Diyizhang Malie Zhuyi Dazibao* (The First Marx-Leninism Big-Character Poster in the Cultural Revolution)', in Liu, Op. cit., 1996, pp. 3–16.

Station on 1 June 1966 and published on the first page of the *People's Daily* the next day.[35] Then, as the main visual medium, big-character slogans were written in red on all available surfaces. Stores, government offices, tea shops, noodle restaurants and various eateries were so completely covered that it was impossible to tell which was which.[36]

Although a piece of handwriting consists of words — a letter, a poem or a slogan — carrying literary meanings, its textual identity could be debased by illegible calligraphy or, indeed, the violent visual impact of the big-character posters of Chinese political movements. When the artistic value of writing overpowers its literary content, the identity of Chinese characters become ambiguous. The word 'anti-writing' has a positive meaning in Chinese visual culture, changing literary words to images. "By subtly suppressing the content of a handwritten text a writer can emphasize the aesthetic value of his brushwork," however, Wu Hung argues; "all traditional calligraphers conducted this transformation in one way or another, but none of them tried to completely divorce form from content. A radical departure from this ancient tradition only occurred in contemporary Chinese art." [37]

From the late 1980s, the most influential Chinese artists, such as Gu Wenda, Wu Shanzhuan and Xu Bing, coincidentally got into 'anti-writing' by producing a large body of pseudo-calligraphy and fake texts, in which they consciously distinguished form from content, and tried to construct a purely calligraphic art. Wu Shanzhuan states, "Chinese character is the most significant one, in terms of either its function that is able to construct people's ways of thinking, or its influence on the national psychology. And its monosyllabic pronunciation and unusual image make it distinguishable among all characters in the global context. If character is the key to the national soul, losing Chinese character is to lock the most powerful soul ever in a safe."[38]

The exhibition *70% Red, 25% Black, 5% White*, which included 76 pieces of work led by Wu Shanzhuan, took place in Zhejiang Academy of Fine Art in Hangzhou in 1986.[39] The title of the exhibition reflects the artists' visual memories during the Cultural Revolution. Based on the proportion of these three colours, the installation

---

35 '*Beijing Daxue Qi Tongzhi Jiechuan le Yige Dayinmou* (An Evil Plot Was Exposed by the Seven Comrades from Peking University)', *Renmin Ribao (People's Daily)*, 2 June 1966, p. 1.

36 Yan Jiaqi and Gao Gao, translated and edited by D. W. Y. Kwok. *Turbulent Decade: A History of the Cultural Revolution*. Hawaii: School of Hawaiian, Asian & Pacific Studies, University of Hawaii, 1996, pp. 89–90.

37 Wu Hung. *Transience: Chinese Experimental Art at the End of the Twentieth Century*. Chicago: The David and Alfred Smart Museum of Art and The University of Chicago, 1999, p. 38.

38 Wu Shanzhuan, '*Guanyu Zhongwen* (About Chinese Characters)', *Meishu (Fine Art)*, 1986, Vol. 8, p. 61.

39 The artist group of the exhibition includes Wu Shanzhuan, Zhang Haizhou, Lü Haizhou, Luo Xianyue, Song Chenghua, Ni Haifeng and Huang Jian, who started their studies in Zhengjiang Academy of Fine Art in 1983.

is constructed by Chinese characters in *heiti* (bold typeface), which was popular in Cultural Revolution propaganda. This industrial style demolishes the poetic aesthetics of traditional calligraphy but revisits the visual identity of Chinese revolutionary slogans.

The work *Hongse Youmo (Red Humour)* (Fig. 24) was created as an installation at Wu Shanzhuan's studio in Zhoushan in 1986, but was not shown to the public until 1998 in the United States. The artist used the format of the Cultural Revolution's big-character poster, but the messages were drawn from the surrounding environment and conveyed the multiple dimensions of contemporary political, social and economical information. The texts written all over the room's walls, floor and ceiling included political slogans, such as "exercise for strength in the class struggle", price notices and popular advertisements such as "newly arrived supplies", newspaper headlines, traffic signs, Buddhist texts, weather forecasts and even some lines of ancient poetry. The big-characters in *Red Humour* were written not only by the artist himself, but also by visitors to the installation. Viewers might sense a playful and happy attitude when seeing Wu's windowless room filled with the absurd combination of nonsense and terror. Nevertheless, the personal experiences of the Cultural Revolution inevitably could be recalled by such a familiar visual environment in which revolutionary and holy ideals or the highest instructions were ironically de-constructed and de-signified.

Gu Wenda's *Pseudo Characters Series* (Fig. 25) investigated the intrinsic aesthetics of Chinese character by displaying a conflict between linguistic meaning and aesthetic pleasure. Calligraphy is usually used for captions and visually served as decoration in Chinese traditional painting. In Gu's work, traditional calligraphic techniques are used to write restructured characters with components upside-down, reversed or wrongly written. The proportion of painting and calligraphy was changed; the huge reversed Chinese characters dominated the picture instead of the landscape itself. As Gao Minglu states, the production of these works demonstrates a paradox: whenever a calligrapher is writing, an aesthetic affectation may override any concern with the text, whilst Gu Wenda became a radical destroyer of the power of traditional writing,[40] and arguably was influenced by the 'big-character aesthetics' of the Cultural Revolution. More directly in Gu's 1987 installation *Guanzhong Zuowei Qizi de Xuangua Qipan de Youxi (A Game in which the Audience Serve as Chessmen on a Suspended Chessboard)* (Fig. 26), large black characters ge and ming (revolution) were reversed and crossed out by red lines, with political and religious meanings. Jason Kuo observes, "this treatment of Chinese characters seems to be the artist's reaction toward the abuses of language by the writers of big-character poster during the Cultural Revolution."[41]

---

40 Gao Minglu, 'From Elite to Small Man: The Many Faces of a Transitional Avant-Garde in Mainland China', in Gao Minglu (ed.), *Inside Out: New Chinese Art*. London: University of California Press, 1998, p. 159.

41 Cited in Sullivan, Michael, *Art and Artists of Twentieth-century China*. London: University of California Press, 1996, p. 264.

In another example, Qiu Zhijie's *Wenshen (Tattoo 1)* (Fig. 27), a large character *bu*, meaning 'no', is written in bright red across the artist's body and the wall behind him. It creates the illusion that his body has strangely disappeared, and the character has become independent, detached from the body and the wall. In other words, this character rejects the ground and makes the person invisible. "The character *bu* was chosen because its structure would be interesting in this piece of work, and it does work very well with my body," said the artist; "as soon as I decided on this big character, I could not think about using any other colour rather than red."[42]

Xu Bing used to call himself a member of the first artist generation of *wenzi gongzuozhe* (literally 'character worker' and generally known as writers or editors; here it means artists focusing on Chinese characters as a visual form). His interest, or rather habit, of making Chinese characters was formed during the Cultural Revolution.

One of the government-enforced curriculum changes was a push to simplify many traditional Chinese characters. The simplified form could be seen as an initial 'cultural' revolution, in which Mao attempted to formalize and popularize the traditional format of writing and, more ambitiously, to prepare a cultural foundation for cultivating the new ideology. In Chinese education, everyone needs to spend several years memorizing thousands of individual characters. Xu Bing recalls his experience of learning Chinese characters at school: "every few months, a new set of simplified characters would be devised by the government; and the previous one, some of which had been considered inappropriate, would be replaced." Therefore, many of Xu's days were spent learning, then unlearning different characters for the same word, a process that made him realize that to change the language, even a little bit, really changes people's thinking. This could also have confused the understanding of Chinese culture in which, traditionally, "characters would be respected as a sanctified creature, and the movement of simplifying Chinese characters actually challenged the root of Chinese culture."[43]

Growing up in the centre of the Cultural Revolution at Peking University, Xu Bing witnessed the movement, including the display of the first big-character poster. When his father, the chair of the History Department in the university, like many other intellectuals, was sent to prison to be 'reformed' through labour, Xu Bing was labelled as 'the bastard son of a reactionary father'. The big-character posters were shrill and angry, denouncing people by name and accusing the targets of being 'capitalist roaders'. Many irregularly simplified or even deliberately wrongly written characters (Fig. 28)[44] in political propaganda became

---

42　Interview with Qiu Zhijie, 26 February 2000, Beijing.

43　Interview with Xu Bing, 21 November 2003, Manchester.

44　For example, the character *qi* in the name Liu Shao Qi, former chairman of China and a political opponent of Mao, could be turned on its side to become *gou*, or 'dog', as a way to insult.

a way to insult opponents, but, later, these inspired the artist's conscious invention of his 'heavenly words'. "At that time", says the artist, "you really felt the power of characters. If you wanted to kill somebody, you did it not by gun but by brush."[45] As a result, Xu enthusiastically dedicated himself to political propaganda in order to rid himself of this blemished family history. "I sat in the Propaganda Office hour upon hour", Xu Bing recalls, "writing and painting big-character posters and leaflets made of tightly written small characters, they all were as carefully and neatly done as professionally printed words. Even the largest slogan posters were perfect on first try. Each character was standard and forceful. I could write them quickly and extremely well."[46]

Since the late 1980s, Xu Bing has learned to enjoy the skills that he acquired, not necessarily from his seven-year study at the Department of Printmaking in Central Academy, but from his 'training' during the Cultural Revolution. He spent many years of intensive work hand-carving more than two thousand wooden type elements (Fig. 29) and printing them on paper. However, none of those characters in the *Book from the Heaven* can be pronounced or understood because the artist invented each one by rearranging elements from original Chinese characters. The installation was composed of three elements: handscrolls, wall panels (Fig. 30) and books (Fig. 31) in the traditional woodblock-printed form. The orderliness of thousands of characters printed in black on white enshrouds the room, masking the wall. Erickson notes that the *Book from the Heaven* has been likened to the big-character posters that appeared throughout the Cultural Revolution for people's daily reading.[47] To the viewers — foreigners as well as Chinese — all semantic significance of the Chinese characters was completely removed from the 'heavenly book', the writing itself. Thus, the artist seems to mock the sacred texts of antiquity.

Wang Jinsong's photographic work *Bai Chai Tu (A Hundred Chai)* (Fig. 32), completed in 1999, witnesses the reconstruction of the city of Beijing. Since the 1990s, the Chinese character *Chai* (to demolish) began to appear — in bold white or spiny red — all over the capital, either on the outer walls of traditional residential buildings or on doors and windows. It was marked for the bulldozer's target, as low-rise buildings made way for those of greater height. The handwritings of *Chai* seem "despotic, truculent and even tyrannical in many cases", discussed the artist; "the impact is not from the literary meaning of the character itself, but the visual format and execution of the writing."[48] Only

---

45 Interview with Xu Bing, 21 November 2003, Manchester.

46 Xu Bing, 'The Living Word', in Britta Erickson (ed.), *Words without Meaning, Meaning without Words: The Art of Xu Bing*. London: University of Washington Press, 2001, p. 16.

47 Erickson, Ibid, p. 44.

48 Interview with Wang Jinsong, 25 March 2006, Beijing.

because of the writing, the character as a sacred image would then be able to demonstrate authority and power, to demolish an architectural space or, as in the turbulent era, to vandalize humanity and bereave one's life.

Man or Mao

On 1 October 1949, Mao Zedong with his comrades ascended Tiananmen, the Gate of Heavenly Peace, which once stood as a gate of the palace of the Qing dynasty. He declared the foundation of the People's Republic of China to the thousands of commoners and soldiers gathered under Tiananmen: "Chinese people have finally stood up!" The appearance of Mao, as the Chinese communist leader, must have added a new political dimension to the former imperial building, reinterpreting the hidden ruling power to finally symbolize the beginning of a new era. At the same time, the gate instantly offered Mao the dual status of both communist leader and feudalistic emperor.

During the Cultural Revolution, the traditional customs, festivals and folk religions were considered superstitious and anti-communist and forcibly removed from people's life. To fill the 'religious void', Mao played the role of the new 'god' and symbolized by a red sun. This popular song extended the metaphors of the chairman:

Sailing on the sea relies on the helmsman,
The universe growing relies on the sun;
Seedlings raising by the moistness of dew,
Revolution needs the thought of Mao Zedong.

Fishes cannot live without water,
Melons cannot live without vines;
The revolutionary masses cannot live without the Communist Party,
Mao Zedong's thought is the endless sun.

Wang Yi suggests that Mao's identity as the red sun was closely related to the healer and the rescuer who would be able to save the people from agony and illness, as well as a world full of evils.[49] Because of the personal cult, the image of Mao permeated the visual environment of the Cultural Revolution. Mao's image far outweighed a representation of a man; rather it presented a new god fabricated by the Chinese revolution. It is estimated that during the Cultural Revolution 2.2 billion of the so-called 'standard portraits

---

49 Wang Yi, ' *"Wanwu Shengzhang Kao Taiyang" yu Yuanshi Chongbai* ("The Universe Growing Relies on the Sun" and the Primary Worships)', in Liu, Op. cit., 1996, p. 128.

(*biaozhunxiang*)' of the chairman (Fig. 33) were produced,[50] and 900 million posters of Liu Chunhua's oil painting *Chairman Mao Goes to Anyuan* were printed (Fig. 34). Those images appeared as Mao's substitute in both private and public spaces in people's lives to provide instant and direct access to the great leader. In another medium, more than 2.8 billion Mao badges (Fig. 35), or four for every man, woman and child in the nation were manufactured during the Cultural Revolution; the total variety of Mao badges has been estimated at over some 50,000.[51] These images were produced, exchanged and displayed as tools for communicating Chinese nationalist ideology to the masses and offering them the opportunity to learn about, conform to and define themselves in Mao.[52]

I argue that reflecting on Mao has been a continuous motif in contemporary Chinese art, with three different perspectives. First, the critical approach of representing Mao's image became an extreme challenge of rebellion for the artists, who had been under his power for many years. In the 1979 Stars exhibition,[53] the *Ouxiang (Idol)* (Fig. 36), a wood sculpture by the self-taught artist Wang Keping, was the most striking work in the show — a daring pioneer work that 'violated' the sacred image of the communist chairman. The sculpture obviously was re-shaped from the image of Buddha, which originally came from India but generally was understood as a sign of Chinese traditional religion; Chinese viewers would immediately recognize the significance of the pentagram engraved above his forehead. The ironic interaction between 'feudal superstition' and the communist ideal boldly revealed the fact that Mao had been worshipped as a new religious idol. In fact, *Idol*, finished in 1978 only two years after Mao's death, was the first to utter what most people did not even dare think. The artist is rather a militant hero, challenging the autocracy of the state.

The next work on Mao with this critical approach did not appear until ten years later in 1988. It is Wang Guangyi's series of paintings *Mao Zedong*. The artist re-pictured the chairman's 'standard portrait', ubiquitous during Mao's political reign, on five large canvases. Two of them in red grids — *Mao Zedong – Hongge (Mao Zedong – Red Grid)* (Fig. 37) — and another three in black grids — *Mao Zedong – Black Grid* — were shown in the 1989 China Avant-Garde exhibition at the National Art Gallery in Beijing. The

---

50 Barmé, Geremie R. *Shades of Mao*. London: An East Gate Book, 1996, p. 8.

51 Lu Na, *Mao Zedong Xiangzhang Shoucang yu Jianshang (The Collection and Appreciation of Mao Zedong Badges)*. Beijing: International Culture Press, 1993, p. 14.

52 For a detailed discussion on Mao badges, see Melissa Schrift and Keith Pilkey, 'Revolution Remembered: Chairman Mao Badges and Chinese Nationalist Ideology', *Journal of Popular Culture*, Vol. 30, Fall 1996, pp. 169–197.

53 The first Stars exhibition opened on 27 September 1979 and was staged in the street outside the National Art Gallery in Beijing. It defined a more unofficial position in the Chinese art world since 1949. See Yi Dan, *Xingxing Lishi (A History of the Stars)*. Changsha: Hunan Art Press, 2002.

original intention of this series was to conclude the artist's "liquidation of humanist enthusiasm",[54] however, after it had been exhibited, Wang Guangyi suspected that "the onlookers, with hundredfold humanist enthusiasm, endowed Mao Zedong with even more humanist connotations" however, after it had been exhibited, Wang Guangyi suspected that "the onlookers, with hundredfold humanist enthusiasm, endowed Mao Zedong with even more humanist connotations".[55] During the Cultural Revolution, the grid was a useful tool for duplicating Mao's portrait to scale avoiding any mistake in proportion. Here, Wang Guangyi brought this hidden grid to the surface, overlying Mao's sombre grey image. In his painting, the warning barrier required people to pause and to think before approaching this deity and forced an objective reconsideration.[56] The grid of thick red lines, on the one hand, could be a superficial symbol of imprisoning Mao or his autocratic era. On the other hand, the grid, as a measuring tool, could show how a man might possibly be 'magnified' and, simultaneously, bring this divine image to a frame rationally analysable and dissectible.

Starting at about the same time as Wang Guangyi, Yu Youhan concentrated on reshaping Mao's imagery for more than eight years. However, instead of defiantly criticizing the former leader, Yu's response can be analysed as the second approach — cynicism — and seems more relaxed. Born in the early 1940s, Yu Youhan experienced the Cultural Revolution while studying at Central Academy of Arts and Crafts in Beijing.[57] To him, Mao represented many things: a great leader of the nation, a symbol of China, the East, a depth of culture or a particular period of history. Sometimes Mao is avant-garde, sometimes conservative.[58] In Yu's series of paintings *Mao and His People* (Fig. 38), the Chairman was positioned in the centre with the gesture appropriated from Mao's famous official photograph of his Yan'an presentation, *Lun Chijiuzhan (On Protracted War)*. Instead of the original patched trousers, Mao's suit was patterned with colourful flowers, which were also spread in the painting and turned into a fabric-like composition or, in the artist's own words, an "unreal and hollow environment".[59] Similarly, floating flowers are applied to the work *Talking with Hunan Peasants (Yu Hunan Nongmin Tanhua)* (Fig. 39) derived from a photograph of Mao taken in the 1950s with a family of cheerful

---

54 For an analysis on Wang Guangyi's notion of "humanist enthusiasm", see Martina Yang, *Semiotic Warfare: A Semiotic Analysis the Chinese Avant-Garde, 1979–1989*. Hong Kong: Timezone 8, 2003, p. 154.

55 Cited in Lü Peng and Yi Dan, *Zhongguo Xiandai Yishu Shi (A History of Contemporary Chinese Art) 1979–1989*. Changsha: Hunan Art Press, 1992, pp. 166–168.

56 Smith, Karen, 'From Mao to Now: Wang Guangyi', in *Wang Guangyi*. Hong Kong: Timezone 8, 2002, p. 10.

57 Central Academy of Arts and Crafts (*Zhongyang Gongyi Meishu Xueyuan*) is the former name of Institute of Art and Design, Tsinghua University (*Qinghua Daxue Meishu Xueyuan*).

58 Interview with Yu Youhan, 9 October 2000, Shanghai.

59 Ibid.

smiling peasants in his hometown village Shaoshan, in Hunan province. Isolated within the red faces, peasants' white teeth somehow lay bare the fallacy of the joyful bliss. As Dal Lago argues, "the exaggeration exposes the farcical quality of political propaganda and the surreal, over-idealized relationship between the leader and the people".[60]

Another strategy employed by Yu is to juxtapose Mao's official images with the icons of Western pop culture, for example, the American singer Whitney Houston or, more generally, a fashionably dressed woman (Figs. 40 and 41). The design clearly presents the artist's personal perception of the leader in terms of his representability of 'Chineseness' as well as the revolutionary era, placing him in the context of contemporary life. A similar juxtaposition is created in Qi Zhilong's work *Xiaofei Xingxiang (Consumer Icons)* series in the early nineties (Figs. 42 and 43). Like bright flowers or charming beauties with seductive smiles, Mao is portrayed as another consumable image in today's urban life. This appropriation of Mao's image is understood as "one of the most generalized and at the same time personalized way[s] to deconstruct ideological pressures".[61]

Li Shan's earliest painting of Mao's portrait could be traced back to the Great Leap Forward movement in 1957, when he was a young propagandist in middle school. In October 1989, the artist restarted to work on the image of the chairman in his painting series *Rouge* but in quite a different way. *Yanzhi* (rouge) is a hue of pink verging on fuchsia, originally, a particular colour associated with Chinese folk art, such as that seen in the Beijing Opera and the New Year painting. Li Shan's painting series *Rouge* is based on two of the chairman's most famous portraits, one taken during the period of Mao's guerrilla activity in the 1930s and the other of a benevolent-looking 'standard portrait'. The image of Mao is understood by the artist as 'cultural imagery' in his works rather than as a political sign. The title *Rouge* is chosen for its symbolism of something superficial but, at the same time, useful for whitewashing the revolutionary ideology and the prospect of people's life.[62] In the series *Rouge*, a mysterious lotus-like flower in the colour rouge is always carried by the lips of the communist leader, who is wearing a red star cap as well as lipstick (Fig. 44). This '*Yanzhi hua* (rouge-ization)' of Mao demonstrates the popularization of the Chairman's portrait and its transformation into a mass icon; the almost vulgar colour rouge eliminates and insults the sacred meaning of the image of Mao (Figs. 45 and 46).

---

60 Dal Lago, Francesca, 'Personal Mao: Reshaping an Icon in Contemporary Chinese Art', *Art Journal*, Vol. 58, No. 2, Summer 1999, p. 50.

61 Li Xianting, '*Qi Zhilong de Zuopin He Yishi Xingtai de Jishixing* (The Work of Qi Zhilong and the Instant Ideology' in *Xiaofei Xingxiang (Consumer Icons)*. Hong Kong: Schoeni Art Gallery, 1994, p. 5.

62 Interview with Li Shan on 4 October 2000, Shanghai.

Does Li Shan's portrayal of Mao have any sexual implication? Dal Lago explores:

> An implicit reference is directed toward male homoerotic desire, traditionally associated in China with the theatrical world because of the convention of men playing female roles (in Beijing Opera). This association — implied both by the use of the colour and by the androgynous, feminized features assumed by the portrait in Li's series — introduces another recurrent trope of the literary recollections of the Cultural Revolution — that of sexual freedom and liberation experienced during this period. 'Gendering' Mao becomes Li's personal way to vulgarize the figure of the leader and bring this sublime object of desire to a more accessible level. The result of this practice is the projection of the artist's sexuality onto the icon, the screen of a feminized Mao.[63]

However, the artist denied that he had attempted to feminize Mao or that the painting was based on any association with the Beijing Opera. Instead, the 'treasonous' representation was explained as transferring Mao to a purely unisex human being, a visual cultural identity for the artist himself.[64] In fact, the artist might have to accept that he depicted a unisex face by the way of inevitably feminizing Mao, who actually is a saviour of the whole nation, more than simply a male. Because of Mao's political and apotheosized status, the feminized version of Mao had objectively constructed a subversive impact. In the meantime, the artist's private expression unconsciously had been revealed by depicting the sign of his own cultural background.

The third artistic approach on Mao is not necessarily by borrowing Mao's image, but by Mao's suit and Mao's book *Mao Zhuxi Yulu (The Quotations of Chairman Mao)*, which have become the metonymies of Mao and which could invite more reflections on the era itself rather than Mao as a person. Actually the so-called Mao suit was first designed for Sun Zhongshan (Sun Yat-sen), the leader of the republican revolution. After 1949, the Mao suit quickly became the most popular dress, conveying both nationalistic and revolutionary significance. Without Mao's image, in Sui Jianguo's *Yibo (Legacy Mantle)* (Fig. 47), the Mao suit is sculptured and monumentalized more explicitly as a political symbol, but the inside is empty; and at the same time, reaffirmed as a "historical subjectivity that manifested both the modernity of Chinese culture and its ability to be self-critical".[65] The artist's 2003 work *Youshou (the Right Hand)* (Fig. 48) is an enlarged right arm up to some 7 metres in length. The sleeve of the Mao suit has an immediate

---

63 Dal Lago, Op. cit., 1999, pp. 54–55.

64 Ibid.

65 Zhu Qi, 'Putting on and Taking off: How the Mao Suit Became Art', in Wu Hung (ed.), *Chinese Art at the Crossroads: Between Past and Future, Between East and West*. Hong Kong: New Art Media, 2001, p. 50.

link with Mao's standard statue shown in public places during the Cultural Revolution, while the deathlike gesture of the bodiless hand demystifies the 'super instruction' of the Chairman.

The *Quotations of Chairman Mao Zedong*, the *Hong Baoshu (Precious Red Book)*, has endured as one of the infamous images of the Cultural Revolution. It was produced in over fifty different languages and the number of copies printed is estimated to be as high as 10 billion.[66] Benewick and Donald argue that the *Precious Red Book* "was the narrative and visual instrument of the largest experiment in the politicisation of society ever undertaken".[67]

To Xu Yihui, the *Precious Red Book* has been the concrete form of a spiritual resource (Fig. 49). More symbolically, the red books are well situated in the flowered altar (Fig. 50), while glazed ceramic has been a perfect medium to reinterpret the visual principle of '*hong guang liang*' — 'red, smooth, and luminescent' — in the Cultural Revolution. In order to produce canonical writings for the new political and religious authorities, the first Qin emperor reduced to ashes most ancient books that were no longer useful. During the Cultural Revolution, the destruction of millions of books led to the worship of a single book. On the one hand, burning Mao's book became another ritual ceremony, exterminating the era of Mao (Fig. 51); on the other hand, in the artist's words, "it could be seen as a kind of process of sublimation".[68]

The cult of Mao was fostered from the moment Mao took charge of the Chinese Communist Party and reached its climax during the period of the Cultural Revolution. During the personality cult movement, Mao was given the title of the Four Greats (*Sige Weida*), namely, the Great Teacher, the Great Leader, the Great Commander and the Great Helmsman. He transcended an image of a human being and became a god of the red sun to receive people's worship. In the post-Mao era, when the revolutionary fervour evaporated, could Mao easily be simplified and pulled down from his throne? As reflected in art, this man seems to have been even more complex and mystifying as a visual icon of the era.

---

66 Cited in Barmé, Op. cit., 1996, p. 207.

67 Benewick, R. and S. Donald, 'Treasuring the Word: Mao, Depoliticization and Material Present', in Robert Benewick, Marc Blecher and Sarah Cook (eds.), *Asian Politics in Development*. London: Frank Cass, 2003, p. 65.

68 Interview with Xu Yihui, 28 October 2003, Beijing.

Conformity or Carnival

In China, "every city, town, or village must have a square for public gatherings"; Wu Hung argues, "big or small, a square is always conjoined with a platform built for the leaders to review the mass assemblies. A square thus becomes a legitimate place for people to meet their leaders, an indispensable joint between the high and the low, the brain and the body."[69] Tiananmen Square became the most representative one within this kind of political space. It is hard to imagine Mao's perception of viewing some 70,000 cheering people from Tiananmen for the first time in the 1949 founding ceremony. Although he ordered a new square to be built shortly afterwards — a square 'big enough to hold an assembly of one billion',[70] — the new square completed after his death could hold only [!] 600,000 people. We have revisited the image of Mao, so what was the identity of the people themselves in the Cultural Revolution, and how do artists approach representations of this collective identity? In particular, how does the Cultural Revolution influence contemporary art in reshaping the people's collective identity?

Since the foundation of the People's Republic in 1949, mass assemblies for either Maoism study or political parade and gathering have become familiar and prominent phenomena in people's daily life and reached the climax during the Cultural Revolution. The word 'collective', then, far outweighs its literal meaning; Instead, it has been interpreted productively based on various sociological and political backgrounds. Without the experience of the Cultural Revolution, one might have a completely different understanding of individuality and uniformity, dispersion and assembly, private and public, family and society. I argue that artists have been exploring these relationships and conflicts and representing the collective identity of 'Chineseness', with a pair of entirely different or almost contrasting approaches.

The concept of 'family' is deeply rooted in the Chinese culture as a small version of 'collective'. Zhang Xiaogang's interest in old family photographs during the Cultural Revolution was the starting point of his internationally acclaimed painting series *Da Jiating (Big Family)* (Fig. 52), which firstly appeared in 1993. There were some common rules for the family photograph in Mao's era. For example, the father is always positioned on the right, mother on the left and child in the middle. The photographer would offer them some criteria for positioning their body, gesturing and even expressions, offering an idealistic model of society. Those family photographs could have been rendered by hand after the studio shot to match the 'standard' aesthetics. During this

---

69 Wu Hung, *Remaking Beijing: Tiananmen Square and the Creation of a Political Space.* London: Reaktion Books, 2005, p. 23.

70 Cited in Wu Liangyong, '*Tiananmen Guangchang de Guihua he Sheji* (The Plan and Design of Tiananmen Square)', in *Jianzhushi Lunwenji (Essays on Architectural History)*, Vol. 2, 1979, p. 26.

revision, many aesthetical and sociological perceptions of the reviser would be added onto the photographic image, with or without the subjects' agreement. "I am always interested in exploring the relationship between individual and the society, i.e. the conflict between simi hua (private) and gonggong hua (public)"; as the artist discusses, "family photography is obviously a private medium, but in China, it has been conformed to a 'public standard' within the society."[71]

In the *Big Family* series, typical costumes, such as Mao's suit, Red Guard uniform, navy striped top and red scarf (Figs. 53 and 54), are appropriated in the works to indicate the historical background and people's spiritual pursuance. However, the artist does not aim to represent any particular individual or family by depicting any personal characteristics; rather, the artist tries to show the collective similarity, images with a mono-appearance, and the reactions or the situations of individuals who were confronting the public social environment. As portraits, eyes in the *Big Family* are considered more vital than anything else, and they have been rendered in detail (Fig. 55). However, the artist states that "the most important expression of the eyes in these portraits is non-expressive or, in Chinese, *zoushen* (literally losing expression, that is, staring blankly)".[72] The light falling on the faces like birthmarks emphasizes the absurdity of the impersonal expressionlessness behind the generation's revolutionary fervour and captures the disappearance of individuality, while the inevitable colour red, which appears reasonably or unreasonably, links comrades' spirits and defines themselves in the context of national collectivization.

The traditional family model will have been changed inevitably by the one-child policy, which has been referred as a 'no-other-solution solution' because of China's huge population and which generated millions of the so-called standard families. As the first photographic work of Wang Jinsong in 1996, *Biaozhun Jiating (Standard Family)* (Fig. 56) comprises two hundred photographs of one-child families. Each of them with its own appearance and personality is seen as the most basic and ordinary element to construct China's whole society. However, the repetition of those families in this monotonic module enlarges the visual impact of the work and at the same time "diminishes the significance of independence of each family and ignores any individual story behind people". The artist comments, "The reality of China is a great system of unification where the appearance of collective dominates in the society in the forms of various movements, either political or economical, and these visual memories and reflections have been offering me vocabularies for my works."[73]

---

71 Interview with Zhang Xiaogang, 30 October 2003, Beijing.

72 Ibid.

73 Interview with Wang Jinsong, 25 March 2006, Beijing.

Artist Bai Yiluo himself worked in a photograph studio for three years, taking identity photos for his clients. People came to the studio with different appearances and social status and, for a normal photograph left a similar impression in the exposure. An identity photo (*zhengjian zhao*, passport photo), however, would have to be presented to the public without all the privacy of a portrait. Therefore, facing the camera or, rather, facing the eventual public, one would conform oneself consciously or unconsciously to 'standard' aesthetics, as an ordinary individual among the social collective.

Three years' work experience in the photograph studio offered Bai Yiluo a large collection of identity photos of various people — including workers, peasants, soldiers, students and intellectuals — to execute his project *People (Renmin)* (Fig. 57). In 2001, 3,600 small-size photographs were sewn together with threads into a 15 square metre sheet, which constructed a surprisingly heroic pattern. The image of each individual perhaps is no longer important but collectively represents "their nationality, social background and their living environment."[74] The people's relationships are visualized and concretized by the threads woven between the photographs, while the rubbed texture implies a mysterious net, covering, caring and connecting the individuals within the collective community.

Growing up in Henan province at the commencement of the Cultural Revolution, Zhuang Hui often travelled around with his photographer father who utilized a technique made popular during the early 1900s, that involved a 180 degrees rotational lens camera to take group photos. It was an amazing experience for the child to understand a camera that could catch such a large number of people with a single click, or in other words, identify the image of assemblies, a significant visual presentation of the era.[75]

In Zhuang Hui's photograph series *Jiti Zhao (Group Photo)* in 1997, the groups that were organized and photographed were sometimes made up of more than 600 persons. The concept of conformability is reflected explicitly not only by the photographic work itself, but also by the execution of the art practice. Zhuang Hui cleverly chooses typical examples of any civil society's institutional framework — organizations of school, work (Fig. 58), public security (Fig. 59) and village residence (Fig. 60) — to preserve this disappearing visual legacy of conformity and places these against the double backdrops of Mao's ideology and China's current economic reformation. The horizontally elongated picture reminds one of the Chinese traditional handscroll, encouraging spectators to 'read' every single character in the photograph. The artist himself is always present, standing at either the far left or right of the assembled group, as the director of the scenery or, indeed, a signature seal in the end of a handscroll — a calculated position of importance.

---

74 Interview with Bai Yiluo, 28 May 2005, Beijing.

75 Interview with Zhuang Hui, 28 October 2003, Beijing.

The question of subject in Zhuang Hui's portraits is even further complicated by his own presence. The answer seems neither to lie in the individuals that comprise the group, nor in the group. As Borysevicz discussed, "Zhuang Hui's presence mystifies the configuration by leaving the subject a tedious sum of the mass, its component parts, and the artist himself. The disciplines of portraiture, self portraiture, and group portraiture merge."[76]

This approach could also include Shao Yinong and Mu Chen's photographic work *Family Register (Jiapu)* (Fig. 61). The birth of the artist couple's son motivated them to learn Shao Yinong's family history as a case study and start the project of re-building a family register. In *Family Register*, the ten sepia-toned photographic scrolls, totalling 38 metres in length, show family members dressed in Mao's suit, paired with their choice of lower garment, to present the conflicting embarrassment created between the past conformity, particularly the collectivist experience during the Cultural Revolution, and contemporary individualities driven by today's market economy. The artists intentionally adapt the traditional techniques of studio photograph to minimize their aesthetic input and resume a certain degree of authenticity and reliability for the *Family Register*. At the same time, it has somehow reconstructed a less realistic or dramatic presentation for both memory and imagination.

Paradoxically, the conformity of people's collective could suddenly become hysteria. To many young artists who experienced the era in their childhood, the Cultural Revolution is not necessarily viewed as tragic, but rather carnivalesque, an entirely different world or even a dream world. Yang Fudong's black and white film, *Houfang – Hei, Tianliangle (Backyard – Hey, Sun is rising!)* (Fig. 62), interprets his revolutionary impression through a dream-like journey. It tells the story of a young man (or perhaps four) who attempt to capture those passing feelings just before waking in the morning. They all dress in the uniform and move as a team but in a somewhat hysterical way (Fig. 63). The artist writes poetically, "when the puppet-like indolence has been punctured by the dancing swords, they communicate within the loving indignation, hurt but never with pain … all the fragments present a discontinuous dream, which might be true, but would only happen within a fleeting moment just before the sun rises."[77]

The performance with dream-like excitement actually reminds us of the assemblies in Tiananmen Square during the Cultural Revolution. When Mao ascended Tiananmen for eight times to inspect his Red Guards in the summer of 1966, the fanatical energy behind conformity was exhaustively expressed. "At five o'clock in the morning,

---

76 Borysevicz, Mathieu, 'Zhuang Hui', in John Clark (ed.), *Chinese Art at the End of the Millennium*. Hong Kong: New Art Media, 2000, p. 252.

77 Artist statement. Text provided by Yang Fudong.

18 August 1966", as the *People's Daily* records, "Chairman Mao dressed in a green Army Uniform with a red star shining on his cap. Chairman Mao came through the Golden Water Bridge in front of the Gate into the masses, shaking hands with the masses ... at that moment, the whole square was suffused, people raised Mao's books in their hands on high, jumped and acclaimed ... and cried out, 'Chairman Mao is coming to us! Long live Chairman Mao ...'"[78] This excitement had been presented throughout all the mass assemblies of celebrations for national anniversaries or Mao's new instructions (Fig. 64). This reflects Durkheim's idea of a "collective effervescence", which "leads to outlandish behaviour whilst people's passions unleashed are so torrential that nothing can hold them. People are so far outside the ordinary conditions of life, and so conscious of the fact, that they feel a certain need to set themselves above and beyond ordinary morality... As a result of collective effervescence, they believe they have been swept up into a world entirely different from the one they have before their eyes."[79] The visual environment of the cult of Mao did not build a solemn religious atmosphere. Instead, it presented a liveliness and boisterousness consistent with Chinese traditional festivities (Fig. 65), or in other words, carnivals with nationalistic excitement liberated or transformed from conformity but, at the same time, within conformity.

Artist Liu Dahong recalled, "I was frequently awakened during the nights by the loudspeakers celebrating a revolutionary success. People would have movements for the revolution every single day and always keep themselves in a state of hysteric excitement."[80] The artist's two-panel painting *Shuangcheng Ji (A Tale of Two Cities)* (Fig. 66) is one example demonstrating this particular feature of the Cultural Revolution. The visual phenomenon, including big slogans, Mao's portraits, mass parades, Red Guard performances, and even the metaphors of the Great Helmsman were appropriated, reinterpreted and recomposed in a dramatic and almost surrealistic way. Another monumental work *Jitan (Sacrificial Altar)* (Figs. 67 and 68) is completed in a Western triptych-like form, which ironically presents a heavenly prospect. The god-like Mao dominates the centre of the painting installation, accompanied by his wife, Jiang Qing, and his pre-nominated successor, Vice Chairman Lin Biao, while on the back of the triptych, the members of the Gang of Four *(Siren Bang)* occupy the holy positions. All these political figures are juxtaposed with the roles of the Model Operas *(Yangban Xi)* and revolutionary representatives within a fairy tale-like scene that offers an absurd performance. As for folk festivals, people dressed in a variety of minority group costumes

---

78 '*Mao Zhuxi Tong Baiwan Qunzhong Gongqing Wenhua Da Geming* (Chairman Mao Celebrating the Cultural Revolution with Millions of Masses Altogether)', *Renmin Ribao (People's Daily)*, 19 August 1966, pp. 1–2.

79 Durkheim, Emile, translated by Fields, Karen E., *The Elementary Forms of Religious Life*. London: The Free Press, 1995, pp. 218–228.

80 Interview with Liu Dahong, 12 November 2003, Shanghai.

to fabricate the prosperity of Mao's era and represent the social environment of mass movement, a continuous carnival or, in Durkheim's term, the "collective effervescence".[81]

The collective in Tiananmen Square was depicted differently in Yue Minjun's 1993 painting *Dakuangxi (Great Joy)* (Fig. 69), in which people are lined up, having the same smirking face and frantic gesture. The lines of collective are to present a kind of "solidified and orderly force", which had been purposely embedded into the artist's childhood memory during the endless collective celebrations and parades.[82] Later in the same year, the artist began to put his own image into the work and sometimes duplicate it to create a crowd effect. While his self-image is constantly repeated, the power of an individual is then exaggerated by the increase in quantity and the generation of collective. For example, in his later works, such as *Taiyang (the Sun)* (Fig. 70) in 2000 and *Maihuai Haoqing (Lofty Sentiment)* (Fig. 71) in 1999, either the red sun or the red sea of flags in the background were employed as a historical and ideological hint, while the hectic laughter infinitely duplicated became a dominant sign of fanaticism. In Yue Minjun's 2003 work *Langman Zhuyi he Xianshi Zhuyi Yanjiu (Romanticism and Realism Study)* (Fig. 72), the beaming collective dashes out from the two dimensional canvas to replace the socialist group statues. The more carefully the original positions and poses of the statues were imitated by the artist, the more cynically the revolutionary ideology and the power from the heroic collective of worker-peasant-soldier are appropriated, represented and then transformed or, indeed, reverted into a carnival.

Yue Minjun's recent *Renshou Zhijian (Between Men and Beasts)* (Fig. 73) can be seen as a further reflection of this revolutionary fervour carried by the people's collective during the Cultural Revolution. The self-image has been even more plasticized with a pair of horns and raised hands moving with different unknown gestures. Had those arms been lifted high some forty years ago for the excitement? Are those images only referring to the artist himself? As outsiders, we could suddenly reveal the terror hidden behind the manic grin.

The same kind of carnival excitement can be found in Hu Jieming's series of photo-manipulated pictures *Raft of the Medusa*. The original painting, *Le Radeau de la Méduse (The Raft of the Medusa)*, was created by Theodore's Gericault in 1819. It commemorates the loss of the French government frigate *La Méduse* and the tragic fate of its passengers and crew.[83] On one level, Gericault's *Raft of the Medusa* looks like a neo-classical history

---

81 Durkheim, Op. cit., 1995, pp. 218–228.

82 Interview with Yue Minjun, 24 March 2006, Beijing.

83 It is recorded as a tragic story. When the ship *La Méduse* sank at sea, its captain and senior officers took the suitable lifeboats and consigned the other 150 persons to a makeshift raft, from which only fifteen survived.

painting; but it is also highly subversive, not depicting heroes with courageous endurance in any conventional sense, but a moment of profound human iniquity. This story would immediately remind those victims of the Cultural Revolution of Mao's famous metaphor, the Great Helmsman. Hu Jieming draws a parallel to events of the Cultural Revolution when tens of millions of Chinese intellectuals suffered atrociously for no good reason. However, by understanding the sadness of this background, Hu's skilful digital hands somehow turned the original into a raft of carnival (Figs. 74 and 75). It carries both revolutionaries and contemporaries, both Maoism and current ideologies from China's market economy, and is steered without direction.

The sails in Hu Jieming's raft are transformed from the red flags, which played an important role during the Cultural Revolution, were distributed through the mass parades and the activity of *Geming Dachuanlian* (Exchange Revolutionary Experience Travel), and permeated the individual cities, towns and work units. As an honoured Red Guard inspected by the chairman at Tiananmen Square, Li Xianting describes his visual memory: "nothing could replace the colour red. It was so red all the time. Red flags suffused everywhere as a slogan says, '*quanguo shangxia yipian hong* (the whole country awash in red)'. It was virtually a red sea. I felt it came as a huge red tide. I was extremely excited and could not help following it."[84] Zhou Hongxiang's *Red Flag Flies* was finished in 2002 (Fig. 76). In this video, the red flag is not only the contextual sign throughout the work but, more importantly, a baton for the performance or a symbol of power authorizing the 'correct' direction, which is stated in the revolutionary saying, "*yiqie xingdong ting zhihui* (all the actions must follow the command)". Most of the slogans appearing in the *Red Flag Flies* were selected from Mao's words, and each of the more than one hundred actors appears only once in the video. The video reinforces the centralization of political power and, at the same time, submerges individuality within a collective identity. As the artist states, "there is no main role in the story, and all people are equal in the performance."[85] The collective unconsciousness is more subtly revealed by Yang Zhenzhong in his *Spring Story* (Fig. 77), a video piece inspired by Deng Xiaoping's *Southern Campaign Speech (Nanxun Jianghua)* in 1992. The execution of the work involves 1,500 workers from the newly built Siemens factory in Shanghai. Each individual has a word or a phrase from Deng's speech to enunciate in the original order so that it ostensibly makes sense as it was intended. "The everyday lives of these people are spent concentrated on specific tasks, like many small jigsaw pieces adding up to a bigger picture of manufacturing achievement, as the small utterances amount to the articulation of some overarching vision. Yang's editing has the relentless mechanical quality of factory activity", as Jonathan Watkins discusses; "through his collaboration

---

84 Interview with Li Xianting, 24 February 2001, Beijing.

85 Interview with Zhou Hongxiang, 12 November 2003, Shanghai.

with the Siemens employees, Yang raises intriguing questions about the role of the individual, and the possibility of individualism, now in a country encouraging rampant foreign (capitalist) investment, but still communist at heart".[86]

In Beijing, Miao Xiaochun uses his camera to capture the neo-collectivization that can be seen as a continuance of the past assemblies. "If the collective fanaticism was political during the Cultural Revolution, it then turns to be economical after the Open-door policy". For example, "everyone would have a little red book in hand. But today, it has been replaced by a mobile handset, which now becomes an indispensable link between 'individual' and 'collective'" (Fig. 78). The artist continues that "one might feel extremely lost, either being abandoned by the revolutionary movement in the past, or today, lagging behind the economical development epitomized by those fashionable electronic devices."[87] In the giant photograph *Qing (Celebration)* (Fig. 79), Miao Xiaochun's digital skill secretly maximized the number of people who are participating in an estate business opening ceremony at Soho Beijing and created an enormous celebratory collective. In the recent work *Chao (Tide)* (Fig. 80), his hard work with computer has been subtly hidden to present an 'untouched' reality of busy Beijing, where individuals are drowned in the moving crowds and traffic or, indeed, in the image of collective with those unknown passing around and those known promoted visually in large scales.

Even in a remote place, such as the Old Silk Road on the north side of the Qilian Mountain, a minority group (Sunan Guyu Nation) can demonstrate a beautiful but fabricated identity of collective. Although the team members in Wang Chuan's *Shaoshu Jiti (Minority Collective)* (Fig. 81) are genuine minorities, the costumes purposefully are borrowed from their past rather than from what is worn today. This instant visual presentation is backed up or, in fact, divulged by the desolate geographical environment to offer an 'authentic' cultural mores of the minority in a collective manner as well as to respond to the curiosity of visitors and the development of the tourist industry.

If public loudspeakers, big-character slogans, and people's gesturing and shouting demonstrated the forceful inculcation through various media during the Cultural Revolution, what has stimulated a collective and identical excitement and fostered another carnival in today's China? In the revolutionary assemblies, people experienced themselves as grander than at ordinary times; they thought they were transformed into a new world and took responsibility to liberate others from the old; they felt, and at that moment really were, assembling for Mao and living a collective life that transported

---

86 Watkins, Jonathan, 'Medium and Message', in *Yang Zhenzhong*, exhibition catalogue. Birmingham: Ikon Gallery, 2006.

87 Interview with Miao Xiaochun, 22 March 2006, Beijing.

individuals beyond themselves. This carnivalesque atmosphere seems to be inherited from the revolutionary era to China's contemporary society, but at the same time, is transformed by different agendas, objectives and beliefs.

Burden or Legacy

The impact of the Cultural Revolution, either dominantly or implicitly, has been demonstrated in visual work through a variety of artistic approaches. Artists either have been depicting the Cultural Revolution itself with various personal experiences or reinterpreting the era by appropriating some identifiable elements as visual vocabularies. Evaluating the various ways of appropriation in the art practice will offer us further understanding of the artists' inspirations and motivations and, more importantly, the significance of the visual legacy or ponderousness of the burden from the Cultural Revolution.

In the 1994 performance *Jiehuo (Borrow a Light)*, Wu Shanzhuan borrowed a light from a security guard for his cigarette. Wu considers artists, in a sense, to be borrowers: "they borrow things but never return them, or borrow things, such as a light, that never need to be returned."[88] However, the questions for those borrowers are: what do you 'borrow' and how do you 'borrow'? The wit of the conscious appropriation and the subtlety of utilizing the visual vocabulary are, methodologically, of vital importance in the representation. However, to some, their unawareness of borrowing could be discovered for a different analysis.

In the arena of contemporary Chinese art after the Cultural Revolution, innovation of visual language was sought desperately by the artists to create a shortcut to distinguish themselves as the avant-garde from the 'conservatives'. Wu Shanzhuan discusses, "it is just like *huashan lunjian* (swordplay, or more generally, martial arts competition at Hua Mountain). Everyone at that moment tried to invent a unique skill to take advantage during the competition. I fortunately found the big-character poster as the strongest visual language of Chinese socialist art, and it is my invention of unique skill."[89] At the same time, Yu Youhan (Fig. 82) and Li Shan appropriated Mao as an iconographical imagery in their works, while Qi Zhilong has been in possession of the Red Guard for many of his large paintings (Fig. 83).

88 Interview with Wu Shanzhuan, 12 December 2003, Hong Kong.

89 Ibid.

Following the famous series *Mao Zedong*, Wang Guangyi also appropriated the great criticism images of the Cultural Revolution in the series *Da Pipan (Great Criticism)* (Fig. 84) that began in 1990. In these works, the artist deconstructs the language of symbols: slogans and images from the worker-peasant-soldier movements of the Cultural Revolution are juxtaposed with the logos of Coca-Cola, Marlboro, Cadbury and other famous consumer brands imported from abroad. This seemingly arbitrary combination of political and commercial symbols creates a humorous and absurd effect that carries with it a biting satire of both the ideology of the Mao era and the blind craze for the Western consumer products prevalent in today's China.

Sui Jianguo's *Legacy Mantle* (Fig. 85) distanced itself from art forms that parodied, ridiculed, criticized or satirized Mao as a political symbol. The artist tells us, "it seems that I was following the guideline of socialist art by discarding all the personalities that might be involved in the practice. In *Legacy Mantle*, I reproduced Mao's suit, just like a carpenter or a blacksmith, by avoiding any personal or artistic rendering."[90] In contrast with a more expressionistic mood, Mao Xuhui started his painting series *Jiazhang (The Parent)* (Fig. 86) in 1989. Without any realistic hint, one might ask who is the parent. But perhaps there is no need to have a certain answer: sometimes it could be a head in a work unit or a principal in a school; and sometimes, of course, it could be the leader of the country. *The Parent* has been a visual record of the artist's reflection on the complexity of politics, autocratic power and the structure of the social system in China. *Quanli de Cihui (The Vocabulary of Power)* (Fig. 87) is a conclusion of the painting series, and the visual vocabularies manifest and reinforce the orthodox authority. Rather than referencing directly any original image from the Cultural Revolution, Mao Xuhui sees the centralized political power as the core of the culture, reflects at an ideological level and responds with his expressionistic style. As he states paradoxically, "the more abstract the painting that I produce, the more explicit the image of 'the parent' can be a symbol in my mind".[91]

In Liu Dahong's surreal drama and Hu Jieming's *Raft*, one can easily recognize those familiar images from the Cultural Revolution, while Zhang Xiaogang and Zhuang Hui's intension seems more implicit. They are not interested in visual signs of the Cultural Revolution, rather, they revisit their personal experiences, appropriating conformable poses and revealing the human conditions of the era. Similarly, Qiu Zhijie inherits the revolutionary gestures in his photograph series *Hao (Fine)* (Fig. 88). The revolutionary ideals of the Mao era are easily recalled from the affected or, in the artist's words, the "fine standard"[92] gestures, while the past faith is mocked in a contemporary context.

---

90 Interview with Sui Jianguo, 31 October 2003, Beijing.

91 Interview with Mao Xuhui, 9 November 2003, Kunming.

92 Interview with Qiu Zhijie, 26 February 2000, Beijing.

From the late 1980s, mainland China witnessed at first a fitful then a nationwide revival of interest in Mao Zedong.[93] This phenomenon, which is termed '*Maore* (Mao-craze)', reflects people's nostalgia not only for Mao himself but also his era. Contemporary art obviously is a participant in the phenomenon, where artists tried to appropriate the past 'god' to satirize and criticize the current reality.[94] When the former leader and the revolutionary ideal were reshaped with popular and cynical vocabularies in a contemporary context, the original sacred significance was deconstructed on the one hand. On the other hand, in a sense, the Maoist ideology, people's enthusiasm and the communist Utopia of the era have been even more mystifying to new generations. Shao Yinong and Mu Chen's *Assembly Hall* and Wang Tong's *Vestiges of the Cultural Revolution* (Fig. 89) quietly present a visual documentation that offers a space for reflections upon the performance at the political events. In architecture design, the revolutionary spirit of the Cultural Revolution and the common memory of the excitement can be seen in today's nightclub, *Hongse Niandai (The Red Era)* (Fig. 90). The designer Liu Jiakun was trying to find some similarities between the revolutionary rebellion and the conceptions of today's new generation, and 'youth', 'passion' and 'violence' became the keywords throughout the design process to bridge the revolutionary legacy to the popular culture of today's youth life.[95]

The Chinese Cultural Revolution, as a political movement, was a disaster for the country. However, at the beginning of the twenty-first century, a different assessment might be possible. The literal meaning of 'Cultural Revolution' is rather positive. It can be read as, and it actually was, an attempt to re-establish the foundation of the Chinese culture. Contemporary Chinese art has developed dramatically since the end of the Cultural Revolution. It can be considered as a visual medium for personal response and, at the same time, as an outcome, including artists and their art, of the revolution. As Li Shan states, "I knew Mao since I was in kindergarten, where I learned my first song, *The East Is Red*, and the very first sentence, 'long live Chairman Mao'. Without Mao, who am I? I am meaningless; without Mao in my art, I would feel rather empty."[96] Indeed, without this particular reference, 'a great revolution that touches people to their very souls', one would have seen a completely different platform of contemporary art practice in China. The influence that an artist received from the experience can be very concrete to every single practice, including the style, the technical skills, the media and the manner of

---

93 Barmé, Op. cit., 1996, pp. 4–5.

94 Li Xianting, cited in Lü Peng, *Zhongguo Dangdai Yishu Shi (A History of Contemporary Chinese Art): 1990–1999*. Changsha: Hunan Fine Arts Publishing House, 2000, pp. 159–160.

95 Interview with Liu Jiakun, 3 November 2003, Chengdu.

96 Interview with Li Shan, 4 October 2000, Shanghai.

execution. Xu Bing argues, "if one tries to distinguish contemporary art in mainland China from that in Hong Kong, Taiwan or other regions, the baptism of the Cultural Revolution would be the key."[97]

It is now four entire decades since the beginning of the Cultural Revolution. The next generation might only be able to read the movement as a 'story' cited in textbooks. If the Cultural Revolution is simply a burden, one day, people eventually would be relieved of it. However, the Cultural Revolution has offered something more, and its influence has been embedded fully in contemporary Chinese culture. In the Post-Mao era, Chinese art has been developed at large in the international platform; through the lens of those sampled representative artists, we see a variety of reflections, reinterpretations and redefinitions of the Cultural Revolution. From a contemporary perspective, rather than a 'desert', the Cultural Revolution can be seen as a cultural complex and, indeed, a significant visual legacy giving birth to the new Chinese art in the context of today's art world.

97 Interview with Xu Bing, 21 November 2003, Manchester.

From Red Guard Art to Contemporary Art

Wang Mingxian

Beginning with the Stars (*Xingxing*) art exhibitions in 1979 and continuing through the 85 Art Movement, modern art in China has evolved over a period of about twenty years. Pivotal in the development of contemporary Chinese art was the period during 1985 and 1986 when a sudden rupture exposed many of the major problems that had arisen in Chinese art over the past 50 years. The emerging new wave has dominated the concepts and style of contemporary art ever since. The art of those two years also presented a sophisticated picture of contemporary Chinese culture.[1] Since the 85 Art New Wave Movement, there have been many contemporary Chinese artworks that tackle the subject of the Cultural Revolution and its art. Representative artists include Wu Shanzhuan, Gu Wenda, Xu Bing and Wang Guangyi who all regard Red Guard art and the socialist experience from a new perspective, creating contemporary works influenced by Cultural Revolution art.

So, from what angle should we view this epoch-making period in Chinese contemporary art? This leads to another question: how should we consider the art movement during the decade of the Cultural Revolution? Of course we can easily denounce this political

---

1 Gao Minglu (et al.) *Zhongguo Dangdai Meishushi (History of Contemporary Chinese Art): 1985–1986*. Shanghai: Shanghai People's Publishing House, 1991, p. 1.

movement, and criticise or mock the stereotypically 'red, bright, shiny, lofty, big and perfect' art styles prevalent during that period. We can even regard them as non-art. However, this 'pseudo-art' was created by many dedicated artists of the time. Mocking them would be equivalent to mocking ourselves. Rather, we should analyse and reflect upon the significance of that period of turmoil, its impact on social psychology, human nature and art outcomes.[2]

I argue that there are three areas of research concerning the influence of the Cultural Revolution art on contemporary art. The first is a historical study of the art of the Red Guards and the Cultural Revolution. The second is a case study of individual contemporary artists and their works. The third is a macroscopic study on the influences of the art of the Cultural Revolution on contemporary art, which is dependent on the results from the first and second areas of research. This paper will briefly review the Red Guard art movement and its influences upon contemporary Chinese art.

The Launch of the Red Guard Movement

The Red Guard art movement is one of the most important movements of the Cultural Revolution period, yet it is largely overlooked by art historians.

The Red Guards were pioneers of the Great Proletarian Cultural Revolution. It was said that, "the revolutionary initiative of the Red Guards has shaken the whole world. ... In the Great Proletarian Cultural Revolution, which was led by Chairman Mao, Red Guards have courageously and steadfastly struggled against those in authority who take the capitalist road, and against all 'ox-demons and snake-spirits (*niugui sheshen*)'; they have become trailblazers in the Great Proletarian Cultural Revolution. ... Red Guards are a new phenomenon on the eastern horizon."[3] Today, Communist Party historians consider that, "The political convictions of the Red Guards were wrong. But most young Red Guards were sincere in following the lead of Mao and the Party Central Committee to take the 'revolutionary rebel' road."[4]

At the same time young artists launched the Red Guard art movement, adding fuel to the flames of the Cultural Revolution. The Red Guard art movement was an important

---

2   Ibid, p. 24.

3   *Red Flag* Commentator, '*Hongweibing Zan* (In Praise of the Red Guards)', *Hongqi (Red Flag)*, No. 12, 1966. English translations: Michael Schoenhals (ed.), *China's Cultural Revolution, 1966–1969: Not a Dinner Party*, New York: M. E. Sharpe, 1996, pp. 43–45.

4   Wang Nianyi, *Da Dongluan de Niandai (Years of Great Turmoil)*. Zhengzhou: Henan People's Publishing House, 1988.

art phenomenon of the period and constitutes one of the three great myths of the Cultural Revolutionary arts alongside *Quotations from Chairman Mao* and political Model Operas. In the 1960s, the world was experiencing dramatic changes; the arts were also undergoing fundamental fission and reconstruction. Red Guard art was a fanatical product of centralised power and modern superstition, as well a 'red modernist' art form. In the present time of cultural diversification and growing familiarity with modern art of the West and East, it is now appropriate to review the Red Guard art movement.

On 16 May 1966 the Chinese Communist Party Politburo issued a circular launching the Cultural Revolution. The big-character poster appearing at Peking University campus on 25 May was regarded by Mao Zedong as the first Marxist big-character poster in the country, and broadcast and published in the press the following day. Mao said:

> Many comrades did not read the articles criticizing Wu Han and did not pay much attention to them ... Articles were written and meantime a Circular was issued on 16 May, but they did not arouse much attention. It was the big-character posters and actions of the Red Guards that drew your attention; you could not avoid it because revolution was upon you. As soon as the poster [big-character poster at Peking University] was broadcast, the whole country will be thrown into turmoil.[5]

On 18 August, a mass rally of a million people took place at Tiananmen Square. It was Mao Zedong's first meeting with Red Guards congregated from all over China. The following morning, the Red Guards went on a rampage in Beijing seeking to eradicate the 'Four Olds (*Sijiu*)', namely, old ideas, old culture, old customs and old habits. The Red Guards filled roads and streets, spreading big-character posters and leaflets, rallying the public with speeches and wildly attacking signs of the 'Four Olds'. Supported by broad masses of workers, peasants and soldiers, they ransacked the city and denounced subjects by making a public display of them or forcing them to wear tall caps. It was a campaign that swept through the whole country; 'revolutionary' ideals of aesthetics were influential above all. In their great manifesto *Declare War to the Old World*, the Red Guards declared that, "We are critics of the old world. We have to criticize and smash all old thoughts, old culture, old customs and old habits, with no exception to any barbers, tailors, photographic studios and old book stores serving the bourgeoisie. We are here to rebel against the old world!"[6]

---

5   Jin Chunming, *Wenhua da Geming Shigao (A History of the "Cultural Revolution")*. Chengdu: Sichuan People Publishing House, 1995, p. 174. English translations: Schoenhals (ed.), Op.cit., pp. 6–7.

6   Cited in Yan Jiaqi and Gao Gao, *Wenhua Da Geming Shinian Shi (The Ten-Year History of the Cultural Revolution)*. Hong Kong: Chaoliu Publisher, Vol. 1, 1989, p. 90.

At the beginning of the Cultural Revolution, the artists of the Red Guard were already in action, posting big-character posters, distributing leaflets, seizing 'reactionary art authorities' to put on public display, and creating propaganda pictures and caricatures. However, it was not until 1967 that the Red Guard art movement began formally, epitomized by the launching of Red Guard art newspapers, periodicals and exhibitions.

Red Guard Art Exhibitions

The Red Guard art reached its climax in 1967. On 5 February 1967, over twenty institutions of higher education in Beijing, together with rebel organizations and the People's Liberation Army (PLA), co-organized the *Smash the Liu-Deng [Liu Shaoqi and Deng Xiaoping] Reactionary Line Caricatures Exhibition* at the Beijing Observatory. Most exhibits had previously been displayed as big-character posters. The preface of the exhibition reproduces bold characters from *Quotations from Chairman Mao*, "To make literature and art serve well as a component of the whole revolutionary machine, as a powerful weapon to unite the people, educate the people, attack the enemy and defeat the enemy; to help the people in one heart struggle against the enemy". The first exhibit was a large portrait of Mao Zedong waving his hand. This work, together with a few others, depicts the heroism of Mao. There was another group of bitter satirical works expressing "revolutionary rebels hate and resent the stubborn elements that uphold the bourgeois reactionary line". In an exemplified caricature, a red hot sun representing Mao Zedong Thought radiates infinitely, while those carrying broken umbrellas are 'authorities taking the capitalist road' and stubborn elements clinging to the bourgeois reactionary line, resisting Mao Zedong Thought and seeking to destroy the Great Proletarian Cultural Revolution. The third group in the exhibition "exposes the counter-revolutionary characters of economism" and depicts revolutionaries responding to Mao Zedong's summon to "take firm hold of the revolution and stimulate production (*zhua geming cu shengchan*)". A representative caricature depicts a train, in front of which is a handful of wildly dancing 'ox-demons and snake-spirits', interpreted as, "the counter-revolutionary economism, and any conspiracies and tricks of the bourgeois reactionary line cannot stop the wheel of historical progress of the Great Proletarian Cultural Revolution". The last group of the exhibition features another caricature: two big hands — inscribed with the characters '*geming zaofanpai* (revolutionary rebels)' — firmly grasping a villain "representing the authorities taking the capitalist road and stubborn elements clinging to the bourgeois reactionary line" and who is perishing under attack by the revolutionary masses. At the exhibition, the 'Jinggangshan Regiment Red Guards' of Tsinghua University also presented their own slide shows *Take Firm Hold of the*

---

7 *Xinhua* News reporter, "Smash the Bourgeois Re-actionist Line", *Qianjun Bang (Heavy-weight Rod)*, No. 2, February 1967.

Revolution and Stimulate Production and Monkey King Conquers the White Boned Demon (new edition).

The *Xinhua* News reported that

> The whole exhibition was filled with a strong revolutionary passion; expressing the boundless love of the revolutionary masses for Chairman Mao and faithfully safeguarding Chairman Mao's revolutionary line; praising the rebel spirit of the unification and seizure of power by the Proletarian revolutionaries. Every caricature, like a sharp spear or dagger, relentlessly attacks the bourgeois reactionary line; thoroughly describes the ugly features of a handful of authorities taking the capitalist road. They reflect the immense significance and the bright prospect looking to the ultimate victory of the Great Proletarian Cultural Revolution.[7]

Obviously, this report was not a conventional art review that analysed the artistic value and visual techniques; rather, it emphasized the significant role of the exhibition during political struggle.

In May 1967, on the first anniversary of the Cultural Revolution, eighty-four revolutionary rebel groups in the capital — including the Workers Congress, Peasants Congress, PLA, Red Guards Congress, and revolutionary literary and art organizations — jointly presented the *Long Live the Victory of Mao Zedong Thoughts Revolutionary Painting Exhibition* (Fig. 91). As reported, "the exhibition is designated to open at the China National Art Museum on 23 May. A mass pledge will be taken on the preceding day to expose the black gang elements of literary and art circles to the public."[8]

On a larger scale, this exhibition featured several hundred prints, caricatures, propaganda pictures and drawings of new quotations. Works in praise of Chairman Mao's revolutionary line include:

- *Progress Successfully alongside Chairman Mao's Revolutionary Line on Literature and Art* by Military and Museum Revolutionary Rebels Group of PLA Military Museum
- *Safeguard Mao Zedong Thought to the Death* by 'Xinghuo Liaoyuan (literarily, a single spark starts a prairie fire) Revolutionary Rebels Group' of PLA Logistic Institute

---

8　*Meishu Zhanbao (Art War Bulletin)*, No. 4, May 1967.

- *Progress Successfully alongside Chairman Mao's Revolutionary Line on Literature and Art* by 'Anti-revisionist Regiment' of the Central Academy of Fine Arts Affiliated Middle School
- *The People's Revolution led by Mao Zedong Thought is the Locomotive of Historical Progress* by 'Mao Zedong Thought Propaganda and Combat Team' of Beijing Motors Section 27 Commune
- *Build the Whole Country into a Large School of Mao Zedong Thought* by 'Red Sun Propaganda Team' of Electronics Revolutionary Alliance
- *Praise the Issuance of the Great Historical Document 16 May Circular* collaboratively by 'Red Rebel Network' of Labour Union of Machine Tool Plant No. 1, 'Red Sun Propaganda Team' of Electronics Revolutionary Alliance, 'Red Brush' of Labour Union of Beiguang Electronic Tube Factory Revolutionary Committee and 'Little Red Soldier' of People's Art Publishing House

Critical propaganda images included:

- *Down with Liu* [Shaoqi] *and Deng* [Xiaoping] by 'Red Rebels Headquarters' of Labour Union of Beijing Silk Factory
- *Down with Liu Shaoqi, Criticise Black Cultivation* by 'East-is-Red Commune' of Labour Union of Beijing Motors Company
- *Smash Totally the Handful of Counter-revolutionary Revisionists* by 'Red Brush' of Labour Union of Beijing Machine Tool Plant No. 2, among others

There were many caricatures attacking Liu Shaoqi in the exhibition, from which the organizing team compiled a catalogue — *Selection of Caricatures from Long Live the Victory of Mao Zedong Thought Revolutionary Painting Exhibition* — and included:

- *Liu's Fishing Tool Store* by East Is Red Art Soldier of Beijing City Publishing House
- *Play Tricks* by People's Publishing House and Zunyi Regiment of Peasants' Literature Publishing House
- *Clippings of Secret History* and *Miscellaneous Scenes* by Little Red Soldier Combat Regiment of People's Art Publishing House
- *Chanting Revisionist Scripts, Axle* and *Revolutionary Heritage* by Red Rebels Soldier of Labour Union of Capital Applied Art Association
- *Ego Analysis on Liu's 'Cultivation'* by Xinghuo Liaoyuan Regiment of the Central Academy of Fine Arts

Among the many provocative exhibits, there was a humorous polychrome sculpture *An Old Couple Studying Selected Works of Mao Zedong* by Red Rebels Column Temporary Revolutionary Committee of Beijing Polychrome Sculpture Factory, depicting a genre scene of an old couple in popular style.

This revolutionary art exhibition was highly influential. The artworks were reported to "have been filled with love and adoration for Chairman Mao, and celebrate the success of his revolutionary line. There were also many whimsical caricatures that denounced the crimes of China's Khrushchev, Liu Shaoqi."[9] This exhibition was regarded as "representing the culmination of Chairman Mao's revolutionary line on literature and art, a glorious celebration of the Proletarian Cultural Revolution, and a joyous occasion in the history of Chinese art!"[10]

As a 'revolutionary' art exhibition, it was reviewed not by professionals, but the masses of worker-peasant-soldier. One of the renowned 'model learners' of the works of Chairman Mao, Wei Fengying, commented that:

> The broad masses have picked up their brushes to praise our dearest great leader Chairman Mao. Each work glitters with the glory of Mao Zedong Thought, showing scenes of our great leader with the masses and of one mind with them. The success of this exhibition echoes with the great victory of the invincible Ma Zedong Thought! This is the result of the living study and application of the works of Chairman Mao by the workers, peasants and soldiers! It is a great victory for Chairman Mao's line on literature and art, and a great victory for the Great Proletarian Cultural Revolution.[11]

Another 'model learner' Li Suwen said:

> This is a solemn declaration to all the revolutionary people in the world, equipped with Mao Zedong Thought, the workers, peasants and soldiers have conquered art. They have picked up their brushes to praise our great leader Chairman Mao! Every painting depicts scenes of our dearest great leader Chairman Mao with and of the masses. They also reflect the devotion of workers, peasants and soldiers in their limitless love for our great leader Chairman Mao.[12]

In the afternoon of 25 May 1967, *The Long Live the Victory of the Great Proletarian Cultural Revolution Touring Art Exhibition* (Fig. 92) opened in Tiananmen Square; it then toured to Beijing's factory suburbs, peasant communes and troops. There were over 150 exhibits, including portraits of Mao Zedong and other paintings, woodcuts, caricatures

---

9　'The Great Alliance of Revolution, the New Art Exhibition of Battles', *Manjianghong (Crimson Flooding into the River)*, No. 4, July 1967.

10　*Meishu Fenglei (Art Tempest)*, No. 1, June 1967.

11　A joint issue of *Meishu Zhaobao (Art War Bulletin)*, No. 5, and *Wuchanzhe Huakan (Pictorial of Proletarian)* No. 3, July 1967, p. 4.

12　Ibid.

and paper-cuts that depicted the glories of Mao Zedong Thought, his famous *Three Old Essays*, the Red Guards and the Model Operas, and commemorated the twenty-fifth anniversary of Mao's *Talks at the Yan'an Forum on Literature and Art*. Major works included the painting *Long Live the Victory of the Proletarian Revolutionary Line Led by Chairman Mao* and the woodcut prints: *Study Mao's Three Old Essays as Motto, Let the New Socialist Literature and Art Conquer All Stages, the Great Proletarian Revolutionaries Grasp the Political Power Firmly*, and *Down with Liu Shaoqi! Criticise the Black 'Cultivation'* (Fig. 93). Another two most influential woodcut prints *Sail with Chairman Mao in Braving Storms and Long Live Marxist Mao Zedong Thought* (Fig. 94), by Shen Yaoyi from the Central Academy of Fine Arts, were also exhibited. This exhibition was organized entirely by the Red Guards, including the Revolutionary Rebels Commune of the Ministry of Railway Fengtai Bridge Construction, Red Flag of Beijing Power Station, Revolutionary Alliance and Red Flag of the Central Academy of Fine Arts, Beijing Commune of the Central Conservatoire, Jinggangshan of the Central Academy of Arts and Crafts, and another Jinggangshan of the Beijing Film Academy.

People were pleased the way in which this touring exhibition served the workers, peasants and soldiers. As a visitor commented, "in the past we had no time to visit any exhibition [in an exhibition hall], but today we can enjoy art on our way home". And the other said, "When we were ruled under the 'Four Olds', literature and art did not serve the workers, peasants and soldiers directly, whilst today, art has been brought to our life," he continued, "This is the first exhibition of this kind for seventeen years after the Liberation, and even the first time in history. Previously, we workers would have no time to visit an art exhibition if it took place only in big museums in the cities, isolated from the ordinary life." Furthermore, in terms of organization of the exhibition, one remarked, "exhibitions in the past were only organised by specialists, who would not present exhibitions to factories or villages. But this time, the exhibition is created by ourselves and comes to our factory, demonstrating the victory of the Cultural Revolution!"[13]

In October 1967, this touring exhibition was ready for a nationwide art exhibition. On the eighteenth anniversary of the founding of the People's Republic, *The Long Live the Victory of Chairman Mao's Revolutionary Line Art Exhibition* was opened at the China National Art Museum. On an unprecedented scale, it featured over sixteen hundred items of classical Chinese paintings, oil paintings, prints, propaganda pictures, clay sculptures and handicrafts. The exhibition team travelled with a number of the exhibits as well as with slides of other exhibits and presented these in villages and mountain regions. An official review of the exhibition reads:

---

13 Ibid.

> These revolutionary artworks were created by the workers, peasants and soldiers, Red Guards and revolutionary artists holding high the great red banner of Mao Zedong Thought and following closely Chairman Mao's great strategy during the Great Proletarian Cultural Revolution. It was created during the life-and-death battle against China's Khrushchev and his fellow leaders who take the capitalist road. The artworks were not only from Beijing, the centre of the Cultural Revolution, but also Shanghai, Guizhou, Qingdao, Wuhan, and from the corps, villages, mines and schools, all parts of the country. More than 70 percent of the exhibits were created by the workers, peasants and soldiers [amateur artists], and reflect their lives during struggle.[14]

Most works of the exhibition are expressions of the 'infinite trust, love, faith and adoration' of Mao Zedong, including *Chairman Mao Stands atop Tiananmen; Chairman Mao Arrives at Jinshui Bridge; Ten Millions of Sunflowers Blossom Facing the Sun; Chairman Mao Stays with the Red Guards; Chairman Mao Established the Party in the Regiment; The Red Sun Brightens up Anyuan; Chairman Mao Stays with Us — Returning from Beijing;* and *Following Chairman Mao, the Whole World is Red.*

Representative pieces are oil works *The East is Red* (Fig. 95), woodcut prints *the Great Historical Document* (Fig. 96), woodcut series *Long Live Chairman Mao,* and the Chinese paintings *Bombard the Headquarters* and *My Big-Character Poster.* The large oil painting, *The East is Red,* uses bright colours to depict Mao Zedong, Lin Biao, Zhou Enlai, Jiang Qing, Chen Boda and Kang Sheng meeting the Red Guards at Tiananmen. *The Great Historical Document* manifests the Chairman issuing the *16 May Circular,* which "sounds loudly the horn of the Great Proletarian Cultural Revolution", with the background depicting Marx, Engels, and Lenin and Stalin, as a representation of the three stages of the development of Marxism. The woodcut series *Long Live Mao Zedong,* by the Red Guards from the Beijing New Normal College, depicts the historical achievements of Mao by highlighting significant events as milestones in the Chinese revolution, from the early establishment of the Communist Party, to the founding of the People's Republic of China, and then to the launching of the Cultural Revolution.

Artists passionately depicted the fervour of Revolution: from popular prints to badges worn by every fighter; from giant mural paintings to window paper-cuts; and from spectacular large clay sculptures to meticulous ivory carvings. One of the most significant exhibits was the sculpture, *Odes to the Red Guards,* depicting the Red Guards destroying

---

14 Art Critic Panel of the Central Art Administration, 'Odes to Chairman Mao's Revolutionary Line: Reviews on the Long Live the Victory of Chairman Mao's Revolutionary Line Art Exhibition', *Xin Meishu (New Art),* No. 1, 1967.

the 'Four Olds' and replacing them with the 'Four News'. This large-scale work is a collaborative work by PLA fighters, Red Guards and revolutionary professional sculptors that "aims to destroy the bastions of bourgeois thought with odes to Chairman Mao's revolutionary line. Only today has the China National Art Museum truly become the propaganda battlefield of Mao Zedong Thought."[15] Astonishingly, the sculpture was completed in only twenty days and considered as "being unprecedented in the world history of sculpture"[16]; it is, of course, one of the prominent pieces in the Red Guard art movement.

Red Guard Art Publications

In 1967, Red Guard organizations exerted their influence on art institutes throughout the country. At the same time, numerous Red Guard art newspapers and pictorials appeared, collaboratively and interactively working with the Red Guard art exhibitions. If the Red Guard art exhibitions were works of both professionals and the many more non-professionals, then it was obvious to have two categories of Red Guard art publications, including newspapers, leaflets and periodicals: one by revolutionary rebel organizations in the art field, and the other by amateur visual propagandists.

The rise of Red Guard art newspapers and periodicals in 1967, especially in Tianjin and Beijing, was almost a miracle in the history of Chinese art. The most influential examples by professionals (mainly art students) are *Art War Bulletin* (Fig. 97) by ten organizations including Xinghuo Liaoyuan Revolutionary Regiment of the Central Academy of Fine Arts; *Red Art* by Revolutionary Alliance and Red Flag Regiments of the Central Academy of Fine Arts; *Crimson Flooding into the River* (Fig. 98) by East-is-Red Commune of the Central Academy of Arts and Crafts; *Red Artist Soldiers* (Fig. 99) by Revolutionary Rebels Committee Propaganda Office of Tianjin People's Publishing House; *Art Soldiers* (Fig. 100); *Worker-Peasant-Solider Pictorial* (Fig. 101); *New Art* (Fig. 102); and *Maps War Bulletin* (Fig. 103) and *Art Tempest* (Fig. 104) by the Great Student Union of the Central Academy of Fine Arts. However, there were many more local and non-professional Red Guard art publications, and it is impossible to estimate the total number of Red Guard publications.

The inaugural issue of *Art Tempest* declared, "all ideas and efforts focus on one thing: seizing power. We are here to drag out 'the big snakes and small snakes, the black

---

15 Ibid.

16 Cai Qing, '*Yongyuan Genzhe Mao Zhuxi Nao Geming: Ping Nisu "Hongweibing Zan"* (Always Follow Chairman Mao to Carry out Revolution: on the Clay Sculpture "the Odes to the Red Guards")', *Xin Meishu (New Art)*, No. 2, December 1967.

snakes and white snakes, the snakes with poisonous teeth and snakes disguised as pretty women in the art field', to seize power for the proletariat, and lighting the art field with the infinitely bright sky of Mao Zedong Thought, turning the land of art into a fertile land of the workers, peasants and soldiers."[17] This demonstrates that Red Guard art publications acted as a sharp sword in the centre of the 'revolutionary' struggle as well as a motet praising the Chairman and his Proletarian Revolutionary Line.

Closely related to political developments, the caricature became the main medium in the Red Guard art publications to criticize Liu Shaoqi, one of the communist successors and whom Mao called a "dangerous figure like Khrushchev sleeping next to us". Examples attacking Liu and his 'bourgeois reactionary line' or 'black cultivation' could be seen in every Red Guard art periodical and general Red Guard tabloid. In *Art War Bulletin* alone, there was a total of 142 caricatures criticizing Liu in the first six issues, and some of those almost were turned into a 'special issue of Liu Shaoqi caricatures'. Even more, the two caricature series, the *Ugly Histories of Revisionist Liu* and *Criticise Black Cultivation* were published in *Crimson Flooding into the River* and *Worker-Peasant-Solider Pictorial*, respectively; and the 120-illustration series *Down with Liu Shaoqi – China's Khrushchev* was published by Jinggangshan Propaganda Office of Red Guards Congress of Tsinghua University. Within the caricature campaign, the appearance of the work *A Swarm of Uglies* by Weng Rulan signified a turning point in caricature style, which had evolved from the humorous sketches of the artist Feng Zikai in the 1920s, to the international political satirical style exemplified by Hua Junwu in the 1950s and 1960s, and eventually to become a weapon in the class struggle. After the publication of *A Swarm of Uglies*, this style of caricature was rapidly adopted and designed as *Reference Materials of Revolutionary Critique Caricature*.[18] These caricatures depicted the central leaders Liu Shaoqi, Deng Xiaoping and Tao Zhu; Qi Baishi or Mei Lanfang of the literary and art circles; and 'imperialists and reactionaries', such as Americans, Soviet revisionists and Jiang Jieshi.

Importantly, the original works of Red Guard art, particularly from the early Cultural Revolution, increasingly become unavailable because they were considered political products and were not preserved. Their visual records in Red Guard art publications, which are also disappearing, become highly valuable as primary sources for future research.

---

17 *Meishu Fenglei (Art Tempest)*, No. 1, May 1967.

18 *Meishu Geming (Art Revolution)*, No. 9, September 1967, pp. 2–3.

Red Guard Contemporary Art

The Red Guard art movement in 1967 was a landmark in the development of Cultural Revolution art. Its second peak was represented by the national art exhibition on the commemoration of the 30th anniversary of Mao Zedong's *Talks at the Yan'an Forum on Literature and Art* in 1972, during which many classic red [revolutionary] artworks were created. In this exhibition, art practice seemed to return to the institutional arena, presenting more sophisticated skills to emphasize themes of celebration; the style of Red Guard art in the first half of the movement had been characterized by a strong rebel spirit, crude yet powerful, and was considered only as a political instrument with no artistic value.

The official publication *Contemporary Chinese Art* comments that Cultural Revolution art was

> Unprecedented in human history, and would be difficult to replicate in the future. It was considered to have been detached from, and to have distorted the basic spirit of Mao Zedong's *Talks at the Yan'an Forum on Literature and Art*. Though it claimed to uphold the spirit, it totally denied Chinese and Western cultures, and was considered an extremely Leftist ideological form of art. Cultural Revolution art was thought to damage Contemporary Chinese art and go against the rules of art so that it almost lost its essence.[19]

Nevertheless, ideas about art and aesthetics have continued to evolve; since the 1980s, Chinese art has diversified. New artists are able to revisit Red Guard art with contemporary concepts and reflect upon the influences of the Cultural Revolution in their own art. During the 85 Art New Wave Movement, for example, in the *Red-Black-White* exhibition by a group of Zhejiang artists, Wu Shanzuan's *Red Characters*, his first work in the *Red Humour* series, has been considered as a representative visual response to the Cultural Revolution. In the paper installation, all interior surfaces from floor to ceiling were covered with red characters and then layers of red paper, some of which were then removed arbitrarily, simulating the big-character posters of the Cultural Revolution (Fig. 24). In the New China Art exhibition of 1989, Wang Guangyi's *Mao Zedong* (Fig. 37) and Xu Bing's *Book from the Heaven* (Fig. 105) also show traces of Cultural Revolution art.

---

19 Wang Qi (ed.), *Dangdai Zhongguo Meishu (Contemporary Chinese Art)*. Beijing: Contemporary China Publishing House, 1996, pp. 24–25.

Reflecting on his practice of the *Book from the Heaven*, Xu Bing stated:

> I understand that I have to seriously work out this project. When one is extremely serious and intensely involved in an act, the power of art will emerge. You cannot just write out some characters, you must logically design your characters, carve them and print them ultimately the absurdity of the act will become intense. The book turns out to be fantastic, like a sacred script. With such a beautiful and serious book, how could one not to read it with content? Every day I used my hands to carve these characters. It's a laborious job. I spent a year creating over 2,000 characters, which were exhibited in an art museum in 1988. Later I had them reprinted in the ancient style by a printing house specialising in the reproduction of ancient books.[20]

On the audience's comments, Xu recalled:

> At the first show in the west over ten years ago, the characters were interpreted from a more political perspective. Some people said that the work was a reflection on big-character posters. In fact, this work was performed with no didactic intention and represents instead a space without a definition. It is filled with contradiction and absurdity. Some said it is de-constructive and anti-cultural, for I have totally de-constructed the whole writing system. It may have involved a disrespectful and mocking attitude to culture. However, from the perspective of an installation, it is particularly respectful to books. When visitors enter the exhibition hall, they fall silent. This is because the space looks like an altar. Some western academics have said that one feels the urge to kneel down in front of it. That places culture on a pedestal but it is also mocking in nature.[21]

Xu Bing created the performance piece *Golden Apples as Gift of Tender Sentiments* (Fig. 106) in 2002, using memories of 'socialist tender sentiments' of a generation as the inspiration for building an art form and language. "It is based on different people intersecting at the point when reality becomes historical fact in China, to arouse awareness of the immense changes in the Chinese society. It is not a change in colour but in quality."[22] If one takes *An Analyzed Reflection of the World* as alluding to the first Marxist big-character poster at Peking University, then *Golden Apples as Gift of Tender*

---

20 *Nanfang Zhoumo (Southern Weekend)*, 29 November 2002.

21 Ibid.

22 Gao Minglu and Wang Mingxian (eds.), *Fengzhou: Contemporary Art Exhibition (Harvest: A Contemporary Art Exhibition)*, exhibition catalogue. Hong Kong: Building Review Publishing, 2004, p. 35.

Sentiments directly interprets 'socialist tender sentiments'. Xu Bing takes the socialist experience as a source of inspiration for contemporary artists claiming that:

> The cultural nutrition and experience constituents of my generation lie not in traditional culture, but the socialist culture or the culture of the Cultural Revolution. Though the Cultural Revolution is gone, its influences can be reflected at a deeper level. Work reflects an artist like a mirror. My works have aroused my recognition about the significance of the relationship between the Cultural Revolution and contemporary Chinese culture, as well as our need to positively envisage this cultural background and its integration into the construction of the macro-culture of the future.[23]

Many contemporary Chinese artists developed energetic artworks that are closely related to Cultural Revolution art, especially Red Guard art. For artists, the Cultural Revolution "provided a visual modality forged from the socialist experience of a certain period", rather than only, "a negative impact on the political and social development of the country".[24] It is sad to see that Cultural Revolution art, particularly Red Guard art, has left few traces. If not preserved properly and timely, these invaluable historical materials and their relevance to art history may be lost forever. Some ten years ago, I proposed the building of a Cultural Revolution museum, which I still insist is important today. This could surely form the foundations for in-depth research on art during the Cultural Revolution, especially the Red Guard art movement, and contemporary Chinese art.

---

23 Ibid.

24 *Wang Guangyi*. Hong Kong: Timezone 8, 2002, p. 54.

The Image of Mao Zedong and Contemporary Chinese Art

Yan Shanchun

Mao Zedong led China in revolution for half a century, during which Chinese societies underwent drastic transformations; at the same time, art in China also experienced the unprecedented reforms in its ideologies and presentations. Bearing the mark of the revolutionary era, Chinese art became a unique chapter in art history of the world. Mao has not been erased from people's memory, even after his death. Maoist thoughts on literature and art, and indeed his image, were the imperative factors in Chinese art movements in the entire later half of the twentieth century.

Some General Issues about Mao's Image in Artworks

The images of Mao Zedong in Chinese art, especially after the Cultural Revolution, are derived primarily from Mao's photographs taken from his daily life. These photographs benefited from the developments of portraiture-making since the invention of photography in the mid-nineteenth century but, more significantly, from the influence of Soviet paintings of communist leaders and the convention for portraiture production.

There have only been two known artists in China who painted life sketches of Mao Zedong: one is Yin Shoushi and the other is Shen Yiqian. Artists' portraits of the

Chairman normally were based on Mao's photographs; he had personal photographers, but not personal painters. Even Liu Wenxi, as one of the most experienced portraitists for Mao, almost entirely relied on photographs for his paintings. Artworks with Mao's image were primarily produced in the forms of *nianhua* (New Year pictures) and *xuanchuanhua* (propaganda prints); subsidiary artworks were oil paintings, *guohua* (traditional Chinese paintings), prints and sculptures. The style of Maoist New Year pictures originated from traditional New Year woodcut prints, while the propaganda prints were influenced by the New Year calendars. At the same time, modern Western woodcuts and Soviet paintings offered suggestions ideologically and aesthetically for the depictions of Mao and his historical moments.

Although Mao Zedong was deified in his portraitures during the propaganda, there was little influence from Western iconographic paintings and Chinese Buddhist art. The propaganda art of Mao during the Cultural Revolution simply used the composition of a generic iconographic painting in which God usually was located in the centre with a golden or yellow background. If the halos in Buddhist and Christian art are merely an abstract but symbolic form, Mao's halo actually depicts the radiating rays of the sun, which had been a metaphor of the Chairman. Although the theme 'the east is red, the sun is rising' first appeared in paintings of the early 1950s, the image of Mao and the sun had not been juxtaposed until the launch of the Cultural Revolution. There are two reasons to exclude the influence of Buddhist and Western religious paintings on Mao's portraiture production. First, the portraitists were trained mainly in revolutionary art academies, such as Lu Xun Academy of Fine Arts and Literature, during the 1930s and 1940s, and would hardly have any relevant experience in religious paintings of folk art. Second, although Mao accepted the idea of personal cult as a political strategy and that, as a Communist leader, he had been worshiped like a 'god', it was not possible for him to acknowledge and promote either the Christian or Buddhist iconography during the propaganda.

Undoubtedly, there are many complicated social and political implications regarding the image of the leader of a great nation. Chinese artists were governed by certain doctrines and conveyed them visually in their paintings. The first issue is that of 'height'. The establishment of the People's Republic marked a new phase for Mao's image making; good examples include Luo Gongliu's *Chairman Mao at Jinggang Mountain* and Li Qi's *Chairman Travelling across the Whole Country*. During a meeting in 1958, Mao suggested that, among the great Marxists, he was the same height as Stalin, if not even taller, and this should be presented that way. Mao complained that, "In the early 1950s, when Chinese artists painted pictures of Stalin and me, I am always shorter than Stalin, as if blindly succumbing under the Soviet power of that time."[1] The 'height problem', in fact,

---

1 Maurice J. Meisner, *Marxism, Maoism and Utopianism* (translated version in Chinese). Beijing: Central Documentary Press, 1991, p. 170.

hid interpretations of political supremacy between China and the Soviet Union. Since the 1950s, China had been using the hierarchical order of Marx, Engels, Lenin, Stalin, Mao to describe the status of the Communist leaders. During the Cultural Revolution, however, Mao was raised above the other four leaders in the hearts of Chinese people, as a figure of ingenuity and sacredness with his great revolutionary achievements.

Li Qi and Feng Zhen worked hard to tackle the issue of height in their collaborative work *The Great Meeting*, which depicts a scene of Mao meeting Stalin in the Soviet Union. At a glance, Stalin, who is in the foreground, appears to be taller than Mao, but according to the principles of perspective, Stalin actually is shorter than Mao when repositioned onto the same horizontal line.

What is interesting is that, following the changes in propaganda strategies, the heights of the leaders in paintings also changed. For example, there are significant differences in the height of Mao and the other four leaders in the work *Long Live the Great Marxism, Leninism and Maoism* by the Shaanxi Art Group, while Mao's height is even greater in Wang Zhaoda's 1968 painting *Mao Zedong Thoughts are the Pinnacle of Contemporary Marxism and Leninism* (Fig. 107).

The second issue of 'size' also reflected the political superiority of that particular historical moment. Influenced by Soviet Socialist realism, the treatment of space in new Chinese oil paintings basically was representational rather than conceptual. Thus, in almost all of the thematic paintings, the figure of Mao conforms to normal visual perception. However, during the Cultural Revolution, this legacy of realistic depiction had been readjusted to meet the needs of the extreme political ideologies and people's revolutionary fervour.

The oil painting *The East Is Red* (Fig. 95) was created in 1967 by the Anti-revisionist Regiment of the Central Academy of Fine Arts Affiliated Middle School under the Beijing Middle School Red Guards' Congress. The chiaroscuro and spatial treatment in the painting primarily are representational, but the arrangement of figures evidently holds some conceptual characteristics. Mao's frontal figure is situated in the centre of the painting, while Lin Biao on Mao's right and Zhou Enlai on his left have smaller figures; Lin Biao is shown with a full-face and Zhou Enlai with a profile. The key members of the Central Group of the Cultural Revolution, such as Chen Boda, Kang Sheng and Jiang Qing, follow but, likewise, in diminishing scale. The portraits of ancient Chinese emperors use diminishing scale as a measurement of hierarchical status of the emperors, while the New Year picture of the sacred horse manipulates both scale and orientation of the figures. Indeed, the hierarchical structure in *The East Is Red* may be mirrored by Western religious art in the Middle Ages, for example, in the Byzantine mosaic work *The Miracle of the Loaves and Fishes*.

The third issue is about 'left or right'. Images of Mao's profile, especially on commemorative badges, are mostly of his left side. This is related to the wide dissemination of Wang

Chaowen's 1950 work, which was generally accepted as the standard model for Mao's relief. In ancient Egyptian, Roman and Greek memorabilia, the orientation of the figure does not appear to hold any specific meaning. Left profile orientations are more common, perhaps due to the convenience of execution by right-handed artists. However, in the Cultural Revolution, the left-orientated Mao as the standard image applied to all visual productions indicates his support for the leftists during the political campaigns.

The Historical Development of Mao's Image

The development of Mao's image can be discussed in four phases: first, from the early 1930s to 1950; second, from 1950 to 1966; third, from 1966 to 1976 (the decade of the Cultural Revolution); and fourth, after the Chinese Economic Reform or, more accurately, since Wang Guangyi's *Mao Zedong* appeared in 1987. Between 1977 and 1987, the artworks of Mao's image appeared indistinctive in style, content and function, and offered little significance in the course of Chinese art history.[2]

During the first phase, the image of Mao was primarily used in a practical manner, for example, as book and newspaper covers, assembly hall decorations, demonstration banners and stamps. They were mostly in the format of woodblock prints because of limited wartime materials, as well as Lu Xun's promotion of the New Woodblock Movement. The image of Mao during this period was rather abbreviated and less adorned, giving the impression of being any leader of the masses, or even a leader of a guerrilla troop. The earliest extant record of Mao's image being used in a publication is *Mao Zedong*, published in *Geming huaji* (Compilations of Revolutionary Paintings) by Red China Publishing House in 1933. At the time, the production of Mao's image usually was unprompted and voluntary on the part of the artists. Although the Central Committee had organized the production of art for some important events, the committee lacked scope and officials to oversee it. This was the situation even for the Lu Xun Academy of Fine Arts and Literature in Yan'an. The representative works of this period include Wang Shikuo's colour woodcut *Picture of Chairman Mao* and Shi Lu's colour woodcut print *Gathering of the Heroes*.

Since the founding of the People's Republic, the artistic production of Mao's images had entered the second phase. In the so-called standard portraits of the Chairman directly

---

2   For further details, see Yan Shanchun, Wang Mingxian and Yang Haocheng, '*Mao Zedong zhixiang yanjiu* (A Study on the Image-making of Mao Zedong)', *Shehui zhuanxing yu meishu yanjin — jinian zhongguo meishuguan jianguan sishi zhounian xueshu yantaohui wenji (Social Transformation and Art Evolution — Collection of Articles at the Symposium on the Commensuration of the 40th Anniversary of the Establishment of the China National Art Gallery)*. Beijing: China Literary Alliance Publishing House, 2004.

governed by the Central Propaganda Department, Mao already exemplifies the charm of a great national leader, who looks not only solemn and dignified, but also amiable and benign. At the same time, the Central Committee and many regional art organizations also established Revolutionary Painting Commissions that stimulated the rise of narrative paintings depicting the historical moments of Mao during revolution. Usually, with the assistance of photographs and influenced by Soviet paintings, Mao would be portrayed plainly and situated near the centre among the mass crowd, showing his affability for the people. These paintings were dominant at the opening exhibition of the National Museum of Chinese Revolution and the Military Museum of Chinese People's Revolution in 1961. Significantly, during the late 1950s, Chinese artists began to explore the possibility of appropriating traditional visual elements into their thematic practice, for example Luo Gongliu's oil painting experiment *Chairman Mao at Jinggang Mountain* in Chinese *guohua* style and Shi Lu's Chinese ink-wash painting *Crusading to Northern Shaanxi*, in which revolutionary motifs were freshly introduced. Other representative works of this period include Wang Chaowen's sculpture in relief *Portrait of Chairman Mao*, Luo Gongliu's oil painting *Chairman Mao Reporting about Rectification at the Cadre Meeting in Yan'an*, Jin Shangyi's oil painting *Chairman Mao at the December Meeting*, Cai Liang's oil painting *The Son of a Poor Peasant* and Peng Bin's oil painting *the Long Impregnable Pass is Really like Steel*.

The third phase can be divided into two parts. During the first half, from 1966 to 1969, there was an overproduction of Mao's images because of the pressing need to deify him. Although this activity was started by the Central Group of the Cultural Revolution, the practice and promotion of the works were organized spontaneously by the masses. The artistic quality of these works varied and the image of Mao had been completely idolized. In many of them, Mao appears to be a star, with his glowing face. The horizon line of the paintings is often very low, and the background usually is unrealistic and theatrical, either with a glorious golden immensity or a red sea of flying flags. This is closely related to wide promotion of stage photos of the political Model Operas. A variety of 'standardized' Mao images, especially in woodcut style, appeared during this period, for example, Shen Yaoyi's *Long Live Chairman Mao – Chairman Mao Portrait Prints Collection* (Fig. 108). These model prints not only satisfied the need for their reproduction in newspapers, leaflets, billboards and posters, but also provided amateur art propagandists with some visual reference that easily could be imitated and appropriated, interestingly, similar to the *Painting Manual of the Mustard-Seed Garden* in traditional Chinese painting practice.

The establishment of the Cultural Group of the State Council in 1971 marked the second half of this phase, when the production of Mao paintings across the country began to be centralized by the government and steered by the Assessor Group and the Adaptor Group, consisting of political leaders and art professionals. An unprecedented quantity of Mao artworks appeared during the following five to six years, and the Chairman became the primary subject chosen for the National Art Exhibitions. Generally, in comparison with the artworks from the previous two periods (1930–1950 and 1950–1966), Mao's image from the third period appeared more prominently with '*hong guang liang* (red, smooth, and luminescent)' and '*gao da quan* (lofty, big and perfect)'. Again, the image of Mao basically was appropriated from photographs, evidently altered and conceptualized for its perfection. Although the composition and appearance of figures were patterned after Soviet paintings of their leaders, the brightness of the colours was different from the Soviet style and showed the characteristics of Chinese oil paintings in the revolutionary era. The representative works of this period include Tang Xiaohe's oil painting *Forging ahead in Wind and Waves* (Fig. 109) in 1966 and, more importantly, Liu Chunhua's oil painting *Chairman Mao Goes to Anyuan* (Fig. 34). In 1968, Liu Chunhua's painting was printed in colour in the *People's Daily*, the *People's Liberation Army Daily* and the journal *Red Flag* and distributed across the country. In addition to appearing in major newspapers and periodicals, the prints of this painting were reproduced in posters of all shapes and sizes — altogether about 900 million pieces. The dissemination of the painting became a myth in Chinese art history, and the sacred image of Mao was widely worshiped. As the artist Liu Chunhua reflected, "the image of Chairman Mao was situated dominantly in the painting. The great image of Chairman Mao is facing towards us, walking towards us, like a glorious sun rising in front of us, and blessing us with infinite hopes."[3]

The return of Mao's image from 1987 onwards can be considered the fourth phase. After the Chinese Economic Reform, following the trend of Chinese avant-garde movements, especially the Political Pop wave, Mao's image re-emerged in the works of Chinese contemporary artists. This approach is related to the advent of Pop Art in the West as well as some Russian and Eastern European pop artworks that appeared in the early 1980s. In this period, Mao's image became more ideographic and, to many, sometimes seemed subversive.

Mao in Contemporary Chinese Art

The nationwide rise of various young artist groups in 1985 has now been labelled by many scholars as the beginning of the contemporary Chinese art movement. The North China Art Group, represented by Wang Guangyi, was a very representative and appealing group, and their slogans and ideas represented the spirit of this new era.[4] Although they did not have a unified mode of visual language or style, they shared a common artistic expressiveness that was dignified, apathetic and solemn.

---

3   Liu Chunhua, '*Gesong Weida Lingxiu Mao Zhuxi Shi Women Zuida de Xingfu* (It Is Our Greatest Joy to Praise the Leader Chairman Mao)', *Remin Ribao (People's Daily)*, 7 July 1968.

4   The North China Art Group was established in July 1984. It was one of the earliest groups of young artists in the form of art salon during the 85 Art Movement, comprising art graduates, literary professionals and also students from science and technical institutes. The founding members were fifteen young artists from the three northeast provinces, including Wang Guangyi, Shu Qun, Ren Jian and Liu Yan.

In 1984 and 1985, the Chinese art scene was dominated by various styles of expressionism. In general, it can be seen as a revival and continuation of the Chinese modernistic art movement from the 1930s that expressed personal feelings and fabricated individual art forms. However, this phenomenon was criticized by Wang Guangyi and his North China Art Group who were seeking for a division of '*da wo* (universal self)' and '*bi an yishi* (utopian idealism)' and establishing a style of 'new civilization' with loftiness, health and humanity.

In Wang Guangyi's painting series of *Frozen Northern Wasteland*, the grid-like composition in grey tones and ideographically depicted figure images all suggest a pristine but dispassionate ambience. Inspired by Gombrich's idea of 'Schema Correction',[5] the artist later developed his *Post-Classical* series, reinterpreting classical masterpieces as the pursuance of utopianism. This painting series appears symmetrical, balanced and stable, and generates an ascendant power of soundness that exists in the history of civilization. To avoid the interference by some specific narratives and thematic forms, Wang Guangyi used grids ideographically in his *Red Logic* series. He believed that the grids were able to represent an enforceable power, diminish the original religious atmosphere and visually indicate a kind of rational analysis. Therefore, one can only 'view', rather than 'experience' religion. According to the artist, the meaning behind the "A, O, X, M, A" in the painting relates to Ludwig Wittgenstein's analysis in his *Philosophical Investigations*.

From 1987 to 1988, Wang Guangyi's grids appeared again in his *Mao Zedong* series, which was first shown in a slide presentation at the Huangshan Conference in 1988. In February of 1989, Wang Guangyi's *Mao Zedong* (Fig. 37) appeared in the exhibition *China Avant-garde* at the China National Art Gallery in Beijing. It stimulated heated controversy and criticism during the assessment of all the exhibiting works prior to the opening and, was permitted for the show after an exhaustive explanation by the curators and was placed significantly in the centre of the second floor gallery, with his *Post-Classical* on the left. The prominent location of *Mao Zedong* obviously indicated the importance of the work and the recognition of Wang's leading position in the avant-garde movement. Just before the opening, *Mao Zedong* was considered to be the most newsworthy work in the exhibition, and the success would be approved by its appearance in the headlines. However, when artists Tang Song and Xiao Lu shot their installation at the opening, this dramatic incident attracted all the attention and also, generated a comparison with Wang's *Mao Zedong*, which was based on the artist's substantial reflections. As Wang Guangyi noted later after the exhibition, "I was very worried at that time that people might only see my *Mao Zedong* politically appealing. I believed that the work *Mao Zedong* would definitely draw the media's attention, with no doubt. But this was not my intention. What I really wanted to achieve through art is to invite people neutrally and critically to

---

5   Gombrich, E.H. *Art and Illusion: A Study in the Psychology of Pictorial Representation*. Princeton: Princeton University Press, 1961.

reveal their own cultural identity and also their curiosity towards the media. I think it was an organic development of my art practice, exploring the special cultural attitude of 'the people', including workers, peasants, soldiers and intellectuals, towards *Mao Zedong*, their leader of the past. The 'humanistic zeal' ignited by *Mao Zedong* reflects my vision that I proposed last year in terms of 'reassessing the humanistic zeal'."[6]

If Wang Guangyi's *Mao Zedong* concluded the study of rationalism in China's avant-garde movement, at the same time, it also marked a starting point for Political Pop Art, including many important works such as Wang's *Great Criticism* series. Two years later, the arrival of 'Mao fever' in mainland China reflected a cultural and psychological complex of the Chinese people: a paradox consisting of respect and deceit, hope and disappointment, expectation and nostalgia. It seemed to have been foreseen by Wang Guangyi and his *Mao Zedong*. In comparison, the image of Mao by the Shanghai-based artists Yu Youhan, Li Shan and Liu Dahong appears less dignified and, in a sense, even cynical; it presents the climax of Political Pop Art.

Since 1990, Yu Youhan had began his unique style of using printed fabric to depict Mao Zedong (Fig. 110). The random patterns in the painting almost look like inferior local handicrafts, but based on Yu's vast experience with abstractionism, those boorish patterns demonstrated his skilfulness and subtlety. Yu Youhan can be claimed as the most gifted of all the Political Pop artists. As Yu discussed,

> I paint Mao Zedong in order to reflect China, history, and also the life that I experienced. But as an artist, these reflections are always visualised in my practice. The Chinese Economic Reform by Deng Xiaoping brought Chinese artists liberty, which allowed me to appropriate the image of Mao Zedong, the most important character in China's modern history, in my paintings. Both my childhood and youth were spent in the Mao era, and I also experienced the Cultural Revolution. During the Cultural Revolution, China was filled with Mao's images. More than a decade after the death of Mao, I decided to revisit Mao in my art practice. When I painted floral patterns all over Mao's monochrome uniform in his standard portrait, I was pleased unprecedentedly. The words that had been suppressed for over ten years in my heart were finally expressed in full on the canvas. Mao's image in my painting consists of a variety of meanings: Mao sometimes represents China, sometimes represents the East, sometimes represents culture; sometimes he is a leader, sometimes an avant-garde, sometimes a conservative, and sometimes indeed, only a series of decorative pattern. When I first began to paint Mao

---

6 Wang Guangyi, 'On the Issue of Originality in Contemporary Art Practice', artist's unpublished notes, 24 June 1990.

Zedong, I did not expect any positive response. However, the paintings were welcomed by more and more people, including not only Chinese, but also foreigners, and even invited to many exhibitions.[7]

Yu Youhan claimed that he had never studied the term 'Political Pop' and did not intend to participate in this particular movement. However, his works with Mao's image had, in fact, become part of the ideological game and raised wide interest from critics, curators and art dealers.

Li Shan is another representative artist involved with the image of Mao during the Political Pop movement. In the *Rouge* series (Figs. 44–46), the artist used the colour *yanzhi* (rouge) — which traditionally suggests sensual and gaudy — to embellish Mao's image as the subversive means for profaning the sacred. When Li Shan skilfully used rouge, blue and black to reshape Mao in a placid and slightly eroticized manner, the image lost the initial revolutionary aura and provoked curiosity for the viewers or, at least,, his former followers. The artist stated: "*rouge*, here, is used as a verb. It is not a methodological intention, but an attitude, to 'rouge-ise' my subjects. 'Rouge-isation' declares constantly that art is neither related to artworks, nor to artists, critics, art dealers, museums, collectors or mass media. Once art is noticed, it will become a cheap copy of its own instantly to be obtained by everyone."[8]

Of all Political Pop works, Liu Dahong's works seem the most narrative in nature. He attempted to combine the legacy of Chinese folk art, such as Chinese New Year pictures, together with Persian miniature paintings and the Netherlands' fable arts from the Middle Ages, in order to establish his unique artistic style between classical and contemporary art, and to express his personal insights on the revolutionary enthusiasm in a utopian fable. Different from the simple style of other Political Pop artists, Liu Dahong's paintings always represent a complex drama, where the various stories of different times and backgrounds intersect each other within a dream-like scenery. In the painting series *Four Seasons* (Figs. 111–114), the hybrid image of Mao was derived from famous revolutionary paintings — for example, Liu Chunhua's *Chairman Mao Goes to Anyuan* and Tang Xiaohe's *Forging ahead in Wind and Waves* — and situated in an entirely irrelevant environment of either a literati landscape or even a Chinese traditional fairy tale, while the communist leader obviously has been depicted as the most absurd character of all.

7 Lü Peng, *Zhongguo Dangdai Yishushi (A History of Contemporary Chinese Art): 1990–1999*. Changsha: Hunan Fine Arts Publishing House, 2000, p. 175.

8 Doran, Valerie (ed.), *Hou Bajiu Zhongguo Xin Yishu (China's New Art, Post 89)*. Hong Kong: Hanart Gallery, 1993, p. 59.

From the founding of the People's Republic, until the immediate transformation into the economic development after the Open Door Policy in the late 1970s, it was inevitable that almost all Chinese people had to pay close attention to the political atmosphere. If the political era is unforgettable, then Mao, who was the most influential Chinese political leader of the twentieth century and whose image permeated people's daily life, has become a cultural identity representing the memories of both glory and sorrow. The rise of Political Pop in China can be seen as a visual response by the artists. Simultaneously, the image of Mao, reshaped in contemporary art, reflects the adjusted attitude of Chinese people towards the past and the present.

Mesmerized by Power

Chang Tsong-zung

When assessing the effects of the Cultural Revolution on contemporary Chinese art, we must take into account the experience of change that came about in China as a result of Mao Zedong's legacy. Of course, forces other than ideological politics were at work to bring about this change — economic factors, modes of production and communication, among others — but the degree of radical cultural shift may be understood only in the context of the power struggles in China's ideological politics since the early twentieth century. The seed for the transformation of China's visual world was implicit in the new ideological visions of society and human order from the beginning, while Mao's Cultural Revolution can simply be counted as the most thorough and uncompromising shift of all.

Two Visual Languages of Power

Learning from the Soviet experience, Mao's revolution adopted new techniques of organization and mass persuasion, with astonishing success. These new techniques of control distinguish it from other dynastic rebellions, making it a 'modern' revolution. In terms of a visual culture, Mao's strategies for compromising deep-rooted traditions to his singular revolutionary aim were especially successful. There is, for example, the famous directive proclaimed at the *Yan'an Talks on Art and Literature* in 1942, urging the production of art "to serve the people", which ushered in a new propaganda art that adapted itself to folk art, parodying its form while subverting its contents and spirit. More subtly, throughout his later career, Mao made full use of his image as a traditional literati scholar, emphasizing his poetry and calligraphy and lending authority and historical legitimacy to his role as a sagacious ruler. It is difficult to divorce images of Mao's poetry in his characteristic cursive hand from memories of the Cultural

Revolution. But Mao's references to traditional culture are always subordinated to strategies of an ideological revolution, with the ultimate goal of converting Chinese culture to a new visionary world order. This is where the legacy of the revolution carries over to modern art: a fascination with modernization, aimed at creating a new China in the image of a utopia invented in Europe, motivated by a religious fervour anxious to convert the uninitiated, but essentially unsympathetic to China's historical tradition.

As its name proclaims, the revolution of culture is what the Cultural Revolution was ostensibly about. It was, of course, also about a jockeying for position and influence in the corridors of power; but the ultimate outcome of this decade-long political movement was the radical transformation of China's national culture. The revolution sought intellectuals and cultural workers as its main target, beginning with everyone in a position of authority, both intellectual and political, down to those at the grass-roots level.

Today, historians generally agree on the devastations of the Cultural Revolution, but it still should be remembered that this was the unfortunate resolution of a trend that had its beginnings half a century earlier, starting with the May Fourth Movement in 1919. From the perspective of the visual arts, the Cultural Revolution was a threshold beyond which China's visual culture took a decisive turn. The denigration of traditional culture and rejection of the historical past in daily life was made complete with this campaign. Since the early twentieth century, official Chinese positions on art and culture have always made the implicit assumption that traditional Chinese culture was deficient, requiring mending before it could better serve China in modern times. As a result, the preservation of culture has been unforgivably neglected since the fall of the last dynasty in 1911. The reason is obvious: it is not possible to truly preserve a material culture of the past unless its intrinsic worth in the present is firmly established. The transformation of China's visual culture, the sweeping changes in cultural direction of its material world, is reflected in its political attitudes in modern times. A sad example is the mindless destruction of the architectural heritage that has been perpetrated on an unprecedented scale up to the present moment — all in the name of modernizing China's cities and towns. What is interesting to note is that throughout this process of transformation, the language of visual culture representing power also has evolved subtly to reflect wider political realities. As the Cultural Revolution was the political movement in which cultural and political issues were made to identify with each other, it is the best example to illuminate issues relating to the visual language of power.

China's traditional visual language of power is primarily the written word — the logograph — and, by extension, the incarnate presence of the written word through calligraphy. The presence of calligraphy in public spaces signifies the presence of its author. This is represented in many ways: for example, in public steles inscribed with carved text; arched gateways over crossroads adorned with commemorative writing; shop signs penned by celebrities; and couplets and plaques made for ancestral halls, temples and reception halls of private residences (Fig. 115). These writings usually are moral in nature and often imbued with personal poetic expression. Local residents would recognize the hand of dignitaries and famous literati who had ties to local history, and they venerated the writing as an image or autograph of a pop star today. The political nature of such public presence was not glaringly conspicuous in the old days as public poetic writing in China was so abundant. The conscious use of imperial writing as official endorsement is evident with the early Qing emperors, who as barbarian invaders of China recognized the significance of such cultural gestures. Even today, we still have numerous imperial plaques given by Emperors Kangxi and Qianlong to important temples and monasteries. This imperial custom of the Qing dynasty may be understood as a new technology in the management of power, and it brought the personal presence of the emperor directly to the furthest corners of his domain.

In the West, the visual presence of power primarily is proclaimed through the art of portraiture, both in the medium of painting and sculpture. Statues of famous figures in European public squares and portraits of the sovereign hung in government offices, post offices and civic halls are prime examples. In contrast, portraiture of representing emperors and dignitaries conspicuously are absent at comparable sites in the traditional Chinese world. Publicly displayed figures usually were confined to religious images. While Chinese families traditionally adorn their homes with the calligraphy of illustrious ancestors, European families display portraits of their forebears. During the imperial era, it was inconceivable for the image of the Chinese emperor to be displayed in public; his symbolic image was the dragon, and any official court portrait that may have been painted was viewed only ceremonially by a privileged few, and always within the palace walls.

Thus, the increasing appearance of portraiture in China since the early twentieth century can be read as an early cultural import signifying China's decision to be modernized or, indeed, Westernized. While political figures only began lending their image for public use after the fall of the Qing dynasty in 1911, the rapidity with which this custom spread throughout the public arena is astonishing. Suddenly, the faces of those in power began appearing on coins, currency notes and stamps; and within a decade, public statues and official portraiture became a common sight in modern public spaces such as libraries, public parks, exhibition halls and civic halls. The introduction of this new visual language represented the inauguration of a new order in the political system. The new figurative portraiture favoured by Chinese leaders was based on the modern European tradition of realism. Here it should be noted that, in Europe, the new academic system of the nineteenth century that canonized the skills of realism displaced the old apprenticeship system of art by founding itself on a new 'scientific' method of observation and representation. Chinese importation of this visual language of power followed a tide of positivist science in Europe; and the use of realist portraiture signified a new cultural turn that sought scientific authority for China's modernizing efforts. Under the aegis of positivist science — this new authority of scientific observation — the art of portraiture established itself as the new artistic authority in China.

Comparing the visual languages of the written word and portraiture, it is obvious the power implied by that of writing is more cultural and oriented towards ideas. Perhaps for this reason, even during the most turbulent period of Mao's era when public writing took the form of slanderous slogans and abusive directives, the 'power of words' still indicated the pre-eminence of ideology. Until the arrival of the culture of the figurative icon, the presence of words reflected a power held in check within a cultural system, bound by examples of historical precedence. The written word is, first of all, a visual language expressive of the cultivation and character of the person in power. With the popularization of the iconic portrait comes a new trend of idol worship, in which the individual in power is no longer dependent on the magic of cultural mores, but manipulated and judged by the more sensational and universal language of image replicated through mass media. This system, when the power of its ruler is not tempered by cultural mores, requires a corresponding system of power-checks. In the new civil societies of Europe, the development of a democratic system with a corresponding legal structure perhaps has been integral and necessary to a society that has cultivated the 'power of the portrait'.

Since the early twentieth century, these two visual languages of power — the written word and the portrait — have had a parallel existence in China, and those in power have used both to their advantage. This situation parallels the undefined state of law and order for most of the twentieth century: a lack of checks and balances in either of the two different systems of governance — namely, the traditional Confucian order emphasizing the rule of culture, on the one hand, and the Western legal system based on the inalienable rights of the individual, on the other — made it possible for rulers to manipulate the system at will. The corresponding rise and fall of influence of these two languages of power in modern China gives a visible measure of the extent of modernization or Westernization over the decades. A disastrous resolution of these two divergent influences occurred during the critical years of Mao's era, especially in the ten years of the Cultural Revolution.

The visual world of the Cultural Revolution is characterized by the proliferation of political slogans. From the vistas of street posters and murals to up-close graphic designs adorning teacups and ashtrays, it was impossible for Chinese citizen to escape being bombarded with political messages. People were steeped in a daily flood of slogans, directives, invectives and moral aphorisms. Political cartoons and propaganda paintings accompanied many of the writings, and one image from which no Chinese national could escape was that of Mao Zedong. Figures featured in propaganda art were mostly the generic worker-peasant-soldier with anonymous grinning faces; the one immediately recognizable face standing out in the anonymous crowd was that of Chairman Mao, occasionally accompanied by a portrait of the comrade currently in favour. Given the extent of its dissemination and the size of China's population, one can safely claim that Mao's use of his own image was the most thorough exploitation of mass media in the world at the time. In this respect, Mao was a paradigm of the modern politician, if one concedes that the phenomenon of exploiting mass media to exert political influence — is one of the defining marks of modern life. On the other hand, as Mao's calligraphy was the most popularly known handwriting of the 1960s and 1970s, its political presence proliferated alongside political slogans. In both the visual language of writing and of portraiture, Mao exploited mass coverage to an unprecedented degree and maximized the effects of both media.

This decisive shift in the visual language of power during the Cultural Revolution symbolizes China's arrival into a modernized/Westernized world. It should be emphasized that this shift also marks the Westernization of Chinese culture as a whole, which, ironically, has been achieved through China's own efforts, rather than under Western political colonialism or economic domination. Looking back over China's history, the great pride of this civilization always has been in bringing culture to other nations: civilizing those less developed in their social and political institutions. Now, in the twentieth century, China has radically reversed its position; it has, in fact, willingly destroyed most of its own traditions and institutions to find itself inadvertently being civilized by the West.

Calligraphy and Power in Chinese Culture

Before the age of the pencil and fountain pen, training in brush calligraphy was something every literate Chinese had to undergo. As such, it is fair to claim calligraphy as the representative 'mass art' of China. Every person faced with paper and writing brush would have been challenged by the task of balancing brush strokes of a word within its square format to make it look attractive. This is nothing if not art training, and mass art training as well. It is useful to ask why such an indigenous mass art was never included in the programme of socialist art, especially for a government that always trumpeted its support for national culture and art for the masses. Since the Communists' early years in Yan'an, calligraphy was never factored into the new formula for art; instead, it was made adjunct to movements concerning language reform and the Romanization of Chinese writing (pinyin). For example, in Yan'an and the other 'red' territories controlled by the Communists before 1949, calligraphy was only regarded as a tool for the Movement of Abolishing Illiteracy and rarely promoted as art training. As an independent form of art, calligraphy was probably too cosy with the traditional literati for the taste of Communist reformers, but as a tool for education and abolishing illiteracy, calligraphy could, in Mao's words, "merge with the new era of the masses". In the 1950s, Mao again reiterated that big-character posters do not carry the stigma of class, just as the vernacular tongue is not bound by class. It seemed to legitimize the popularized use of the traditional brush in visual propaganda. Consequently, with the phenomenon of Mao Zedong's calligraphy and novel script forms being widely disseminated, especially during and after the Cultural Revolution, new developments in the culture of handwriting appeared.

Taste in calligraphy changes with the times, and this 'period taste' is reflected in the current choice of masters who are adulated; but the norm of calligraphy — the model texts copied by students — have always converged on the several great masters of the Jin and Tang dynasties. As a result, the criteria for beauty has remained relatively stable throughout the centuries. During the Cultural Revolution, the most popular script styles were the styles of Ouyang Xun, Liu Gongquan and Yan Zhenqing, all from the Tang dynasty, even as the content of calligraphy copybooks was changed to revolutionary messages. Novel scripts invented during the Cultural Revolution period, such as the New Wei script, popularly used for big-character posters, also found their way into model copybooks. As a mass movement, the sheer quantity of hand-written calligraphy that appeared in public postings during the Cultural Revolution probably exceeded that of any other period in the twentieth century. As personal expressions charged with political zeal, big-character posters and small-character posters of the period should be studied as a representative artistic phenomenon. As the writings were mostly created as slogans and posters, the relatively anonymous calligraphic styles of Black Script and Art Script were often preferred. This stylistic tendency indicates a change in the nature of power in China's visual culture.

In the traditional world, when handwriting marked a presence of power, the personal touch gave it flair and personality. With the stiff and relatively impersonal Black Script and Art Script becoming the norm, a different kind of power entered calligraphy: more impersonal, collective in strength and wielding an authority of a more bureaucratic nature. The source of this type of impersonal bureaucratic power can be retraced to the collectivist politics and mass propaganda that appeared with the Industrial Revolution, later made famous by communism. It also should be noted that both the democratic states and the socialist world have chosen to defer to this new authority: anonymous and bureaucratically impersonal. Amid the sea of calligraphic writings, the one individual whose calligraphic personality was always identifiable and distinctive was, of course, that of Chairman Mao. Apart from the chairman, few local leaders made their presence through a recognizable calligraphic style. The hand of Guo Moruo, Kang Sheng and several other national leaders were repeatedly sought for logos of governmental departments and official institutions. Shu Tong was popular in Shanghai, and his calligraphy adorned Shanghai public signs and train stations. This phenomenon further illustrates the close ties between public calligraphy and political power.

During the ten years of the Cultural Revolution, there was little diversity in entertainment, and calligraphy became a popular form of private amusement. Mao Zedong's calligraphy was copied widely as it was considered the height of contemporary artistic achievement. Mao style calligraphy had practical uses as well, especially when his poetry was frequently enlarged or adapted for various applications. Traditionally, only masters who had made important contributions to the development of the art of calligraphy have been considered suitable paradigms for students, and these masters only appeared during ages when Chinese culture achieved major breakthroughs. Traditionally, the choice of a calligraphic paradigm rarely takes into consideration the station of the artist, as calligraphy represents the higher authority of culture. Therefore, the choice of imperial calligraphy as a study model was extremely rare, the gifted twelfth-century Song dynasty Emperor Huizong being the only exception. Although Mao's calligraphy has not yet been issued as a model copybook today, it still is popular and widely published

(Fig. 116).[1] Mao's anointment as a calligraphic paradigm effectively reverses the view on history, as it symbolically disavows the authority of historical wisdom and claims that the height of cultural achievement may be found in the present, not just the past. This may be elucidated by the case of an 'intellectual' argument during the Cultural Revolution on the authenticity of Wang Xizhi's *Lanting Xu (The Preface to the Orchid Pavilion)*, written in 353.[2] As a piece of calligraphy that historically has been upheld as one of the highest achievements of Chinese art and, hence, considered sacred by Chinese scholars, this argument challenged the foundations of Chinese visual art, while allowing a political leader's calligraphy to surreptitiously enter the cultural imagination of the nation. When political power can begin to vouch for a civilization's highest cultural paradigm, this signals the end of a traditional China governed by moral and cultural models.

After the Cultural Revolution, public spaces for calligraphy rapidly receded, and an even greater challenge to handwriting today has been posed by the technology of computer keyboard input methods.[3] The world of the internet and contemporary communication have further entrenched the use of keys in place of handwriting. However, even though calligraphy as a visual language of power may never regain pre-eminence, it remains deeply embedded in cultural memory. It is impossible to predict the fate of logographic writing, except that it still will remain a form of fine art for the foreseeable future. It is interesting to note that, even today, political and cultural leaders continue to practice

---

1   In 1999, a mainland Chinese calligraphy magazine conducted a survey of the most important calligraphers of the past century, and the selection committee put Mao Zedong in seventh place, demonstrating the continued strength of his influence. Even today, thirty years after the end of the Cultural Revolution, many consumer brands have continued to use Mao's calligraphy for their logos; famous examples include the Red Flag sedan car and Chung Hwa cigarettes.

2   Mao's official scholar, Guo Moruo, claimed that *The Preface to the Orchid Pavilion*, which has been copied by almost every single self-respecting artist since the seventh century as the supreme model of fine calligraphy, was fake and could not have come from that period. This seemingly obscure intellectual dispute was blown up to a major political incident, and many calligraphy authorities were wheeled out and forced to take a stance in support of the allegation. The exercise was political in nature, and its intention was nothing short of undermining the foundation of calligraphy aesthetics, with wider implication for the acceptability of historical wisdom. Whatever Guo Moruo's intellectual merit, the unpronounced intention of the debate was to establish the greater authority of contemporary knowledge over the past and discredit the intrinsic value of historical paradigms.

3   Romanizing Chinese into an alphabetic form remains the easiest input system to learn, but that solution would spell an eventual death sentence to the logograph. In the early 1980s, Taiwan scholar Zhu Bangfu invented the Cang Jie input system, which takes into consideration the character radicals. The Cang Jie system is sympathetic to the written word and was soon adapted for simplified characters in mainland China as the Five Strokes system. In spite of these inventions, a truly elegant solution for incorporating character radicals into the keyboard has not yet been found, which means the new generation of Chinese will neither visualize nor conceive the logographic form in the way originally intended if they continually write Chinese on the computer. Furthermore, the core of the computer continues to be operated in alphabetic form, while Chinese words remain stored as images; this means a truly Chinese computer has yet to be built. These are major cultural projects — national projects that require the mobilization of talents from the highest governmental level.

calligraphy, and the urge to develop a recognizable personal style remains a means to further assert their authority. When Hong Kong reverted to Chinese rule in 1997, the most vivid visual impression made on Hong Kong people probably was not the elaborate handover ceremony, but the single piece of calligraphy presented to the city by President Jiang Zemin, which reads: "Hong Kong will have a better tomorrow".

Power of the Word in New Chinese Art

In the Chinese art world, a new cultural wave swept the country at the end of the 1970s, characterized by freer expression of personal sentiments, rebellion against authoritarian doctrines in social life and, in general, a demand for greater autonomy in the private sphere of the individual. The artistic phenomenon of the 85 New Wave, in particular the period between 1984 and 1987, has come to represent the visual manifestation of this cultural turn. At its climax, this movement claimed over 300 art groups — large and small — across China. Each was represented by a special artistic agenda with its own vision of new Chinese culture. The autonomous nature of the movement, the infectious enthusiasm of the artists and its wide geographical reach make the movement an exceptional case amid the endless cultural-political campaigns that characterize Communist Chinese history. The movement is largely remembered for its idealism, creative energy, liberating experience and collective dedication within every art group. The latter point is a phenomenon that deserves closer scrutiny, as, ironically, the demand for tight collective cohesion is tied here to the experience of personal liberation, which brings to mind the appeal of many early Communist mass movements, in particular those at Yan'an in the 1930s and the beginning of the Cultural Revolution in 1966. In these experiences, devotees are drawn to an idealistic cause significant for society and humanity as a whole, and the sacrifice of individuality is felt as liberation through dedication to a greater public cause. Although by nature contemporary art goes against the spirit of mass movements, the 85 New Wave still echoed lessons learned from Mao Zedong's political campaigns. Artists organized themselves around manifestoes and ambitiously mapped out both their own futures and that of society.

Significantly, the project of modernity became an inherent link between the idealism of the artists and the ideology of Communist politics.

The quest for utopia, faith in modernity, subversion of tradition and desire to stimulate social change are not only important features of the 85 New Wave, but also the legacy of Mao's revolution. The artists intuitively understood and articulated the mission of modernity in their own ways. They embraced early European modern art second-hand through poorly illustrated magazines and sought to reinvent Western modernism on Chinese soil; at the same time, they all exhaustively learned the cultural strategies of Mao. As contemporary Chinese art was born under the ghost of the Cultural Revolution, the revolutionary figure of Mao Zedong over-shadowed and secretly was revered by the most radical artists. Artists fought against the bureaucracy and absurdity of the system, yet it was also clear in their minds that this was a world fashioned by the master of subversion. Artists understood that they had entered an historical vacuum as the result of a failed social experiment; it was now their mission to catch up with modernity and fulfil the dream lost by the previous generation. The sense of immense possibility and the lack of sentimental cultural baggage instilled a heroic vision for artists in the 1980s. Challenging and subverting the past with sweeping gestures was standard training for all who grew up in Mao's China; this now became a natural strategy for the New Wave artists. However, with both the European model and Mao's revolutionary 'cultivation' beforehand, there was always a suspicion that the rebellious spirit of modernism and pursuit of individual liberation of the 85 New Wave was a re-enactment rather than an adventure. In this context, the written word has been significant in contemporary art practice for being an indigenous development deeply entrenched in China's cultural memory. Among the pioneers, the most illustrious are Gu Wenda, Wu Shanzhuan and Xu Bing.

Gu Wenda, like many of his ambitious peers, trained himself in modern art by rapidly reviewing important Western art movements and imitating their styles. He first was attracted to surrealism and dada, then made works around themes of chance and strategy. In 1984, Gu arrived at his monumental calligraphy. He called them 'error words' and 'mis-written words'; they are writings suggesting mandates, political and otherwise, but they were written with characters containing wrongly written components or misused vocabulary. Since the early twentieth century, the issue of language reform has been a sensitive topic debated heatedly in cultural political circles. The 'simplification' of the traditional written word to the currently accepted form, approved in the 1960s, was made possible only with Communist totalitarian will, and many still regret that the radical change in the composition of characters disregard the issue of etymology. What Gu did was to strike at the heart of Chinese cultural taboos and stir up broken memories of historical lineage embedded in the language. In breaking taboos, he releases powerful disruptive energy, which elevates his calligraphic writing to a level of monumentality: the content of the text hints at grand mandates, and the writing is embedded in a cloudy ink-wash containing sketches of landscape that suggest mysterious oracles appearing from heaven (Fig. 25). As the artist titled one of the works, *Totem and Taboo* (Fig. 117), the work is totemic and challenges hidden taboos. Breaking the taboo of word correctness shakes the foundation of Chinese culture and recalls the power of Mao's revolution.

Gu Wenda's subversion of taboos extended to artworks involving the human body. After moving to New York in 1987, he worked on projects using soiled tampons, his own semen, menstrual blood and human hair. Like Mao, Gu instinctively crossed over from the logographic word to the human figure in the quest for statements about power. In the series, *United Nations*, are works created as monuments for nations of the world, each exposing a dark past, an embarrassing historical event or a cultural taboo. For China's *United Nations* monument, created in 1997, Gu returned to the written word and made panels of hair incorporating fake Chinese words, juxtaposing nature (hair) and culture (writing) (Fig. 118). Gu further developed the idea into an on-going series of artworks involving hair panels that incorporated fake Chinese words as well as alphabets from various cultures such as Latin, Sanskrit, Hindu and Arabic (Fig. 119).

Wu Shanzhuan, again inspired by the Cultural Revolution, satirizes the contamination of public space by slogans of any form, whether it is political, commercial or simply gibberish. In his famous *Big-Character Posters and Small-Character Posters*, first launched in 1985, Wu parodied the phenomenon of the visual 'red sea' of the Cultural Revolution by papering a room with slogans containing mundane messages, commercial notes and public commands, mostly on red paper (Fig. 24). Wu illustrates how the visual world of ideological slogans in big-character and small-character posters has continued into the post-revolutionary world, now striking at the heart of everyday life. This major work intuitively understands the significance of public writing in Chinese civilization as representing the presence of power. Wu's 1985 work *75% Red, 20% Black, 5% White* pokes fun at the pseudo-science of political ideology and points to the terror of compulsory ideological conversion using humour, or *Red Humour*, according to the artist. By taking ideological logic to the extreme, Wu exposes its absurdity but, at the same time, reveals the hypocrisy of modern life, when everything eventually becomes equally ideologically charged under the guise of commerce and democratic indoctrination. His *Supermarket* series (1991), the *Bird Before Peace* series (1992), and even the recent *Thing's Right(s)* series — that began in 1994 and parodied the United Nations' mandate for human rights by extending it to benefit all inanimate things — all underlie a radical position arrived at from the experience of a civilization that has completely usurped itself. Another major contribution Wu made to the art of the written word was by introducing the fake word in 1986, which he called Character Figure. He painted a vocabulary of non-words that he claimed had autonomous existence and represented non-signifying presences. The idea of the unintelligible word later found monumental manifestation in Xu Bing's *Book of the Sky* in 1988.

Xu Bing is celebrated for his *Book of the Sky* (Figs. 29–31), which has the advantage of having an impressive presence in any exhibition hall. Xu was trained as a woodcut printmaker, and carving the movable print-types of non-words became an example of exquisite printmaking, echoing small woodcut prints he previously had created. The traditional thread-bound format of the *Book of the Sky* surprises the audience when they discover the text is illegible, while the impressive workmanship also gives the work an aura of monumentality. This work immediately became a landmark in Chinese art, and Xu's subsequent works continued to reflect on issues of writing and language. In 1993, he made a work using braille, *Brailliterate*. His next major work in this vein was *English Square Word* (Fig. 120) in 1996. Xu created a calligraphy copybook in traditional format. It shows how to write a funny-looking text (with a soft Chinese brush) that turns out to be English. For this, Xu invented a system for writing the Latin alphabet that resembles Chinese radicals, so that it becomes possible to re-compose English words in a square-word format. This work is exhibited as a classroom complete with a supply of manuals and copybooks for audiences/participants, whose learning is assisted by a video demonstration. This project of *English Square Word* is both art installation and mock subversion — an actual possibility for a new script. A Japanese software company, in fact, has developed in conjunction with the artist a new font for *English Square Word*. On the surface, the artist has played with the system of signification, cross-cultural contextual analysis, and understanding and language in general. At a deeper level, Xu has challenged the written word's central role in China's rooted sense of order and hierarchy, in which the training of calligraphy aesthetics and cultural order are bound together. With his *English Square Word*, Xu brings home the satire of traditional Confucian faith in spreading culture through disseminating the Chinese language. In *English Square Word*, the cultural discipline of calligraphy is preserved, but both the language and culture have been replaced through foreign conversion. Or, it can also be read as an ironic fulfilment of this Confucian ambition by bringing the discipline of calligraphy, if not China's culture, abroad.

After 1990, China's new generation of artists has continued to reflect on the written word in new ways, but few have achieved an in-depth understanding of traditional culture. One of the most exemplary is the inventive artist, writer and curator Qiu Zhijie. His most famous early work in this regard is *Copying the Preface of Orchid Pavilion One Thousand Times* (Fig. 121), for which he made a thousand copies of this calligraphy classic on the same sheet of paper until it turned into a black mass. In studying power and order, China's tradition of copying masterpieces of calligraphy can be read as the basic discipline of attuning to cultural paradigms — the pillars of Chinese tradition. *The Preface of Orchid Pavilion* by Wang Xizhi is undisputedly the most celebrated piece of writing in this tradition, and its position is further enhanced by the fact that Wang Xizhi has been upheld as the sage of calligraphy since the seventh century, so that his calligraphy represents not just good art but also the cultural lineage itself. Copying Wang Xizi represents attuning into China's cultural order, and copying his work until it becomes a gestural exercise on a black surface highlights a message of discipline and order, showing how one's individuality may be formed by grasping the rules of a master narrative. In addition to this work, Qiu has created a number of others that reflect on discipline, order and freedom. These include his 1996 work *April 8th* (Fig. 122) in which he asked various non-specialists to provide calligraphy as a template for a calligraphy training kit, calling into question the nature of cultural authority. *Heart Sutra* (Fig. 123) uses special neon to illuminate alternately his calligraphy of the Buddhist Heart Sutra and a real heart preserved in formaldehyde, juxtaposing two modes of presence that both proclaim power. For a light-hearted work, Qiu has taught himself to write calligraphy backwards, beginning with the last stroke of a word and going backwards to the beginning of a stroke, so that he can reverse the video record of the process and give the appearance of erasing a piece of writing while the brush goes down the text. This is a clever trick, but it comments on the aesthetics of calligraphy, which traditionally has depended on an established approach to the creative process of brush writing. In a recent on-going project, *Light Calligraphy* (Figs. 124 and 125) that began in 2005, Qiu writes with an electric flashlight in dim settings so that, when photographed under long exposure, the text written in light and its surroundings merge to compliment each other, bringing to mind the old customs of writing colophons on traditional landscape paintings. This and other innovations by Qiu open up new possibilities for calligraphy in the modern age, maintaining the currency of spontaneous handwriting at a time when its existence is threatened by electronic keyboard instruments.

Power of the Icon in New Chinese Art

One interesting phenomenon of the early 1990s that brought back the ghost of the Cultural Revolution was an unexpected nationwide fever for Mao Zedong. As a discredited period of history, the Cultural Revolution was identified with Mao's follies, yet with the new Mao fever all was strangely forgiven and forgotten. The sufferings caused by ideological blindness and egotistical aggrandizement was swept aside by memories of Mao the idealist and visionary of new China. The decade-long public taboo about the Cultural Revolution after Mao's death in 1976, during which its memories stirred up nightmares and protests, suddenly broke out into eulogies and glorified affirmation, as though a double personality was always hidden in the public memory (or amnesia) of Mao's era. Reasons for this about-face are complex; public discontent with current social injustice was apparently the main reason, but the long suppression of a significant period of history was probably the more important factor. The twenty-eight years of the Mao era were marked by an endless chain of political campaigns and purges. It would have been impossible to survive this period without somehow identifying with it and coming to terms with reality. To have denied this history for over a decade would have meant suppressing simultaneously an important part of one's personal history, which needed an opportunity for affirmative review and redress; this opportunity appeared with the aftermath of the Tiananmen Square protests in 1989. To stand up for Mao was perhaps not just a protest for idealism and social justice, but also an affirmation and recovery of a period of personal history that had been negated too crassly due to its inextricable ties with public life. In a discussion of China's visual language of power, the return of Mao and his icon in the early 1990s meant a massive resurgence of a singularly political image of power. For artists of the early 1990s, the sophisticated tool of contemporary art meant a more self-conscious exploitation of imageries of power. Artists of the Political Pop genre glorified Mao with the cosmetics of irony and parody, often exposing additional dimensions of power hidden in sexual politics and cultural values. Yu Youhan re-painted Mao's iconic images covered with cheerful floral patterns, hinting at vital powers and festive celebration. Li Shan touched up Mao's features to reveal a sexual allure that merges political power with sex appeal. Wang Guangyi revisited the iconic images of worker-peasant-soldier to denounce product brands but, in fact, affirmed their appeal while seeming to criticize the material decadence represented by consumer brand worship. There are also others whose art reviewed the memory of Mao Zedong in historical perspective. Feng Mengbo sees Mao's era as a festive childhood memory, so it comes naturally to Feng to translate Mao's politicized cultural campaigns into the video game world of today. Liu Dahong goes under the skin of ideology by elaborating the hidden links between Judeo-Christianity and Communism, establishing a basis to unravel the roots of modern China's utopian vision. With Liu Dahong, the mythology underlying ideology yields up its grip on the mind to the liberating imagination of art, and, through his efforts, the myth of modernity again is being absorbed into China's history of dynastic revolutions.

With these post-1989 artists, the legacy of Mao for contemporary art found another generation of heirs. In the 1980s, the excitement of subversion created an adulation of power; in the post-1989 era the affirmation of a derailed history legitimized artists' sharing of a political orthodoxy. In the 1990s, the human figure fully re-asserted itself in contemporary art as an icon of power, gradually gaining popular acceptance towards the end of the decade. The celebrated family portraits of Zhang Xiaogang's *Bloodline* series appeared in 1993, giving art a haunting reminder of ancestral portraits that in the old days were only displayed during worship. The most intense of this series date from the mid-1990s, and they evoke the darkness of a common history, keeping a public secret too painful to disclose. Other successful painters of a younger generation, such as Fang Lijun, Liu Wei, Liu Xiaodong and Zeng Fangzhi, each created iconic figures that found ready imitators. Their imageries now have become public icons through followings in mass culture and the art market.

In retrospect, figurative artists of the post-1989 era have mapped out a terrain of figuration that now forms a perception of the Chinese body widely accepted by the cultural world, making the transition from the archetypical iconography of Mao's era to contemporary art. When Fang Lijun, Liu Wei and Liu Xiaodong first appeared in the late 1980s, they were considered as having defected from the glowing ideals of modernism by the avant-garde. Having been trained academically in the Central Academy of Fine Arts in Beijing, they shared an educational background that represents the artistic orthodoxy of the People's Republic, noticeably, not of the traditional China. The influence of Western art education is dominant in most art academies since the founding of the People's Republic. Fang Lijun, Liu Wei and Liu Xiaodong are the successors of the 85 New Wave; they are also the new image makers developed by China's orthodox academy, who, in the late 1980s, were still strapped to their original mission of modernization. In the early 1990s, the spirit of their art was deemed cynical and infected with malaise, when, in fact, they were more focused on the mundane, sometimes unsavoury, aspects of daily life, from a personal and cynically light-hearted perspective. By turning away from the polemical, idealized visions of their predecessors, they produced images that successfully captured the mood of the time and, together with artists like Zhang Xiaogang, thereby fixed the image of the body for the Chinese imagination. Unlike the Political Pop artists, the figure created by these painters is not larger than life; this figure is from the ranks of common life that does not ask to be adulated, but stands out like personalities from a novel or a film.

Fang Lijun's grinning bald people drew imitators from the very beginning, testifying to their iconic attraction. His development over the 1990s is interesting, particularly as it radically departed from the cynicism by which he was first characterized. The jubilant colours that started to appear in 1993 became his principle palette from the mid-

1990s; together with the happy people that converge and rise up to an unseen source of attraction, the paintings could be a contemporary rendering of Great Leader eulogy (Fig. 126). His increasingly monumental works even suggest some form of religious salvation that comes from above: out of time, lifted from reality, just like the utopian paradise of the Communists. In Fang's work, one sees a return of the ghost of Mao's vision and a return of the triumvirate of peasant-worker-soldier in new costumes.

The development of modern Western art on human body was only canonized by Chinese art institutions in the early twentieth century and, more importantly, finally introduced to the entire nation through Mao's political machinery. Liu Wei's development has taken a different path by which he developed his investigation of human sensuality into a thoroughly subversive view of the integrity of the body. In the mid-1990s, his erotically aggressive female body began to rot from internal disintegration, and, eventually, burst out into corpuscles and fluids that point to irreparable internal damages (Fig. 127). A few years later, other artists even brought a cadaver into the exhibition hall or displayed processed body parts on shelves as tinned food. One wonders whether this recent turn to desecration of the body reflects an intuitive disavowal of the European legacy of the body. If the body today has become the primary icon of power, this radical development perhaps should be viewed as the truly subversive act in art.

Liu Xiaodong continues to study the seediness of the reality through acute observation and his handsome strokes on canvas, while the power of the icon can be consolidated with every single revealing detail of people's daily lives. Zeng Fanzhi's intensely emotional work is autobiographical in nature, and his recent paintings, using a wild chaotic brushwork, represent a successful attempt in breaking away from his academic training. Generally speaking, the figurative icon has taken on the full spectrum of the visual world and is adapting vigorously to change. It is interesting to note that most of these artists, on occasion, refer to the visage of Mao Zedong, as though they all remember this as the source of legitimacy for their own art. Perhaps this represents an unpronounced acknowledgement of the legacy that cultivated them, and this acknowledgement, in turn, is shared by the public who now enthusiastically endorse their art.

The entangled relationship between the figurative icon and the written word in contemporary art has evolved in a fashion parallel to that in the public sphere of visual culture, although in both quarters it is apparent that the written word has been crowded out by number and a gradual loss of mass appeal. Figurative icons have the added advantage of support from the powerful moving image that provides a narrative dimension to figurative imagery in which the written word previously excelled. However, a different type of literacy has been introduced by the digital world, and another class of literate power elite in China will doubtless preserve the power of the word in ways other than calligraphy. Still, in whatever direction Chinese visual culture develops, there is no way around the figure of Mao, who forcibly directed China along a path of modernity that was deeply influenced by his understanding of Western technological power, burning bridges behind him as he crossed them.

Why the Manic Grin?
Hysterical Bodies:
Contemporary Art as (Male) Trauma in Post-Cultural Revolution China

Katie Hill

"In my experience of living, the last paranoia for the helpless could be found only in art, although art is no longer important to me."[1]

— Wang Chuyu

---

1   Wang Chuyu, in 'Hua Tianxue', Ai Weiwei, Feng Boyi (eds.), *Bu Hezuo Fangshi (Fuck Off)*, exhibition catalogue. Shanghai: Eastlink Gallery, 2000, p. 124. Wang Chuyu is an artist living in Beijing. One of his works in 2002 involved cutting his thumb and smearing blood onto the Constitution of the People's Republic of China.

Introduction

> ... the ghost of hysteria, vanished if not banished from the horizons of twentieth-century psychoanalysis, has never stopped coming back, in every kind of guise and disguise.[2]

To think about the Cultural Revolution as a period of hysteria is nothing new. We are all familiar with images of hysteria during the Cultural Revolution, which epitomizes a period of political hysteria in recent Chinese history. Crowds of Red Guard youth shouting Mao slogans and waving the little red book are synonymous with the image of revolutionary China at its most extreme and occur in parallel to the mass movements of liberation in the West, Paris 1968, Beatlemania and images of screaming teenagers. It even could be said that images such as these examples (and there are many more) are iconic visual documentations of the historical era following the immediate post-war period of the 1940s. In the 1960s, fanaticism was a key aspect of mass cultureacross East and West. In the study of representation in modern China, this is important to bear in mind. The complex relationship of these cross-cultural phenomena challenges the notion of the Cultural Revolution as an isolated decade of extremism. What underpins much contemporary art in China is an historical legacy of the Cultural Revolution as it has come to define China in its *aftermath* between its *representation* (crowds waving red flags; blunt, strident political slogans; big-character posters and structured violence) and the reality of fragmented childhood memories, split families and enforced ideological obeisance through the repeated recital of Mao quotations.

Out of this rather broad backdrop, this paper attempts to situate a specific form of hysteria, represented in paintings and performance art from China produced in the 1990s. One of the key features of figurative paintings in China during the 1990s is that of psychological expression. This was an important turn in Chinese art, when the body was first represented through an emotional lens. Briefly, in the 1980s there was a move away from the political into the human; yet the conceptual framework of painting was still relatively underdeveloped, as it followed a Socialist Realist structure that aimed to depict society in positive terms. Here my main focus is on the manifestation of a kind of hysteria, which can clearly be seen in paintings of the late 1980s and early 1990s, with specific reference to the laughing face in works by Yue Minjun, Yang Shaobin and Zeng Fanzhi. A series of paintings was produced in the early 1990s following an earlier work, Geng Jianyi's 1987 painting *A Second State*, which seemed to precede a wave of similar imagery in painting that focused on an expression of apparent vacillation between pain and laughter, a moment of agony and ecstasy. The effect of politics on the human body

---

2 Bowlby, Rachel, 'Never Done, Never to Return', in Sigmund Freud and Joseph Breuer, *Studies in Hysteria*. London: Penguin, 2004, pp. vii–xxviii.

is shown here in the close relationship between the physiological as manifested in facial expression and bodily posture. The paintings may be read as a unified narrative of post-traumatic expression, which gives the impression of an artistic movement intent on revealing a state of mind for China, by the depiction of self with the face and also in the depiction in (predominantly male) groups.

I argue that these paintings, made in the context of a recent political trauma in 1989, can be read on the back of Cultural Revolution history. In that period, trauma was built into the political structure in the form of public humiliation sessions, mass violence and destruction of historical buildings, artworks, books and religious icons. In a twisted ideological logic, during 1966 and 1967, 'humanist' and 'compassion' could become hideous insults; 'destruction' could become a term of immense praise.[3] In other words, trauma itself officially was condoned — indeed promoted — to carry out the furthering of the revolutionary process. The period of the 1990s is peculiar as it is highly paradoxical, consisting of severe political repression as well as a continuous movement towards fostering international trade and contact with the Western world. The phrase commonly used for this is: 'walking towards the world' (*zouxiang shijie*)'. I suggest that this split state of politics is reflected in the emotional effect of ideological stagnation and globalization, a legacy that continues today. These paintings serve to represent a subtext of emotional experience, contrasting sharply with a vast body of realist sentimental depictions of oriental, feminized China, including those by highly commercial artists, such as Chen Yifei, which were produced in the 1980s and 1990s. They present a cultural interpretation that promotes the negative, painful aspect of experience, pushing a cultural critique with subversive connotations. Other later work, such as that of Sheng Qi whose recent photographic series depicts his self-mutilated four-fingered hand, uses the body in a more conscious construction of trauma as image or icon. His work applies the notion of historical trauma placed together with collective memory and personal experience. Other work actively producing images of trauma is live art, such as Zhang Huan's *65 kg*, which promotes the physical body, and video work, such as Xu Zhen's *Rainbow* (Fig. 128), which depicts a person's back being slapped violently. The theme of trauma is pursued further in exhibitions, such as Shu Yang's recent *Internal Injury*,[4] which overtly articulates the theme in its curatorial framework. The early work of Zhang Huan is discussed here, as it can be seen as the first example of work producing an aesthetic of the traumatized body, in which the artist's own body is made to undergo extreme physical and psychological exertions. The encapsulation of beauty and pain through the human body is what makes his work distinctive during this period.

---

3   Mitter, Rana, *A Bitter Revolution: China's Struggle with the Modern World*. Oxford: Oxford University Press, 2004, p. 209. Mass violence was perpetrated against individuals in the summer of 1966, resulting in more than 1,700 murders in Beijing in one month alone.

4   Shu Yang, *Internal Injury*, 798, Beijing, July–August 2006.

In paintings from China, the depiction of the manic grinning face exerts a powerful psychological force that displays a state of helplessness. Hysteria not only is shown through the facial expressions of certain paintings but also in the many depictions of groups of bodies, whether in grotesque orgiastic activities that appear violent and threatening or in association with flesh depicted as red meat.[5] In the paintings of Geng Jianyi, Yue Minjun, Yang Shaobin and Zeng Fanzhi, the artists seem fixated on single-image types, which are repeated again and again in ghastly succession. This leads to the question of what they might mean beyond the endless limited historical explanations of the 'new China' manifested in 'new Chinese art' describing individualism. Beyond presenting new subjectivities, an examination of the paintings, regarding their relationship to contemporary China in psycho-social terms, might reveal a deeper understanding of contemporary art in China and its broader historical, social, aesthetic and psychological contexts.

Grinning Faces in Repeated Succession

When looking at paintings from the late 1980s and early 1990s, a visual narrative emerges through which the grin/grimace appears as a central theme in individual work and also collectively. Geng Jianyi's well-known oil painting *A Second State* (Fig. 129), showing four grinning faces, was made in 1987.[6] It depicts faces — earless and seemingly cut out of the void — as suspended signifiers rather than real physiological faces, caught between the plastic and the real. The grinning face here is purely conceptual, removed from its physical context and displaying, one might say, a state of pure psychology, which is a suspension of the real. The title *A Second State* directly refers to Freudian terminology — "*condition seconde*" — referring to a state of hysteria in which the patient is not "in the normal state".[7] It, therefore, defines itself as removed from normality.

The striking painting in large scale is rendered more powerful by the duplication of the grinning face. The image has a plastic quality, which changes it from the possibility of being realistic and gives it the appearance of a rubbery mask with no frame beneath it. The faces are essentially unframed masks, expressions not attached to bodies and seemingly without any context against a black background. The unsettling nature of

---

5   See for example, Zeng Fanzhi, *Meat*, in Doran, Valerie (ed.), *Hou Bajiu Zhongguo Xin Yishu (China's New Art, Post 89)*. Hong Kong: Hanart Gallery, 1993, p. 148.

6   The translation alternates between 'second state' and 'second situation'. 'Second state' would appear to be closer to the idea of 'trance' or state of mind and fit Freudian terminology as suggested.

7   These examples, such as Fraulein Anna O. in 'Case Histories' recur, in Sigmund Freud and Joseph Breuer, *Studies in Hysteria*. London: Penguin, 2004, pp. 46–50.

the grinning expression is created by its wilful persistence — its manic obsessive-fixed expression that is unflinching and yet cannot be deciphered. Looking closely, the eyes are screwed up and, therefore, actually hidden and the face creased into a grin or grimace, vacillating between pleasure and pain. This grimace appears the same in many paintings, with eyes closed so the mouth dominates the field of vision and the implied sound, of course, is rendered mute in the medium of paint.

Yue Minjun's work (Fig. 73) is well known for its trademark grin that shows all teeth. Here the face is disturbingly schematic. As in *A Second State*, it is impossible to get past the dominating manic expression that denies reading real emotion by presenting an overbearingly hysterical attitude. The paintings are hideous and compulsive, uncomfortably grotesque in their wilful repetition and vacancy. In Yue's work, the size of the heads is unnaturally large in relation to the puny body, and the faces seem interchangeable, as though mechanistic. Yue's figures are unfeeling in their hysterical state, not pitiful but obnoxious and menacing. The aspect of cloning is important as a sense of threat is created in numbers, the grotesque association of mass ignorance and irresponsibility. Yue's painting is highly controlled, clean cut and unfeeling in its precision, accentuating the unnaturalness through cartoon-like composition and drawing on photography, design and the tele-visual.

Yang Shaobin's work is more humanistic, the faces represented in more physical terms. The men's faces are connected to the pink flesh and grotesque gestures and postures of their bodies, and there is a stronger sense of social cohesion in their close fleshy physicality. His later work pushes the grotesque body much further so that paint and body become intermingled into an explosion of splattered colour and flesh, which accentuates the powerful materiality of art and body alike.

Zeng Fanzhi's work again features grinning heads, but the mask series, for which he became known, seems to be about duplicity itself. The gestures of the men are expressions of pretence, as they cross their legs in shabby-looking suits and awkwardly place their huge, unwieldy hands, revealing their state of discomfort. His painting is acute social observation, which likely is derived from realist techniques but is taken much further, freeing up representation of the figure through a fluid manipulation of paint.

All the paintings discussed have a peculiarly concentrated depiction of the open-mouthed grimace, which is sometimes masked and often cloned into replicas of types. The singularity of these images exerts an obsessive quality. The manic grin is a prominent feature that borders hysterical laughter and grief — an adult version of a child who does not know whether to laugh or cry. It is both threatening and vulnerable, implying a state vacillating between confidence and weakness. Any possible narrative is suspended in a primarily psychological state of being that seems to imply a blockage of expression, an inability to diffuse emotion and a paralytic fixation. Masks, clothing and vacant contexts exaggerate the feeling of cultural depravity. In the performance work that makes actual use of the human body, the materiality of the body comes to the fore, and the psychological state is highlighted through the real presence of the body and its heaviness and human vulnerability. The paintings of the early nineties produce a complex picture of how the body reacts and how it subsequently portrays itself. Their fixed silent screams and the later bodily manifestations of the burdened body produce its own spectacle as self/artist/marginalized persona.

Hysteria and Its (Western) Historical Context in Culture

The hysteric, as depicted in art, can be seen as descriptive of society as well as constituting the artist's own obsession — a cultural critique that, nevertheless, rebounds onto itself in an act of power and narcissism. The use of the term hysteria in this context may be seen as a leap in terms of historical and cultural references, since the word is rooted in classical Western culture and, in the modern context, associated with Western psycho-analysis, specifically developed by Freud whose well-known case studies of female hysterics form a fundamental basis for Western psycho-analysis.[8] For centuries, hysteria was associated with a principally female condition from its etymological roots meaning 'uterus', first coined by Hippocrates.[9] As Janet Beizer describes, the hysteric as male subject, however, goes back more than a hundred years in literature. Beizer's excellent synopsis of the history of hysteria as discourse throughout many centuries shows that the departure from association of hysteria with the womb to that of the brain only occurred in the late nineteenth century, and, even then, there was a tenacious clinging to the notion of hysteria as principally female. Beizer's discussion of Flaubert, who describes himself as a hysteric, illustrates that the use of the term relating to males is by no means completely unprecedented. In nineteenth-century France, male cases of hysteria were diagnosed as pertaining to those on the margins of society: "workers, vagabonds, and déclassés, these men were not only marginal (and therefore assimilable to women) but were also, as if in echo to the most ancient of uterine theories, virtual incarnations of mobility".[10]

The connection between nineteenth-century France and contemporary China might appear oblique; nevertheless, there is a strong resonance in cultural terms, with rapid urbanization and huge waves of migrancy becoming key components of social transformation in China during the past two decades. The theme of artist as migrant also

---

8   The case studies can be read in Sigmund Freud and Joseph Breuer, *Studies in Hysteria*, Penguin, 2004. It is worth noting that the word 'hysteria' is transliterated in Chinese as it has no native translation as such. The word '*xisiliya*' is very much a foreign term, imported from the English word. This situates it in the construction of modernity through the readings of Western writers, particularly in the early twentieth century.

9   Beizer, Janet, *Ventriloquized Bodies: Narratives of Hysteria in Nineteenth-century France*. Ithaca: Cornell University Press, 1994, p. 4.

10 Ibid., pp. 6–7.

has rich connotations in the Chinese context and often has been identified, particularly in the case of Zhang Huan's work. The development of artist communities on the fringes of Beijing is a phenomenon that has resulted from the influx of artists from the provinces flocking into the cities and forming new cultural environments. The Freudian discourse of hysteria through his case studies has become fundamental to the development of psycho-analysis in the twentieth century. In the 1980s, Freud was among the many sources of modern thought taken up by Chinese intellectuals. As Beizer points out, "in the mid-1980s, the hysteric was being rediscovered by literary and cultural critics on both sides of the Atlantic and was often recovered in feminism's name as a figure emblematic of revolt against the patriarchy: as a cult figure."[11] This cult figure of rebellion against the patriarch fits well with the new subjectivity of Chinese artists at the turn of the 1990s, when the assertion of a strong, self-determined identity came into being. Many works of art during the late 1980s to the early mid-1990s dealt with the subject of the patriarch Mao, showing him barred (Wang Guangyi), dissolved or abstracted (Yan Peiming) or as a backdrop to social life or degenerate youth (Liu Wei), symbolizing, above all, his status as a past icon, no longer at the forefront of people's lives. The lost patriarch, loss of the father figure and lack of a substitute role model is, in Freudian terms, at the root of hysteria and, therefore, a prime condition of modernity, particularly where women are concerned (in traditional terms).

Hysteria as Language of Discontent in Contemporary China

By locating late twentieth-century visual culture in China within this discourse, a possible reflexive relationship is suggested between the subject as it is portrayed and the producer's own cultural milieu. Recent feminist analyses of hysteria in the fields of comparative literature and cultural studies support my use of it, at least in the context of contemporary art. In my own analysis, I maintain that it is the dominance of a certain kind of male culture, stemming from Mao who is gender specific and evident as a dominant theme in contemporary art and the art world in China. The specifically Chinese context also would bear witness to extensive themes in the early decades of the twentieth century; Lu Xun stands out as the most obvious critical figure, describing the hysterical reactions of the Chinese people in such writings as *Madman's Diary* and *Ah Q*. These themes returned in China in the 1980s when Freud was recognized and translated as part of the rush for Western theory known as '*Wenhua Re* (Culture Fever)'.[12] The historical link between the Cultural Revolution and the May Fourth Movement, in terms of its obsessive and destructive nature, is astutely observed by Rana Mitter: "The Cultural

---

11 Ibid., p. 2.

12 Jing Wang, *High Culture Fever, Politics, Aesthetics and Ideology in Deng's China*. London: University of California Press, 1996, p. 10.

Revolution in China was largely caused by the obsessions of one man concerned both with the purity of his revolution and his own personal position. However, the patterns of thought that defined the path he took were largely ones that had shaped him in May Fourth. Mao's Cultural Revolution is an explicable end-point of the darkest side of May Fourth — obsession with youth, destruction of the past, arrogance about the superiority of one's own chosen system of thought — without the enlightenment of the original — cosmopolitanism, critical enquiry and universalism."[13]

Recent scholarship has made sense of the position of hysteria in the broadest context, aligning it to a late twentieth-century condition of discontent and, more specifically, to a "malady of representation".[14] This is a useful reading in the context of late twentieth-century art in China. The transition from the 1980s to the 1990s was, it could be argued, a transition from a humanist visual language epitomized by the search for self — '*ziwo biaoxian* (self expression)' and '*xungen* (root-searching)', frequently discussed in Chinese literary theory — to a new subjectivity seeking to distance itself from those humanist values and creating a visual language that foregrounded the artist as subject.[15] Paintings and performance art in China in the 1990s mark a moment of cynicism in Chinese culture, following the humanist explorations of the 1980s. In the words of Gao Minglu, the paintings "might refer to the artist himself in a gesture of indifference, self-mockery, and powerlessness — as a figure called a '*pizi*', or 'riffraff'."[16] While this is true, I would take the analysis further by suggesting that the depiction of a hysterical state reveals something beyond the artist's intention, producing, inadvertently, a subtext of agony that is real but not always controllable.

The nineties was a decade when cultural production seemed to take on a particular expression of social alienation, and more extreme work that used real body parts as material came to the fore at the end of the decade and the turn of the twenty-first century. This type of work, such as Zhu Yu's *Eating People*,[17] caused a shockwave of revulsion, which appeared to prove the depths of depravity that the 'new China' could

---

13 Mitter, Op. cit., 2004, p. 208.

14 Bronfen, E., *The Knotted Subject. Hysteria and Its Discontents*. Princeton: Princeton University Press, 1998, p. 40.

15 See Martina Köppel-Yang, *Semiotic Warfare: The Chinese Avant-garde, 1979–1989, A Semiotic Analysis*. Hong Kong: Timezone 8, 2003, pp. 69–71.

16 Gao Minglu, 'From Elite to Small Man: The Many faces of a Transitional Avant-Garde in Mainland China', in Gao (ed.), *Inside Out: New Chinese Art*. London: University of California Press, 1998, p. 156.

17 See image of this work and others using human body parts in Ai Weiwei and Feng Boyi, Op. cit. This catalogue shows a range of images of artworks that can be seen as displaying the hysterical body, abounding in images of abused bodies and grotesque distortions of nature made from animal and human body parts.

display. The delving into morgues to produce artworks highlighted the ethical distance from the West and also showed how the rapid rise of capitalist practices in China was matched by a certain anarchy, which allowed artists access to the darker sides of society with impunity. Chinese artists and critics confidently could announce that they were able to produce more extreme work than Damien Hirst, the arch bad boy of Britart.

The Emergence of the Body

In China, the body appeared as a 'locus of the self' and an index of subjectivity for the first time in art in 1986. In the context of a highly competitive art world in which artists compete for recognition, the use of the body can be a powerful tool for literally making the artist visible, as both work of art and persona, by integrating the relationship between the artist and the work that is produced. Although the body in contemporary Chinese art has been a central theme in art practice, until recently, its history has not been sufficiently analyzed. Recent works of art in China have focused on the mortal body as material flesh through the controversial use of real human and animal body parts.[18] Performance art necessarily uses the body as its material. In China, performance has emerged since the 1980s as the most radical form of art and, as Amelia Jones says, perhaps more than any other art form has postmodernist implications through Its use of the 'real', acting as a form of cultural agency between the physical and material aspect of the human body and the audience.[19]

When talking about the emergence of the body in art since the 1960s, Amelia Jones says: "the body, which previously had to be veiled to confirm the Modernist regime of meaning and value, has more and more aggressively surfaced during this period as a locus of the self and the site where the public domain meets the private, where the social is negotiated, produced and made sense of."[20] In China, this has been an even more intensive process, since the historical period of rapid economic development and prolific cultural production initially was compressed. From 1986 until the mid-1990s, the body indeed became more and more visible, until its appearance in performance and painting in the 1990s had a strong physical presence, which, paradoxically, exerted a psychological force.

---

18 See Ai Weiwei and Feng Boyi, ibid.

19 Jones, Amelia, 'Survey', in Tracey Warr and Amelia Jones (eds.), *The Artist's Body*. London: Phaidon Press, 2000, pp. 16–47.

20 Jones, ibid., pp. 20–21.

Work by Zhang Huan and Ma Liuming involves the body in radically new forms within the context of Chinese history and culture. As younger artists from the generation of the 'China avant-garde' who were born in the sixties, these two artists enter the cultural scene at a different moment. In Zhang and Ma's work, the artist's persona in the 1990s became an important feature, and the imagery of the work was bound up with the imagery of the artist as constructing an identity in and through the artwork, which is the body itself.

Since the early 1990s, there has been a prevalence and preference for mainland Chinese male artists to perform artworks using the nude body, frequently involving masochistic elements with forms of physical endurance or body puncturing. Zhang Huan's early work produces startling imagery in which "the conflict between the body and the external environment is the way to prove the existence of the self."[21] This work is about the environment and its effect on the human body and makes use of the body as bearing the symptoms of spiritual oppression, combined with a rawness that gives it a certain immediacy in contrast to more sophisticated performances. The titles of his performances are reduced to numeric measurements: *12 Square Metres, 65 kg and 25 mm Threading Steel*. These are three works in which the body is pushed to extremes, illustrating an exaggerated version of the human condition and highlighting the physicality of human existence, which, in turn, has a profound spiritual effect.

In *12 Square Metres* (Fig. 130), performed on 31 May 1994, Zhang Huan sits naked for an hour on a public toilet in the village, covered in a visceral liquid of fish and honey that attracted flies. In an interview, Zhang describes the experience thus: "I just felt that everything began to vanish from my sight. Life seemed to be leaving me far in the distance. I had no concrete thought except that my mind was completely empty. I could only feel my body, more and more flies landing and crawling over my nose, eyes, ears, forehead, every part of me. I could feel them eating the liquid on my body. Some were stuck but did not stop eating. I could even tell that they were more interested in the fish liquid than the honey because there were more flies on the left part of my body, where that liquid was. The very concept of life was then for me the simple experience of body."[22] Zhang Huan's work *12 Square Metres* carries this theme into the everyday life of present day China, conveying the demands of the body in a filthy, fly-ridden environment of everyday small-town life. In this work, a self-conscious feeling of the alienation of modernity is conveyed through a single naked figure, his abject physical

---

21 Zhang Huan, in Qian Zhijian, 'Performing bodies: Zhang Huan, Ma Liuming, and performance art in China' (interview), *Art Journal*, Summer 1999, p. 68.

22 Zhang Huan, Ibid., pp. 65–66. *12 Square Meters* was performed in Dashan Village in the suburbs of Beijing, which was renamed Beijing East Village by Zhang Huan.

body trapped in a filthy confining environment, inhabited by flies that literally feed off his flesh. The body appears both sexualized and politicized, portraying a masculinist display of muscle-power, which has an impressive aura. The image shows a close-up sideways view of the artist, his head shaven and his skin glistening with the honey and fish substance. On his left wrist is a heavy silver bracelet, and a silver ring is on his thumb — the jewellery his only adornment. This work, although ostensibly about the effect of the environment on the body, immediately is apparent as a work about image itself, specifically the image of the artist. It could even be seen as a self-portrait of the artist caught in a moment between modernity and post-modernity. The alienated figure with his shiny muscle-bound body has a monumental feel of existential angst of modernity, and yet, this image is an icon of what could be termed 'post-modern China'. It could not have been made in the 1980s.

The work *65 kg* (Fig. 131), by Zhang Huan, was performed in July 1994 in Beijing. In the words of Sheldon Hsiao-Peng Lu, "the artist was naked and bound to a horizontal bar with ten iron chains three meters above the ground. Beneath the horizontal bar, and placed on a stack of white mattresses, an electric stove heated an iron plate. A doctor drew 250 millilitres of blood from the artist. The blood was then slowly dripped onto the heated plate. It burned immediately, and the room filled with a strong, pungent smell. This performance of self-abuse lasted for an hour and a half."[23]

In a third work entitled *25 mm Threading Steel* (Fig. 132), which took place in 1995, Zhang Huan lies naked on the floor on a construction site on the third underground level of a sky-scraper in Beijing. Here his naked body lies underneath a stream of sparks coming from an industrial machine, the body of the artist looking dangerously close to the red hot burning sparks as they fly over him, 25 millimetres, as the title of the piece indicates. Zhang describes how the construction workers were reluctant to let him do the performance as "they were afraid that the grinding wheel would cut my body into pieces if an accident occurred."[24]

In these three works, the body is placed under the most extreme form of physical challenge, which might be seen as masochistic. The performances themselves are witnessed by small audiences, perhaps up to twenty people. Photography becomes a vital part of the work as it is the transmitter of the performance act through image, and the resulting images become the work. The body in the first piece, *12 Square Metres*, is construed narcissistically as a shining muscle-bound body of flesh, which creates an aura of heroism and magnitude. The use of a real, impoverished environment is employed as

---

23 Lu, Hsiao-peng, 'Global Postmodernization: the Intellectual, the Artist and China's Condition', in Arif Dirlik, and Zhang Zudong (eds.), *Postmodernism in China*. London: Duke University Press, 2000, p. 156.

24 Zhang Huan, Op. cit., p. 68.

a kind of studio backdrop. In *65 kg*, the body is dislocated from its usual gravitational mode. There is deliberate cruelty in its positioning — bound in iron bars, hanging from the ceiling, devoid of its physical power and at the mercy of its essential biological or material aspect. The weight of flesh and bone and the literal flow of blood, which is forced out through the drip, is an outward display of the inner body. The audience, integral to the image of the piece, are seen to be watching this enactment of pure physicality, which is the manipulation of the body by the artist's own means. The mind has brought this on, rendering the physical body as flesh and muscle, powerless and at the hands of others. In *25 mm Threading Steel*, the body is brought even closer to pure physical danger; this very simple piece of work juxtaposes or puts together the actual physical human body and the crude industrial machine that endangers it. Here the artist's body is almost invisible as it is viewed necessarily through the stream of flying sparks of red-hot metal. In these works, there is a strong physical presence of the body in its naked form, a macho self-image, which is highlighted through the acts of self-suffering it is made to undergo.

The visual communication of the male body in work by Chinese artists suggests a complex relationship with its environment. The legacy of hardship was experienced by artists of this generation, in the period following the Cultural Revolution when they grew up. The male body in the work of many artists can be read as a belated evocation of the Maoist/homo-social ideology and the social and cultural legacies of the Cultural Revolution that remain inherent in the political structure today, despite many years of market reform. The body can be seen as a stark example in cultural production of an emergent male liberation, which indicates an erosion of the sharp division between public and private in the transformation of society during the development of a market economy.

Conclusion

The paintings shown have a peculiarly concentrated depiction of the open-mouthed grimace, which is sometimes masked and often cloned into replicas of types. The singularity of these images exerts an obsessive quality. The narrative is suspended in a primarily psychological state of being that seems to imply a blockage of expression, an inability to diffuse emotion and a paralytic fixation. Masks, clothing and vacant contexts exaggerate the feeling of cultural depravity. In the performance work, which utilizes and activates the human body, the materiality of the body comes to the fore and the psychological state is highlighted through the real presence of the body and its heaviness and human vulnerability.

Sheng Qi's work *Universal Brand Happy Chicken*, shown at the season *Fortune Cookies* at the Institute of Contemporary Arts in 1997, can be seen, retrospectively, through the framework of inhumane abuse of the body, alongside the kind of sanctioned abuse of animals in a global economy. With props of supermarket (ready-to-cook) chickens and tables laden with syringes, Chinese medical materials, rubber gloves and a pot of boiling 'soup', he proceeded, slowly and painstakingly, to manipulate a chicken over his body, later injecting it with coloured dye, then finally standing on the table and urinating at length over it. From such performances, it is possible to see the male body as both victim and oppressor at a particular moment in history, perhaps reflecting previous decades in China of oppression, terroristic reality and strong patriarchal nationalism dominated by models of monumentality and power. Sheng's photographic work (for which he has become known since then) features his own mutilated hand holding up small black and white photographs from the past against a red background. The work is a symbolic and aesthetic construction of bodily trauma and memory. The image of trauma in this work becomes more important than the trauma itself. The most extreme work found in the exhibition *Fuck Off* — work by Zhu Yu and others using real body parts of humans and animals — might be seen as the ultimate sickness, where hysteria is manifested in seemingly inhumane forms, a transferral of hysteria onto the manipulation of nature and its moral consequences. This seems a far cry from the Cultural Revolution and yet, a long hidden history of the painful legacy of that period. This 'post-human' work questions the sanctity of the body and vacillates between colluding with horror and critiquing it.

In the twenty-first century, a more sophisticated artistic discourse has developed in which the use of body 'as hysteric' is employed quite deliberately within, and because of, this discourse. The legacy of the Cultural Revolution, by any means, has not passed by, as individuals who are actively attempting to revive and activate historical incidents involving brutal abuse of civil rights against individuals are prevented from showing their work or telling their stories.[25] What is shown through artwork, however apparently apolitical, nevertheless reveals traces and expressions of an environment that is otherwise unreachable, as it becomes more and more taboo to associate anything negative with China. Live art is unique as the only art medium that continually can produce a meaningful form of resistance in a society that retains a fragile balance between capitalism and political control. To return to the words of Janet Beizer, "to apprehend the phenomenon that I call the hystericization of culture, we must focus here on a historical moment experienced as anchorless and uncentered: a moment of crisis related to the razing of political and social structures and, more significantly, the demolishing of a symbolic system. The body of the hysteric — mobile, capricious, convulsive — is both metaphor and myth of an epoch: emblem of whirling chaos and cathartic channeling of it."[26]

---

25 The individuals I refer to must remain anonymous for their own protection.

26 Beizer, Op. cit., pp. 8–9. I am grateful to Scott Wilson from the Institute of Cultural Research in Lancaster for his positive response to my paper delivered at Birmingham Institute of Art and Design, in May 2004, and for his pointing me in the right direction for sources of hysteria in Cultural Studies.

I_t I_s N_{ot} M_{erely a} M_{emory}

Shao Yinong and Mu Chen

The Cultural Revolution of the 1960s is often known, in a literary sense, as '*shinian haojie* (ten years of catastrophe)'. To the many Chinese who were involved in the Cultural Revolution, its influence perhaps has had a more far-reaching and profound effect than if it had been a war. The slogan of the Cultural Revolution was "smash the old world; establish a new one" — the ideal and motivation of those revolutionary years. The devastation of the Cultural Revolution was not solely the destruction of temples and ancestral shrines to this end; the grief that remains is not only a memory of being criticized. By forcing the breakage of a whole culture, the Cultural Revolution may be an unrecoverable disaster. In the several decades since the new world that has been established by the revolution, it seems to resemble a sand castle that has collapsed after being swept by a modern wave of 'rectification'. The people have had to combat a new economic tide. Although the tragedy of the Cultural Revolution enables us to be alert to the bewitchment and deception of the new, it is difficult to distinguish the truth: the new and old have been obscured by revolutionary, commercial and stylish packaging. Through works of art, we can only attempt to differentiate and analyze elements within the mist of reality and history and use images to present personal thoughts.

In the spring of 2000, we prepared the equipment for a small portable photographic studio: a box of clothes, a 450-watt lamp, a soft box, two background lamps, two cameras, a tripod, blue background paper and gifts for the elderly and children. This began our photographic journey of family portraits for the artwork *Family Register* (Fig. 61).

We can trace my (Shao Yinong) ancestry back to my great grandfather, Shao Fuyuan, who was a long-term labourer. His son, my grandfatherwas married to my clever and capable grandmother; the family quickly became prosperous and had nine children.

My grandmother bought land and built houses becoming a big landowner within the neighbourhood. During the Land Reformation (*Tugai*), the garden and farmland were confiscated, and, during the Cultural Revolution, the old mansion and shops were seized. My grandmother only was allowed to live under the veranda; she waited here until the property was returned to her in the 1980s, when the mansion had been in disrepair for many years. My grandmother's descendants moved to different places. Those who were wealthy built their own small modern houses; others, facing greater financial difficulties, established families in the village.

When we returned to the Shao ancestral home, we found uncle Shao Jiayuan, the first figure to appear in the *Family Register*. He was ninety-six years old at the time and the oldest member of the family. Uncle Jiayuan had been tried for demonstrating and had been accused of being a rich farmer and counter-revolutionary from the Land Reformation to the Cultural Revolution. Furthermore, his 'problematic style' made him hard to get along with. His son, Shao Ronggui, the second figure to appear in the *Family Register*, publicly denounced his father during the Cultural Revolution. His father was an honest and upright man, pleading guilty to charges of having a bad attitude and was imprisoned several times, the longest lasting six months. Uncle Jiayuan was the third son of my grandfather. His wife had been the fiancée of his elder brother, and, after his brother's early death, the grandmother ordered her son's fiancée to marry uncle Jiayuan. However, uncle Jiayuan was in love with a girl in the village, and his love for her remained throughout his life. This 'unregistered' love was considered a 'problematic style' or 'immorality' during the Cultural Revolution.

My father is someone we always think about. He had many stories: one was about clothes that were used in our work *Family Register*. In the early years of the People's Republic, my father gave my grandfather and grandmother and each of my three uncles a Chinese Zhongshan suit (later known as Mao suit) to unify the worlds of the old and young. This was a patriarchal action that showed care. The older generation automatically used to think and act this way and it was my father's revolutionary behaviour for several decades. We presented this kind of typical method of care in the *Family Register*. However, it was difficult for us to find a Zhongshan suit; there was no trace of these in the shopping malls of Beijing. It almost seemed as if they existed only in our memory and had vanished from daily life. Eventually, we found them among the old clothes in the Panjiayuan antique market. As we brought these grey, blue and army-green suits home, we sighed with sadness. When Dr. Sun Yat-Sen overthrew the Qing dynasty in 1911, he had designed this suit as a symbol of his belief in the revolution. The suits had been popular for several decades in the new China but now were abandoned to a corner of the city, being sold, ironically, in an antique market, at RMB 3 yuan each.

When we began to photograph *Family Register*, we used the oldest style of group photo to get all the family members together. All the stories that had happened to them in history were to be were wiped away and treated as if they had never happened. We thought their stories might be hidden their stories inside the suit and used it to unite them and remind them of their history. bring them back to a period of unification. At the time of the Cultural Revolution, men and women, young and old, all sang the same song, walked with the same step, wore clothes of the same colour and followed the same orders without objection. My family included those who had been landlord, wealthy farmer, counter-revolutionary, revolutionary soldier, head of rebellions, peasant, worker, or teacher, scholar, artist, merchant, salesman, and laid-off worker; each identity represented a different kind of life experience. To us, the small family unit is huge and compact, and is the liveliest specimen of Chinese society. On calm faces that showed little personality, this family contained another history, on their calm faces, with no personality. One action, and one uniform created a sense of collective intimacy that seems to represent a nation's systemic power. Simultaneously, this kind of simple *Register* provides a visual footnote in the study of sociology and anthropology.

In 1966, the year that the Cultural Revolution began, I was five years old and studying in primary school. At that time, in a land of 9,600,000 square kilometres, everyone heard the same broadcasts and the whole nation saw the same Model Operas. Thus, everyone's memory of the assembly hall is almost the same; however, the most significant memory of the scene varies with each individual. For example, my father never forgot seeing two counter-revolutionaries being killed at the chairman's platform, and my brother remembered his first love of a schoolmate at the backstage. What I cannot forget is the decorated mourning hall of Chairman Mao. The assembly hall of the local primary school was twenty metres away from my home and became the busiest place during the Cultural Revolution. I remember on one day, when the adults were out writing slogans and big-character posters and students were parading in the streets, my mother asked me to stay at home and recite the multiplication table. The wall outside of the school was being covered by the big-character posters, and, eventually, they reached the windows of my home, located on the second floor. If I stretched out my hand, I could easily touch them. At night, the school continued with criticism meetings. A colleague of my mother's once took me to a criticism meeting in an assembly hall that was crowded with people. At that time, no one wore clothing made with printed material, hence, the whole hall looked like a sea of blue. On the stage people were wearing boards around their necks and tall pointed hats, resembling rocket launchers and; some were standing and some were kneeling. In fact, I did not know what was going on. I noticed that a woman was wearing a white porcelain badge on her chest, illustrating the famous painting *Mao Goes to Anyuan*. The badge looked remarkably beautiful on her blue clothing. Once the criticism session began, the whole hall was in an uproar, and when people became restless, I immediately grabbed the woman's badge. This was my first souvenir badge, and I kept it until my graduation from university. I also remember another day when the revolutionaries ordered all landlords and their families to assemble in the square outside the primary school. Covering over half the square was a pile of the 'four olds' that had been found while searching the landlords' homes, including a tap, a prop for traditional festivities, clothes, books and furniture. It was dark when we had been rushed to the square, and people began to light a fire. The fire was so large that everyone's face could be clearly seen. My grandmother held me in her arms so that I would not be afraid. When I returned home, the ground had been dug up with a lot of fresh earth turned over. At that time, I had no idea why. Later when I grew up, I realized that they had been searching for my family's account books and treasures.

During the process of taking photos for the *Family Register* project in April 2000, we returned to our ancestral town, a place called Gexian, where there were houses with exquisite Qing dynasty carvings, an elegant ancestral hall of the Republican period and a simple but grand hall of the Cultural Revolution — all surviving harmoniously with each together. The incompatible struggles and one's enthusiasm and suffering no longer existed, but what was left were the different architectural styles. This resembled the four great leaders now printed on the 100 yuan banknotes, using a motif to erase and reconcile historical disputes. My grandfather previously had opened a shop in Gexian. Unexpectedly, the shop front was a large Soviet style hall with several European style columns and three arched doors. The grand entrance with blue bricks and black tiles was rather dazzling. At the door was a pond. The black surface of the water, littered with rubbish and waste products, held a reflection of the hall. The hall had not been used for a long time and the door was locked. We pushed open the door slightly and peered through the crack. It was empty and had an unpleasant, mouldy smell. Since that time, whenever I pass an abandoned assembly hall, I have a memory of that historical period that never goes away. The discovery of the assembly hall arouses thoughts of a new empty space — a memory of a familiar, yet unknown, space deep inside our heart. Regardless of the slogans, songs, applause, or cheering in a place full of emptiness, a deathly stillness still prevails. History and our hearts are related, and, as we move forward, history will appear.

The history of the Chinese Communist Party, as recorded in textbooks, novels and films, has been defined by the constant political congresses in China, while the attendance of Mao Zedong decided whether one congress should be considered significant enough to be recorded in the history of the Party. Since the establishment of the People's Republic, all of Chinese society has become politicized. Meetings have become more important, not only for the political life of the Party, but also for the common people, making decisions on the fate of the nation and individuals.

The journey for the photograph series *Assembly Hall* started with these two approaches. We began in Ruijin in Jiangxi province and continued along the route up to Yan'an in Shaanxi province, where the 7th Congress took place in 1945. In November 1931, the first conference of the Chinese Soviet Republic was held in Ruijin for which the Party had built a large hall. Later, it was destroyed in the civil war, and restored again after the People's Republic was established. Another route took us from Changting, Gutian, Xingguo, Ningdu and up to Zunyi, Yan'an and Xibaipo. As important revolutionary sites, each of these clearly is marked on maps. Similar to other scenic spots, they already have become tourist sites. The halls were restored to how they looked in the past, newly renovated with old displays that can be fully introduced by some well-trained tour guide. For the past three years, we have followed the routes of the Red

Guards' Exchange Revolutionary Experience Travel (*Geming Dachuanlian*). We first went to the revolutionary shrines and the historical areas to search for the assembly halls. Although they had different names in different places — assembly hall, conference hall, club, or cultural palace — they were each repositories of our mutual collective memories. The main difference between the assembly hall and the other buildings was that the former had a holy platform for the chairman, which divided the space into two: the stage and the auditorium. Those who approached the stage from the auditorium might change from being a public member to either being glorified or the subject of counter-revolutionary contempt. On the stage, the seats were identified with names in anticipation of a performance. In the auditorium, the masses shouted slogans with their arms raised. The history of the People's Republic has been filled with ceaseless political campaigns. Each of the banners used in each conference can be recorded, together with those used at assemblies — for criticism, struggle, sermon, denunciation, debate, report, and honour — and form a comprehensive history of the new China.

With the structural shift, in the 1990s, from a political society to an economically driven one and the decline of the collective economy and state-operated enterprise, the bustling assembly halls became desolate and empty. As large but derelict buildings, the majority of these assembly halls were demolished before or after our photograph-taking. Those left in villages became warehouses, factory buildings, schools or cattle depots or were entirely abandoned, while those in the city were converted into restaurants, dancing halls or skating rinks (Figs. 17–20). A few were preserved as assembly halls and theatres, but their luxurious decoration diminished the political resonance of the past. In today's climate of demolition and transformation, these buildings, full of period characteristics have become increasingly rare. We often lamented that we could not take photos fast enough to keep up with the rapidity of demolition. In one case, the assembly hall of Number Fifty School in Qinghai, the workers were removing the roof when we found it. We took a photo when the workers went for lunch; only the wood beam of the building was left. Under the gloomy sky, the red banner at the chairman's platform looked a bit sad. If we had arrived one day later, perhaps we would not have seen anything of the building.

During the demolition campaign throughout China's economic development, assembly halls, as the product of collective life and socialist environment, were abandoned and demolished. As intellectuals and artists, our instinct is to restore them. The assembly hall served as a revolutionary place for several decades. They embody the history and reality of Chinese society, existing in whatever memories, introspection or research we have. We used images to record them, the negatives capturing details of each disturbance. Our principle was to take simple and direct records. No matter how tired and excited we were, our method of execution was fixed. We took centred, symmetrical, levelled, accurate exposure photos, changing films mechanically. By repeating our actions, we grasped the deadly stillness. Only when all remained quiet, could people notice the things left on the chairman's platform and feel the scenes and hear the sound of warm applause, excited and indignant criticism, void oaths, boring reports and also the joyous revolutionary songs above the halls.

In the same spatial area, we perhaps played different roles under different historical circumstances. Gexian town had an ancient one-hundred-year old ancestral hall. After the liberation, it became a school. Although the building was old and dilapidated, the exquisite carving on the beams and wooden brackets could still be seen. Several columns were carved with characters in two layers. The uppermost layer had Cultural Revolution slogans, but since that layer was beginning to peel off, it revealed the words beneath, which were mostly the moral teachings and persuasions of Confucius and Mencius. The building seemed to be eroding naturally. The ancestral hall had been used for one thousand years, abandoned for fifty years and then replaced by an assembly hall for another thirty or forty years of uproar and glamour, only to become desolate. In one village, there were two halls that previously were used to enlighten the spirits: one advocating Confucian ideas of loyalty and filial piety and another transmitting the thoughts of Mao Zedong. They both now are abandoned. We tried hard to differentiate and analyze the characters on the columns and to appreciate the carving, which cannot be reproduced today. We Chinese people should be proud of our ancient civilization, yet we always try to forget and wipe out or rewrite our history. The scene that appears in reality seemed like those dappled columns on which history could be uncovered, layer by layer.

As time has passed, traces of the Cultural Revolution have become fewer and fewer. Some things that are left have become collectible and re-valued as cultural relics. However, even in today's economy-driven society, there are times when one will be reminded of the time when politics confronted the collective unconsciousness. The more intensely inner feelings clash with reality, the more memory of the Cultural Revolution can creep in. Memory has different levels. Memory may be a story of our own experience, someone else's story, a kind of sound or, indeed, images. For us, the initial memory of the Cultural Revolution is contained in photographs from newspapers that we collected when we were young and the colours of those distinctive propaganda paintings.

'Revolution' suggests a kind of magnificent and explosive colour with full of energy to release. While we were dealing with either a comrade, friend or an enemy, or during struggles even between one's own left and right foot, left and right hand or mind and matter, there is no option other than to execute revolution within the atmosphere of this stimulating colour. Revolution is able to completely destroy something in a way that war is not. One who grew up during the Cultural Revolution used to love the explosive colours that were carried by propaganda paintings, red flags or souvenir badges of Mao Zedong, and which generated excitement from seeing blood. I always dream of red Mao badges in a cave, on a mountain slope or among books. That kind of red is never forgotten: every time I had red powder put on my cheeks for the performance in the chorus, I felt my face turn red and hot; when I wore the red scarf for the first time, I constantly admired the red floating in front of my chest.

In the series *Axis of Memory*, we enlarged scanned photographs until the images began to blur completely into colours. We then painted the memory colours into it. Each small square seems like a luminous screen. In the work *Red Sea* (Fig. 133), the Chinese 'carnival' style reappears. The warmth of the festival celebration and the red fire reach a climax. The memory of the Cultural Revolution's colour is embodied in *Fairy Tales in Red Era* (Fig. 134). These standard photos are not photos for identity cards, but for displaying on an honour roll in a show window. They are enlarged to the same size as standard images of Marx, Mao Zedong, Zhou Enlai, Zhu De, Liu Shaoqi and Deng Xiaoping in an assembly hall. We have seen photos of leaders and revolutionary models as we grew up. Now we want to take photos of ourselves to display on the walls. We colour the negatives of black and white photos by using the nearly pure pigments — colours belonging to our childhood. From the faces of handicapped children, we experience sorrow and loneliness in our innermost being.

In our colourful world, on the one hand, we like colours that show elegance and, on the other hand, we like colours that show violence. We have been deeply affected by dye artworks of the past few years. Two contrasting Chinese colours exist in our mind. One belongs to our memory of revolutionary China, full of explosive colours and the colour red that bleeds with excitement, while another is a dreamland of literati, where we find the Tang poetries and the Song paintings, geniuses and beauties, and the elegance of classic colours. One is filled with red flags in the sky, amid cheering and enthusiasm, extremely intense in feeling, and the other is a scene filled with plums, orchids, bamboos and chrysanthemums against high mountains and flowing waters, poetic and peaceful. In our artworks, time and space are often interwoven and overlapping. They show our ideology instead of genuine reality. In *Childhood* (Fig. 135), *Axis of Memory and Fairy Tales in Red Era*, two techniques are repeated: the 'republican dye technique' and the 'revolutionary dye technique', as they are called. We are obsessed with the hand-made dye colour technique because our colour is no longer the original colours, rather they are the colours from our memories. Colouring the photographs does not draw attention to itself, but the unnoticed relationship that changes or emphasizes the original image. At the same time, it also internalizes and individualizes material reality. Reality can become history, negotiating the interchange between reality and unreality through dye colour; it also links the Cultural Revolution and China's traditional culture.

We and our artworks return to the past, time and time again. This is neither because we love the past nor that it represents the time of our childhood. This rupture in our memory requires more reflection. If we do not have enough time to envisage this seriously, the destruction and devastation of our culture will become even greater. And, therefore, we use our visual work to record and depict broken histories, to establish a space that can accommodate different periods and to urge for an artistic response in the conflict between memory and loss.

Glossary

Lu Xun	鲁迅	1881–1936	Wang Tong	王彤	b. 1967
Luo Gongliu	罗工柳	1916-2004	Wang Xizhi	王羲之	321–379
Ma Liuming	马六明	b. 1969	Wang Zhaoda	王肇达	b. 1943
Mao Xuhui	毛旭辉	b. 1956	Weng Rulan	翁如兰	b. 1944
Mao Zedong	毛泽东	1893–1976	Wu Changshuo	吴昌硕	1844–1927
Mei Lanfang	梅兰芳	1894–1961	Wu Shanzhuan	吴山专	b. 1960
Miao Xiaochun	缪晓春	b. 1964	Xu Bing	徐冰	b. 1955
Mu Chen	慕辰	b. 1970	Xu Yihui	徐一辉	b. 1964
Nie Yuanzi	聂元梓	b. 1921	Xu Zhen	徐震	b. 1977
Ouyang Xun	欧阳洵	557–641	Yan Han	彦涵	b. 1916
Pang Xunqin	庞薰琹	1906–1985	Yan Peiming	严培明	b. 1960
Peng Bin	彭彬	b. 1927	Yan Zhenqing	颜真卿	709–785
Qi Baishi	齐白石	1864–1957	Yang Fudong	杨福东	b. 1971
Qi Zhilong	祁志龙	b. 1962	Yang Shaobin	杨少斌	b. 1963
Qiu Zhijie	邱志杰	b. 1969	Yang Zhenzhong	杨振中	b. 1968
Shao Yinong	邵逸农	b. 1961	Yao Wenyuan	姚文元	b. 1932
Shen Yaoyi	沈尧伊	b. 1943	Yin Shoushi	尹瘦石	1919–1998
Shen Yiqian	沈逸千	1908–1944	Yu Hong	喻红	b. 1966
Sheng Qi	盛奇	b. 1965	Yu Youhan	余友涵	b. 1943
Shi Lu	石鲁	1919–1982	Yue Minjun	岳敏君	b. 1962
Shu Tong	舒同	1905–1998	Zeng Fanzhi	曾梵志	b. 1964
Sui Jianguo	隋建国	b. 1956	Zhang Huan	张洹	b. 1965
Sun Zhongshan	孙中山	1866–1925	Zhang Peili	张培力	b. 1957
Tang Xiaohe	唐小禾	b. 1941	Zhang Xiaogang	张晓刚	b. 1958
Wang Chaowen	王朝闻	1909–2004	Zhao Yannian	赵延年	b. 1924
Wang Chuan	王川	b. 1967	Zhou Chunya	周春芽	b. 1955
Wang Guangyi	王广义	b. 1957	Zhou Enlai	周恩来	1889–1976
Wang Jinsong	王劲松	b. 1963	Zhou Hongxiang	周弘湘	b. 1968
Wang Keping	王克平	b. 1949	Zhu De	朱德	1886–1976
Wang Mingxian	王明贤	b. 1954	Zhuang Hui	庄辉	b. 1963
Wang Shikuo	王式廓	1911–1973			

Chinese Terms

biaozhunxiang 标准像 standard portrait

dazi bao 大字报 big-character poster

gao da quan 高大全 lofty, big and perfect

Geming Dachuanlian 革命大串联 Exchange Revolutionary Experience Travel

geming zaofanpai 革命造反派 revolutionary rebels

gonggong hua 公共化 public

guohua 国画 traditional Chinese painting

heiti 黑体 bold typeface

Hong Baoshu 红宝书 Precious Red Book

hong guang liang 红光亮 red, smooth and luminescent

huashan lunjian 华山论剑 swordplay or, more generally, martial arts competition at Hua Mountain

Jiehuo 借火 Borrow a Light

Lianhuan Huabao 连环画报 Serial Pictures Gazette

Lun Chijiuzhan 论持久战 On Protracted War

Mao Zhuxi Yulu 毛主席语录 The Quotations of Chairman Mao

Maore 毛热 Mao-craze

Mao zhuxi wansui 毛主席万岁 long live Chairman Mao

nianhua 年画 New Year picture

niugui sheshen 牛鬼蛇神 ox-demons and snake-spirits

pipan xianshi zhuyi 批判现实主义 critical realism

Po Sijiu 破四旧 Smashing the Four Olds

quanguo shangxia yipian hong 全国上下一片红 the whole country awash in red

Renmin Huabao 人民画报 *People's Pictorial*

Renmin Ribao 人民日报 *People's Daily*

Shangheng 伤痕 Scar

Shangheng Yishu 伤痕艺术 Scar Art

shangshan xiaxiang 上山下乡 going to mountains and countryside

shinian dongluan (haojie) 十年动乱（浩劫）a ten-year turbulence (catastrophe), literary descriptions of the Cultural Revolution, 1966–1976

shiyan yishu 实验艺术 experimental art

Sijiu 四旧 Four Olds, namely, old ideas, old culture, old customs and old habits

simi hua 私密化 private

Siren Bang 四人帮 The Gang of Four, including Jiang Qing 江青, Wang Hongwei 王洪文, Zhang Chunqiao 张春桥 and Yao Wenyuan 姚文元

Sige Weida 四个伟大 Four Greats as the compliment to Mao Zedong, namely, the Great Teacher, the Great Leader, the Great Commander and the Great Helmsman

Tugai 土改 Land Reformation

Wenhui Bao 文汇报 *Wenhui Daily*

Wuyiliu Tongzhi 五一六通知 *May the Sixteenth Circular*

Xiang Jiu Shijie Xuanzhan 向旧世界宣战 *To Declare A War against the Old World*

xiangtu xieshi 乡土写实 rustic realism

xinghuo liaoyuan 星火燎原 a single spark starts a prairie fire, developed from a verse of Mao's poem

xuanchuanhua 宣传画 propaganda print

Yangban Xi 样板戏 Model Opera

yanzhi hua 胭脂化 rouge-ization

yiqie xingdong ting zhihui 一切行动听指挥 all the actions must follow the command

zhua geming cu shengchan 抓革命促生产 take firm hold of the revolution and stimulate production

zoushen 走神 literally losing expression, means staring blankly

<h1 style="text-align:right">Index</h1>

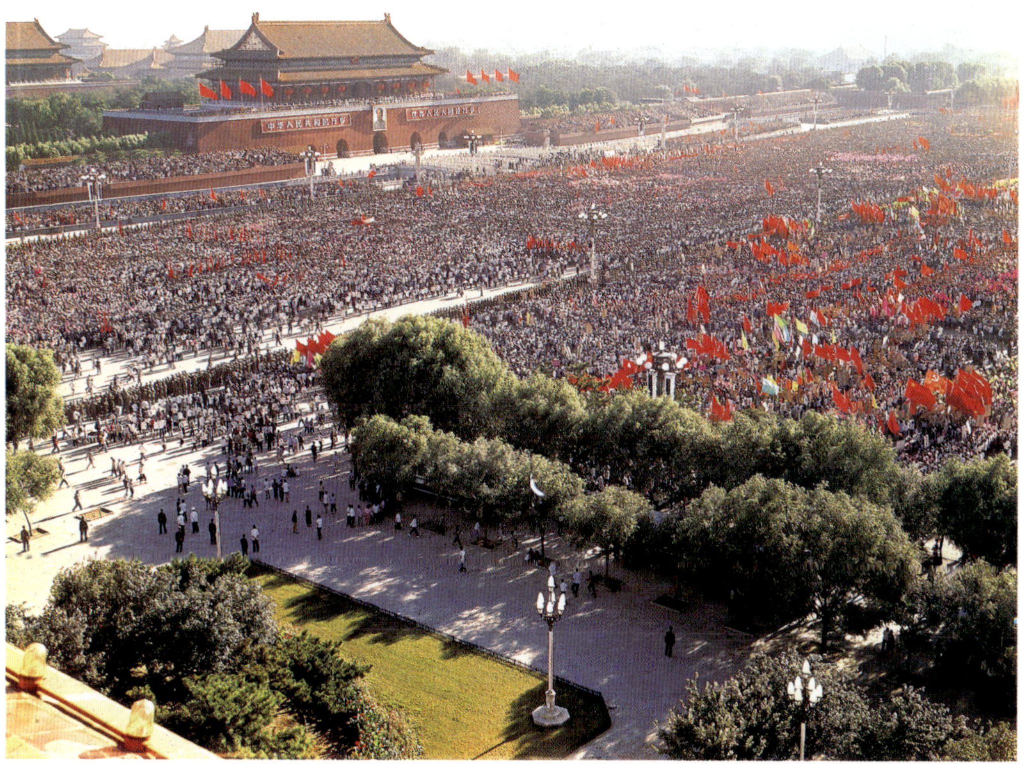

1. *The millions of people attending the gathering pledged their determination to carry out the Great Proletarian Cultural Revolution under the leadership of the great leader Chairman Mao,* Renmin Huabao 人民画报 (*People's Pictorial*), Vol. 9, 1966.

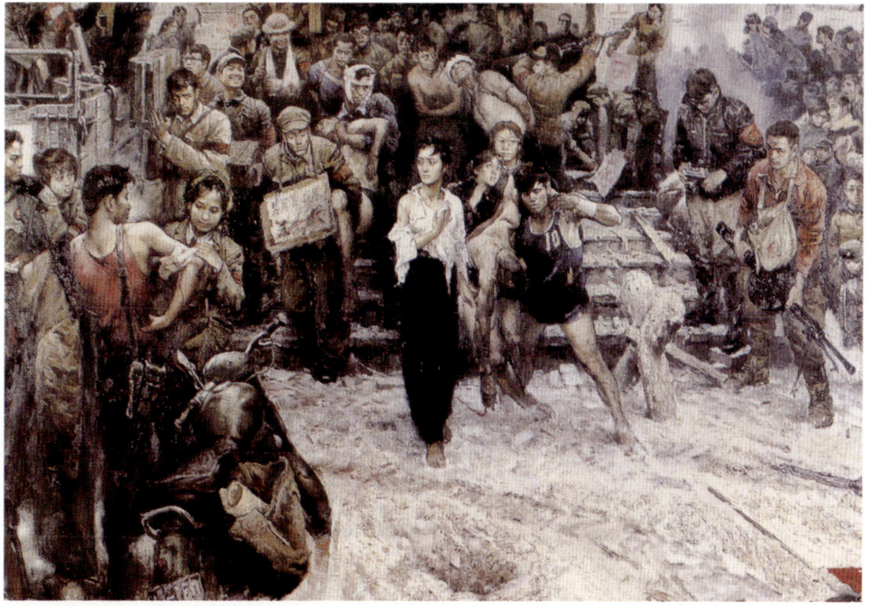

2. Cheng Conglin 程丛林, *Yijiu Liuba Nian Mouyue Mouri Xue* 一九六八年某月某日雪 (*Snow on X Month X Day, 1968*). Oil on canvas, 196 × 296 cm, 1979.

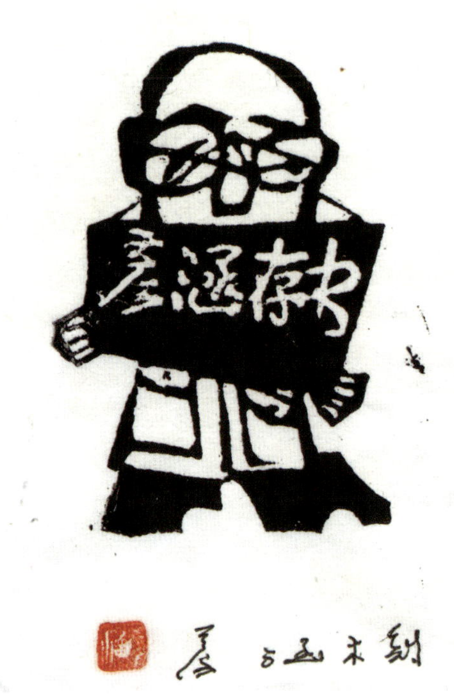

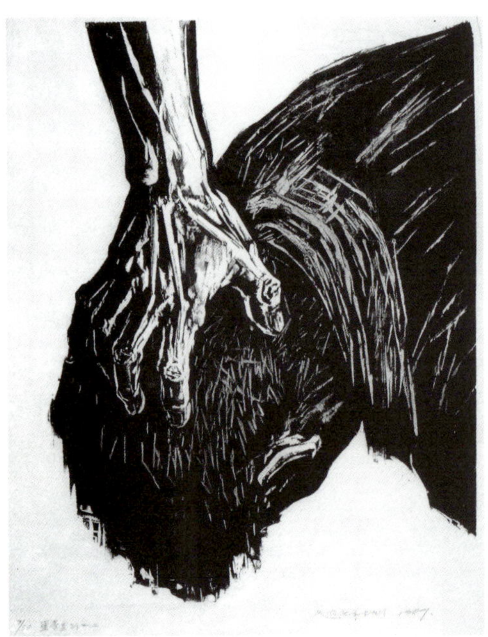

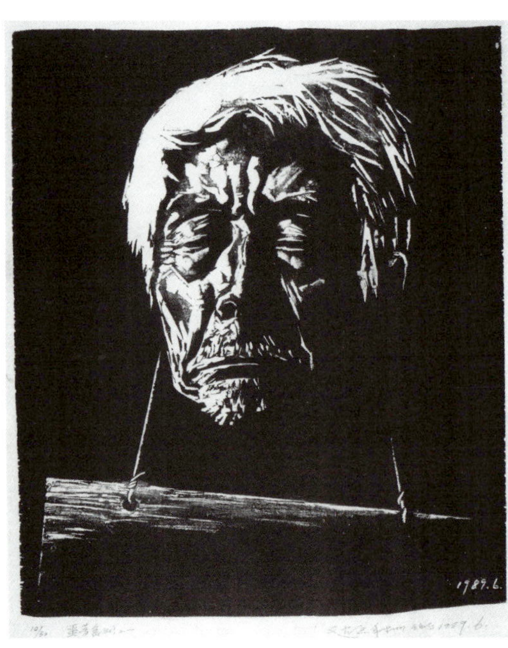

3. Yan Han 彦涵, *Cangshu Piao* 藏书票 *(Book Collecting Stamp)*, 1980s, 8 × 12 cm, collection of the author.

4. Zhao Yannian 赵延年, *Emeng Xilie Zhiyi* 噩梦系列之一 *(Nightmare No. 1)*, 1989, woodcut print, 57 × 48.5 cm.

5. Zhao Yannian 赵延年, *Emeng Xilie Zhier* 噩梦系列之二 *(Nightmare No. 2)*, 1989, woodcut print, 59 × 47 cm.

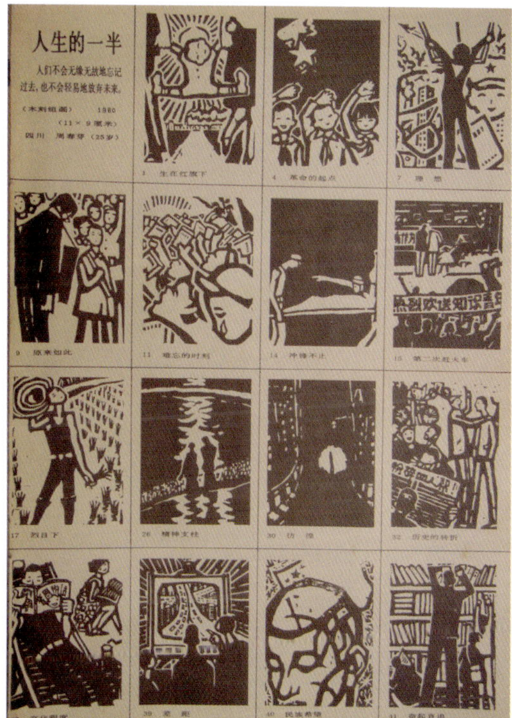

6. Zhou Chunya 周春芽, *Rensheng de Yiban* 人生的一半 *(Half of the Life)*, 1980, reproduction of woodcut print, 15 pieces, 11 × 9 cm each.

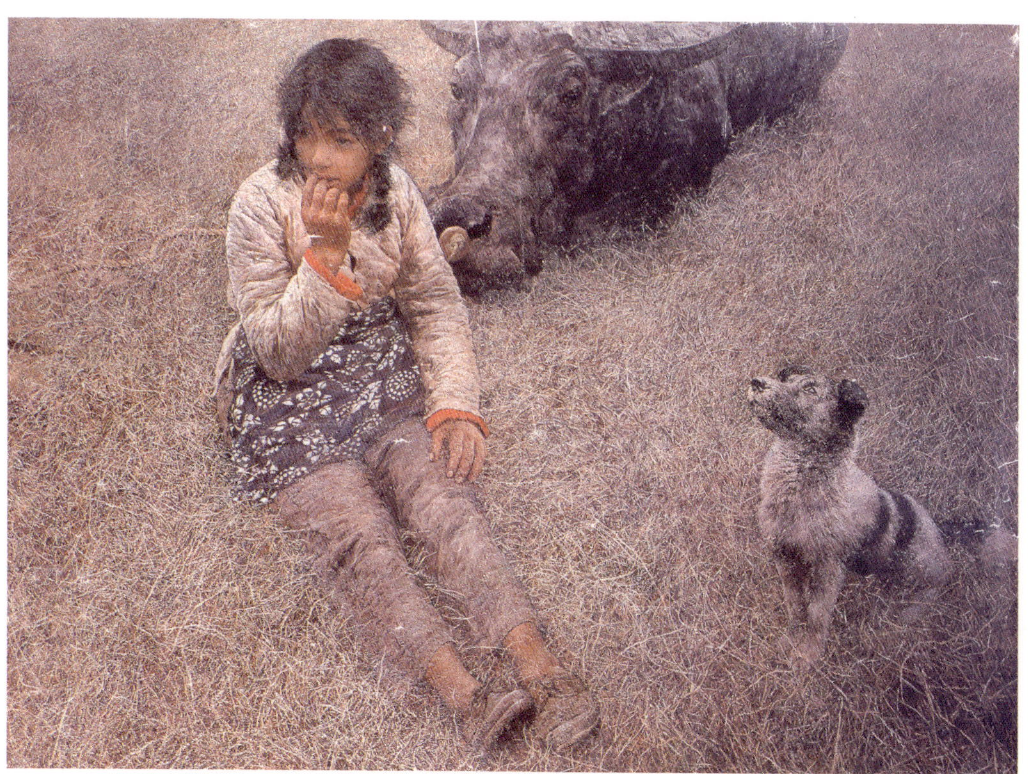

7. He Duoling 何多苓, *Chunfeng Yijing Suxing* 春风已经苏醒 *(Spring Wind Revivified)*, 1982, oil on canvas, 95 × 129 cm.

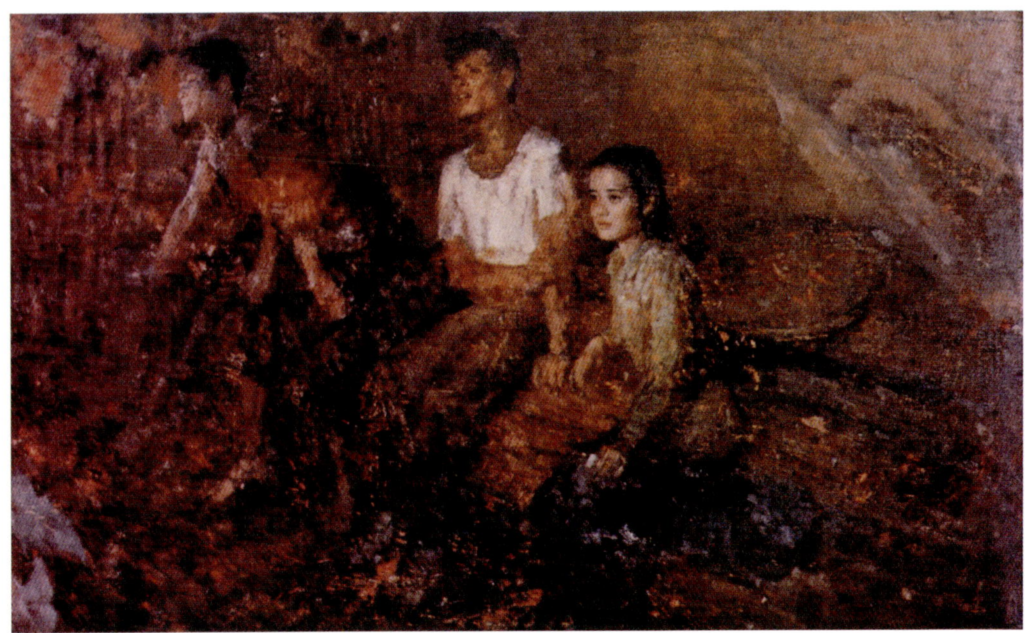

8. He Duoling 何多苓, *Woman Ceng Changguo Zheshou Ge* 我们曾唱过这支歌 *(A Song We Used to Sing)*, 1980, oil on canvas, 102 × 171 cm.

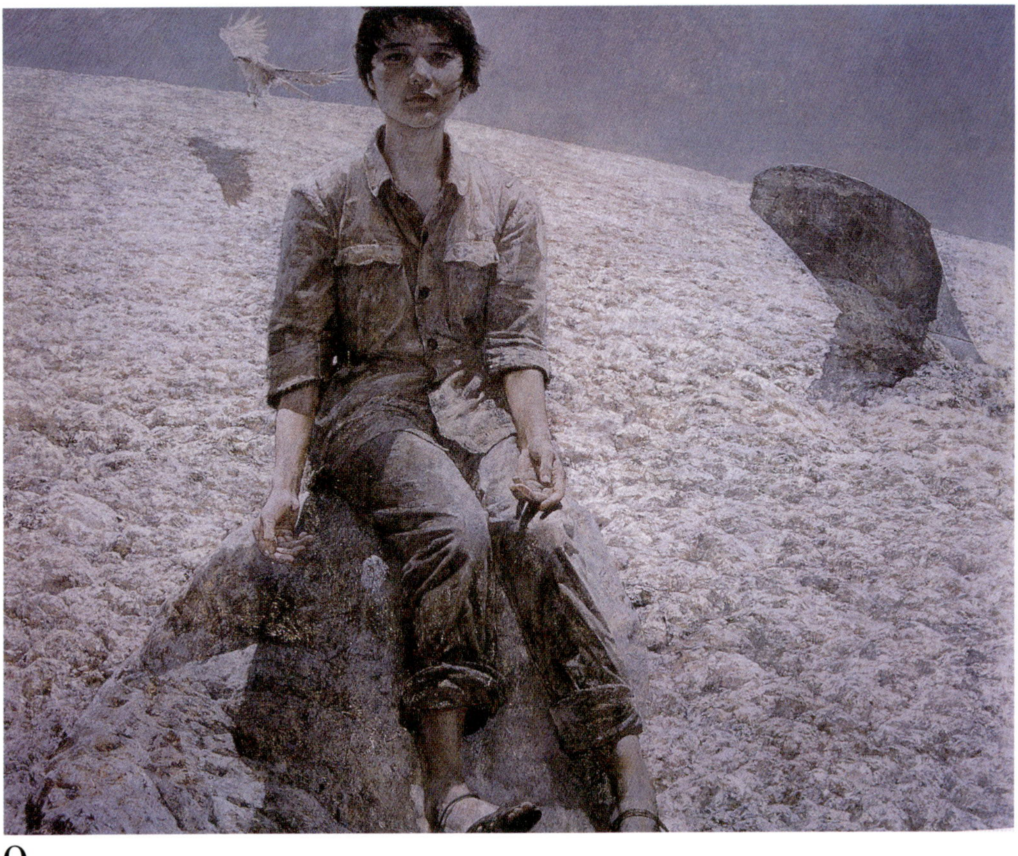

9. He Duoling 何多苓, *Qingchun* 青春 *(Youth)*, 1984, oil on canvas, 150 × 187.5 cm.

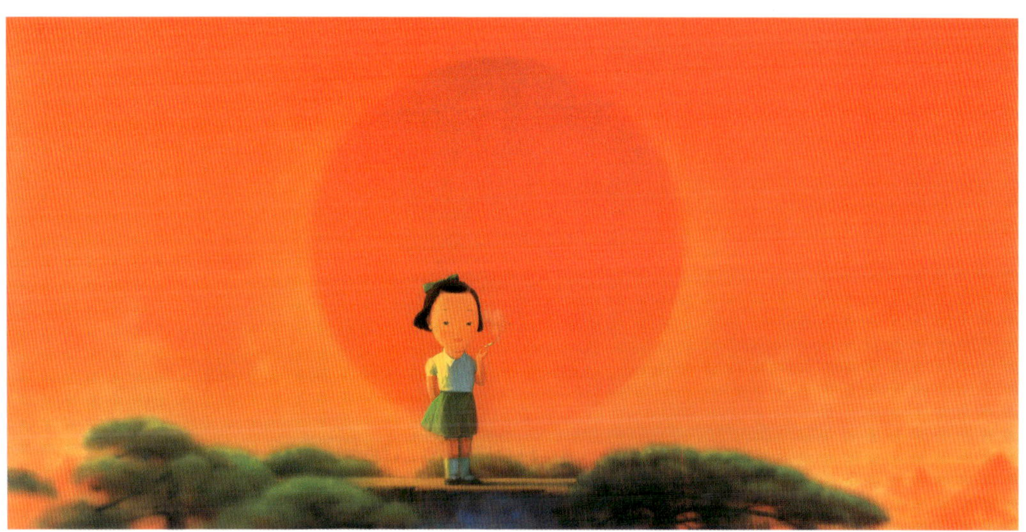

10. Liu Ye 刘野, *Yan* 烟 *(Smoke)*, 2002, oil on canvas, 180 × 360 cm.

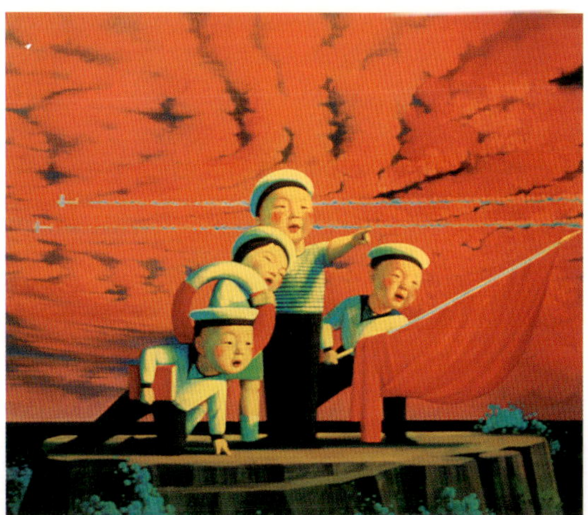

11. Liu Ye 刘野, *Xiwang* 希望 *(Hope)*, 1998, oil on canvas, 60 × 45 cm.

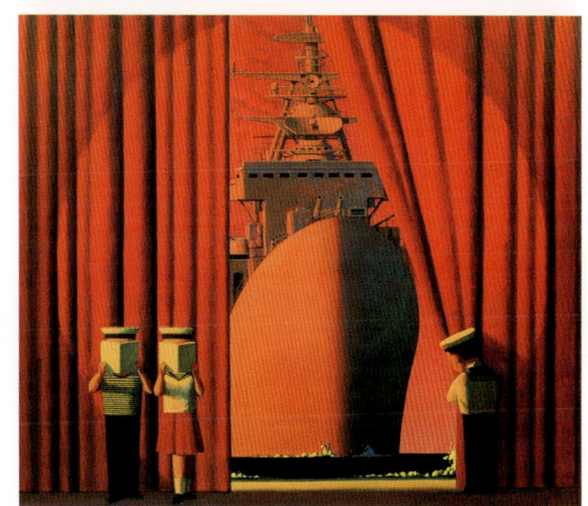

12. Liu Ye 刘野, *Wuti* 无题 *(Untitled)*, 1998, oil on canvas, 170 × 200 cm.

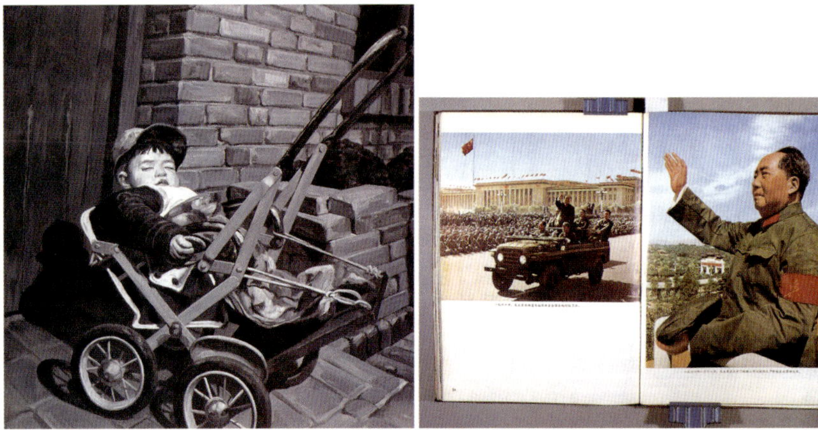

13. Yu Hong 喻红, *Muji Chengzhang* 目击成长 *(Witness to Growth): Six Months Old, 1966,* 1999, oil on canvas, 100 × 100 cm, and photograph from *China Pictorial, No. 11, 1966, P. 55*.

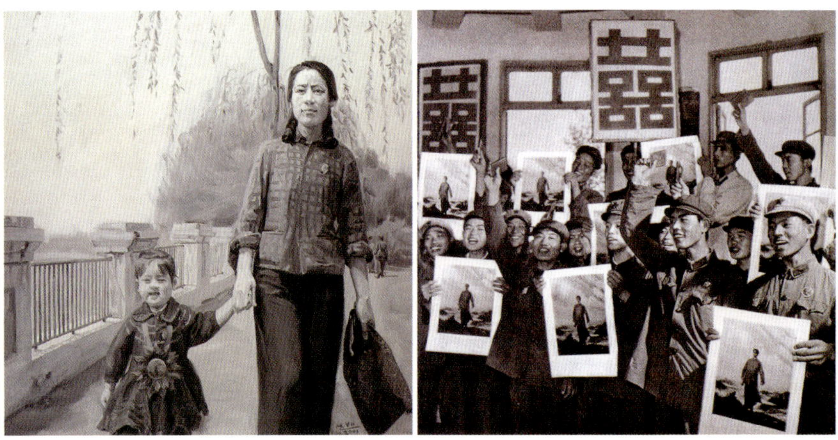

14. Yu Hong 喻红, *Muji Chengzhang* 目击成长 *(Witness to Growth): Two Years old, 1968*, 1999, oil on canvas, 100 × 100 cm, and photograph from *China Pictorial, No. 9, 1968, P. 13*.

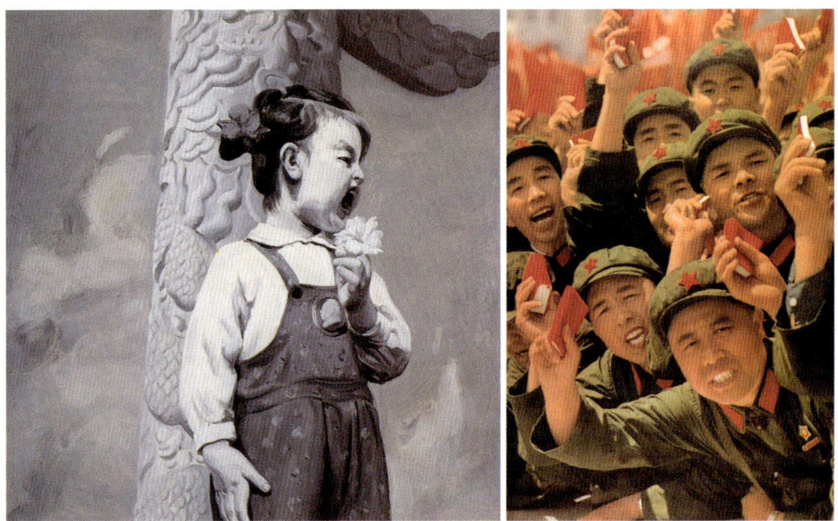

15. Yu Hong 喻红, *Muji Chengzhang* 目击成长 *(Witness to Growth): Four Years old, 1970*, 1999, oil on canvas, 100 × 100 cm, and photograph from *China Pictorial, No. 7, 1970, Back Cover*.

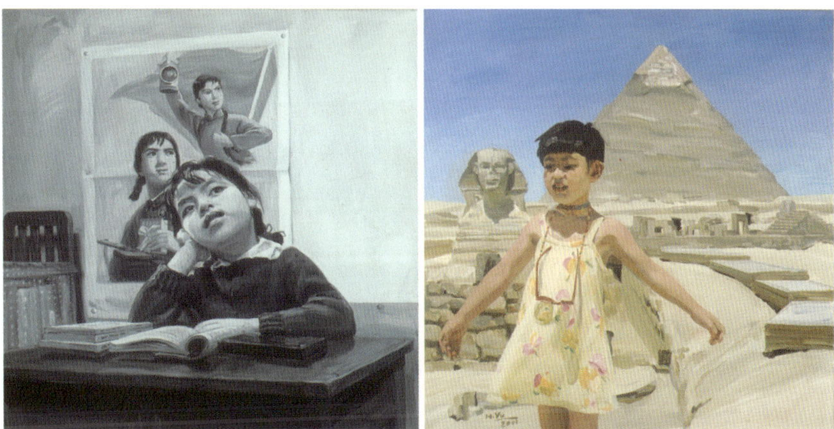

16. Yu Hong 喻红, *Muji Chengzhang* 目击成长 *(Witness to Growth): Six Years old, 1972*, 1999, oil on canvas, 100 × 100 cm, and *Four Years old Liu Wa, 1998*, 1999, oil on canvas, 100 × 100 cm.

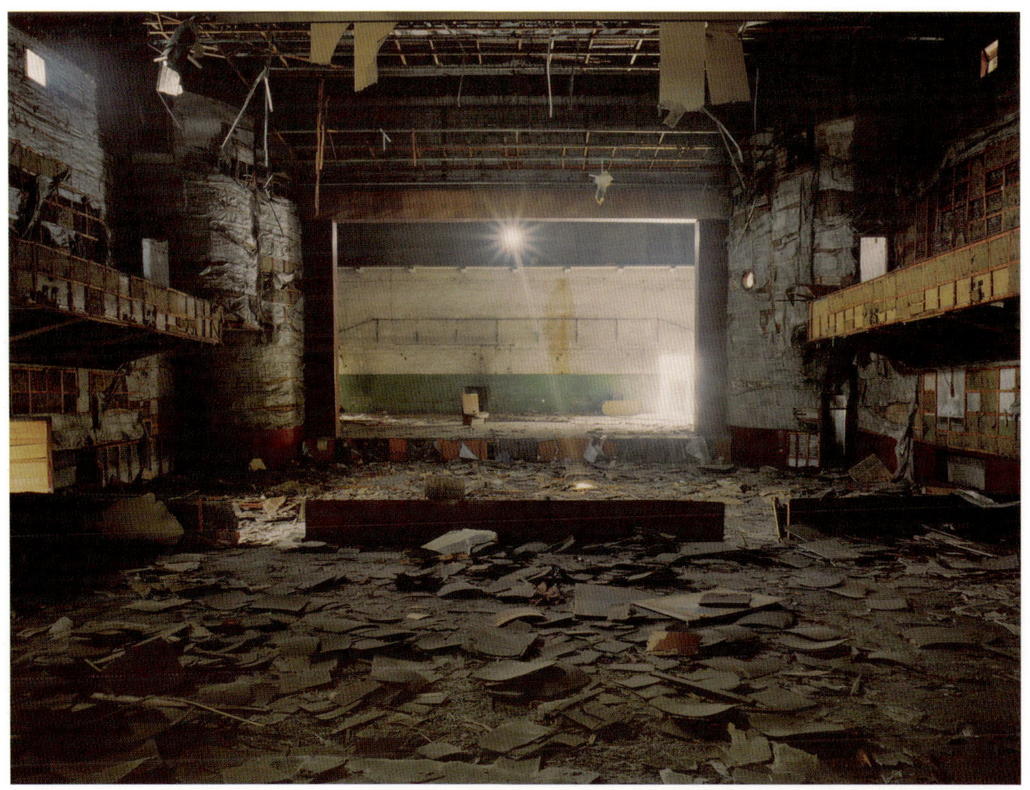

17. Shao Yinong 邵逸农 and Mu Chen 慕辰, *Da Litang* 大礼堂 *(Assembly Hall): Shenbian* 沈变, 2002–05, photograph.

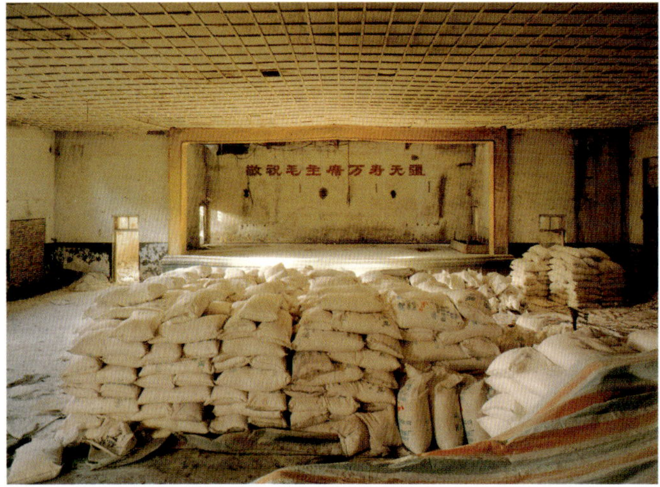

18. Shao Yinong 邵逸农 and Mu Chen 慕辰, *Da Litang* 大礼堂 *(Assembly Hall): Kuangshan* 矿山, 2002–05, photograph.

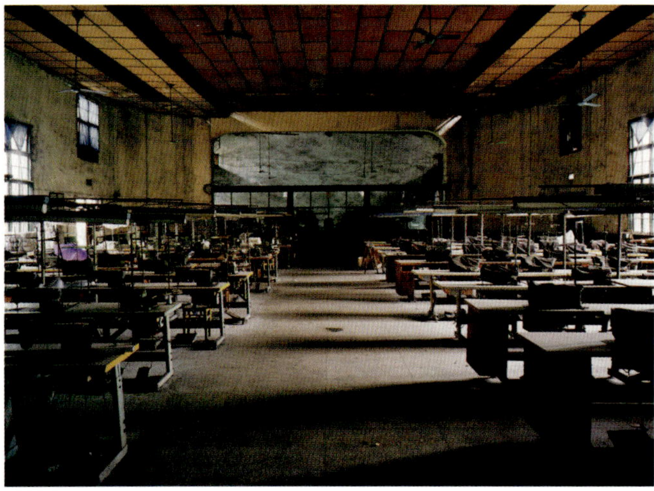

19. Shao Yinong 邵逸农 and Mu Chen 慕辰, *Da Litang* 大礼堂 *(Assembly Hall): Anyuan* 安源, 2002–05, photograph.

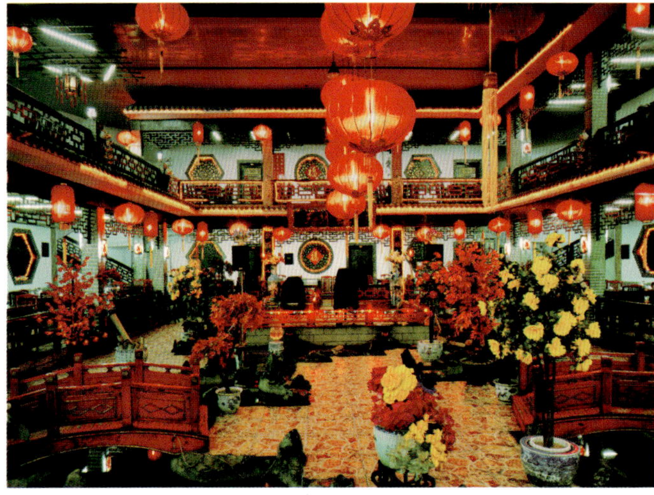

20. Shao Yinong 邵逸农 and Mu Chen 慕辰, *Da Litang* 大礼堂 *(Assembly Hall): Xiaoqiao* 小桥, 2002–05, photograph.

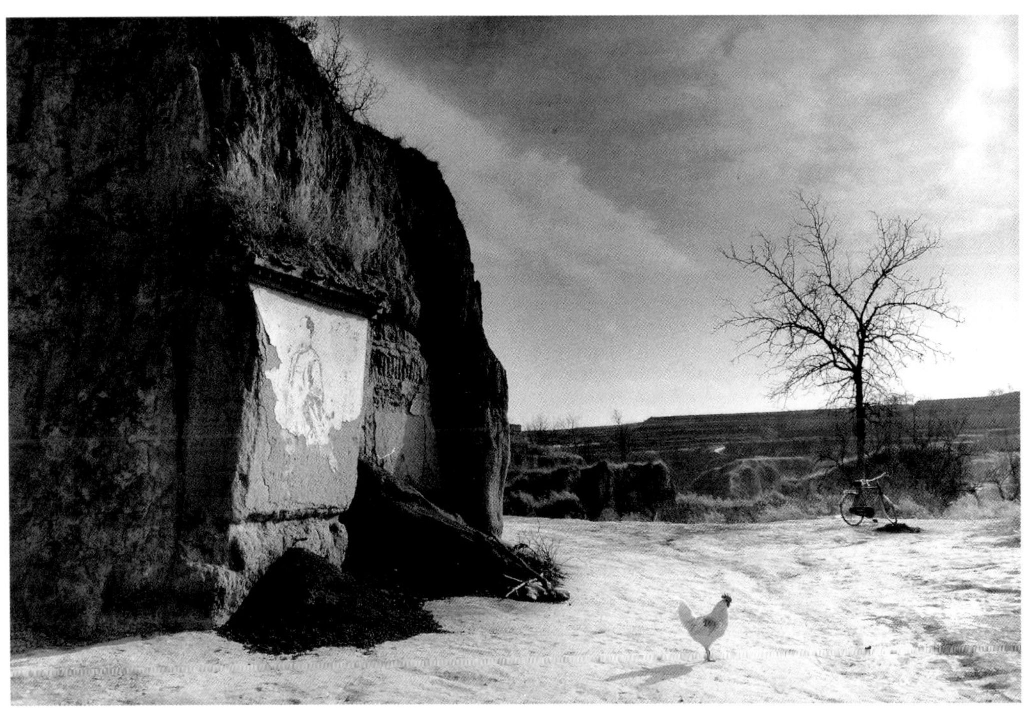

21. Wang Tong 王彤, *Wenge Yijing* 文革遗景 *(Vestiges of the Cultural Revolution): Mengjin County*, Henan, 1996, photograph.

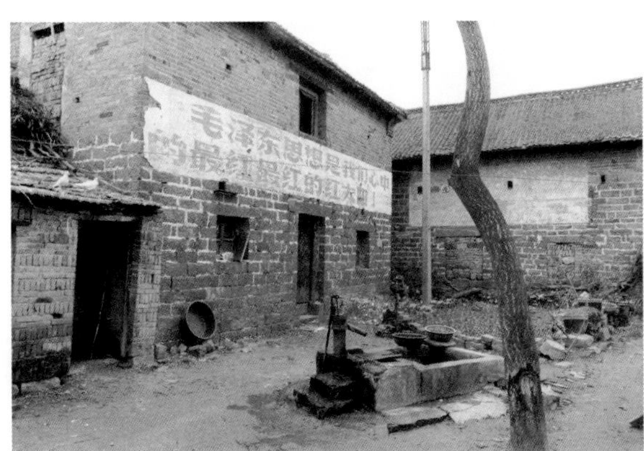

22. Wang Tong 王彤, *Wenge Yijing* 文革遗景 *(Vestiges of the Cultural Revolution): Jia County, Henan*, 1997, photograph.

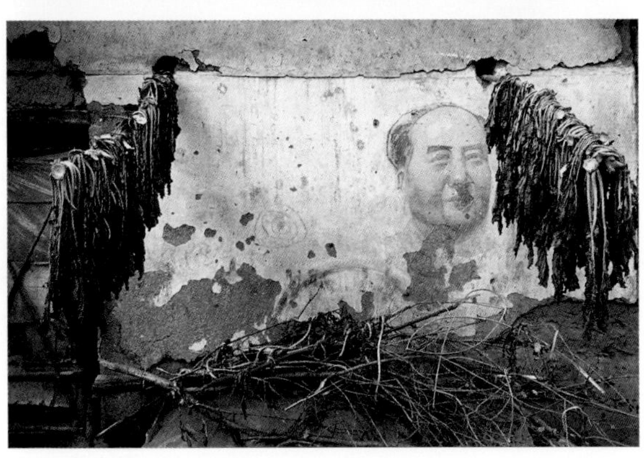

23. Wang Tong 王彤, *Wenge Yijing* 文革遗景 *(Vestiges of the Cultural Revolution): Lushan County, Henan*, 1996, photograph.

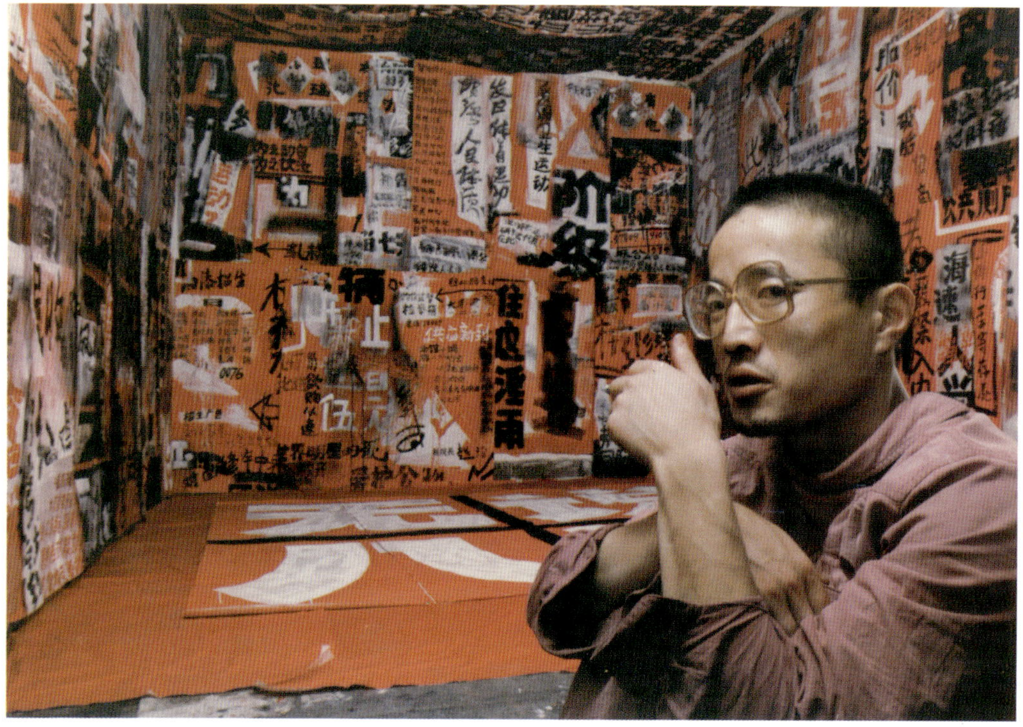

24. Wu Shanzhuan 吴山专, *Hongse Youmo* 红色幽默 *(Red Humour)*, 1986, installation with works on paper, dimensions variable.

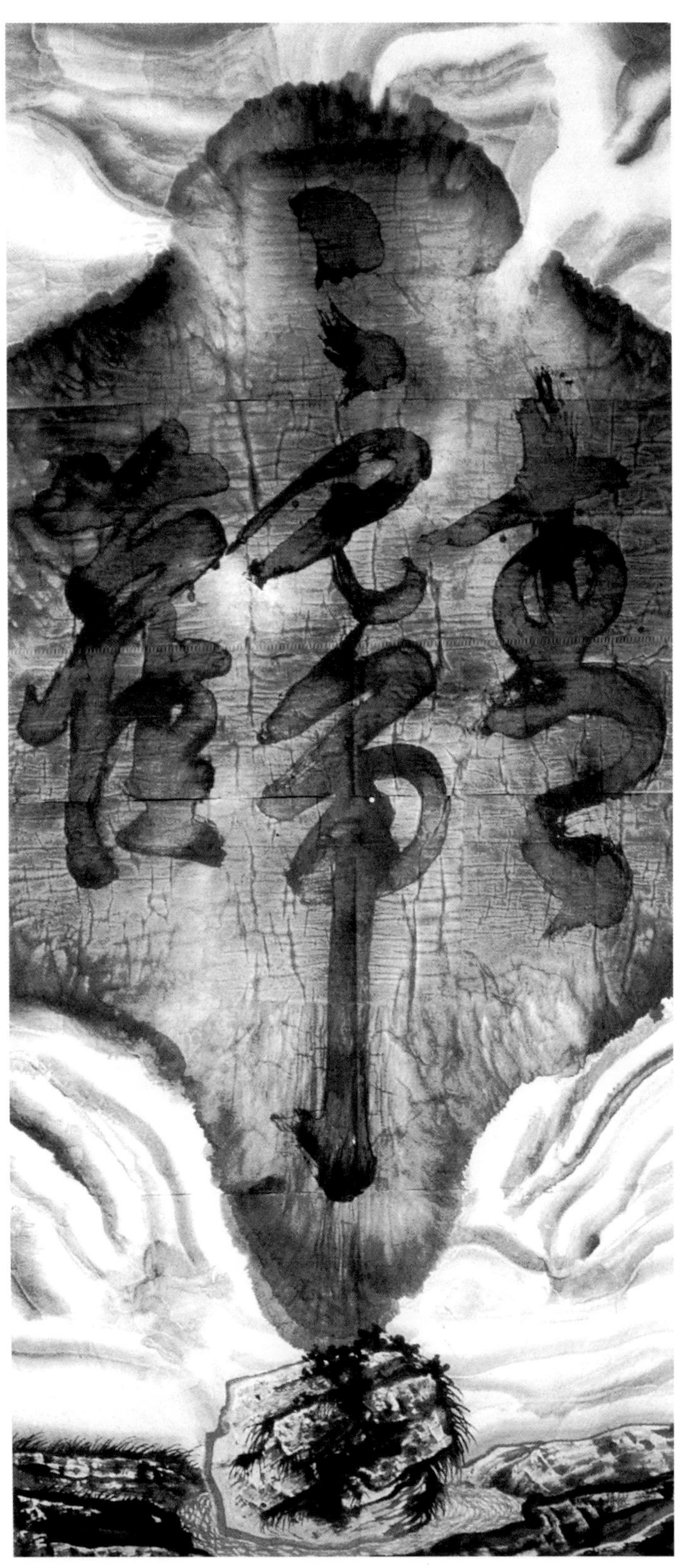

25. Gu Wenda 谷文达, *Pseudo-characters Series: Contemplation of the World* (one of three hanging scrolls), 1984, ink on paper, 247 × 183 cm.

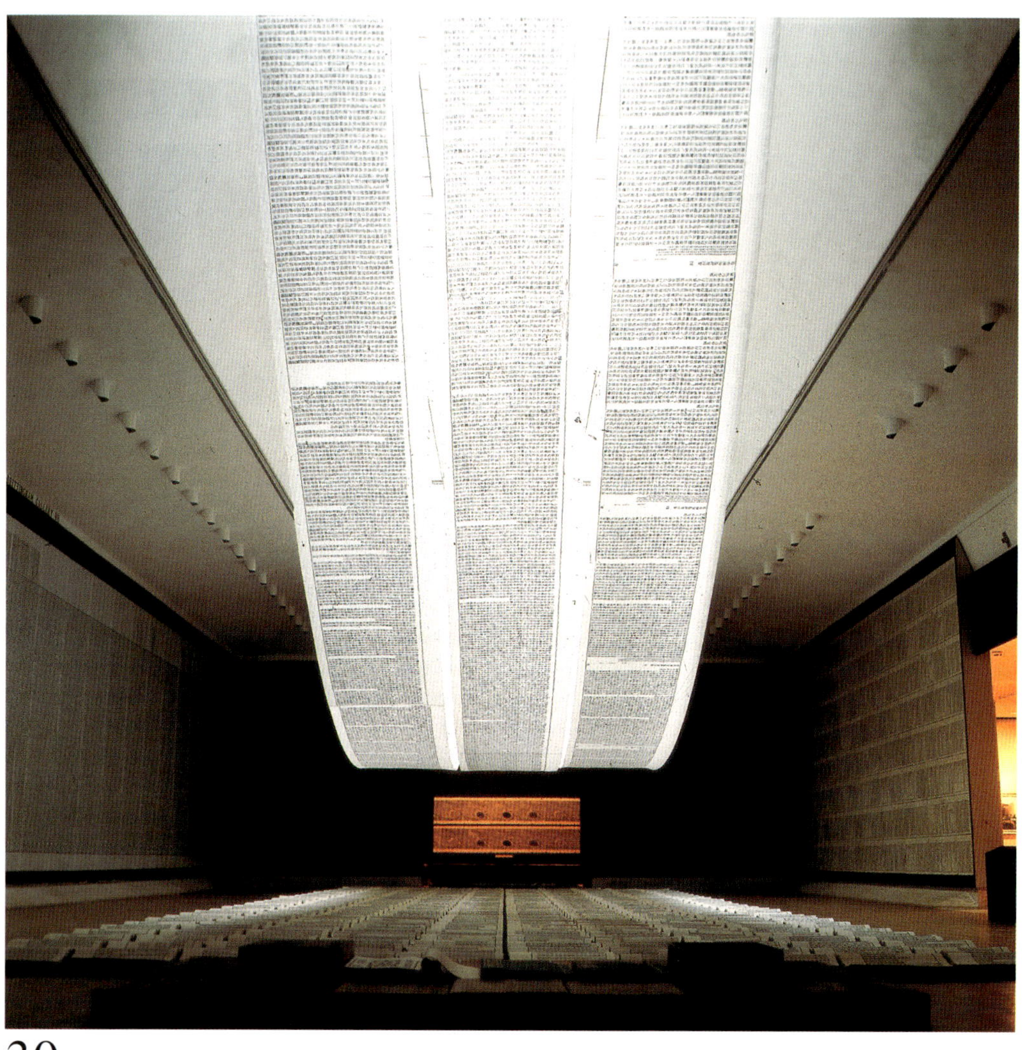

30. Xu Bing 徐冰, *Tianshu* 天书 *(Book from the Heaven)*, 1991–92, installation view, dimensions variable.

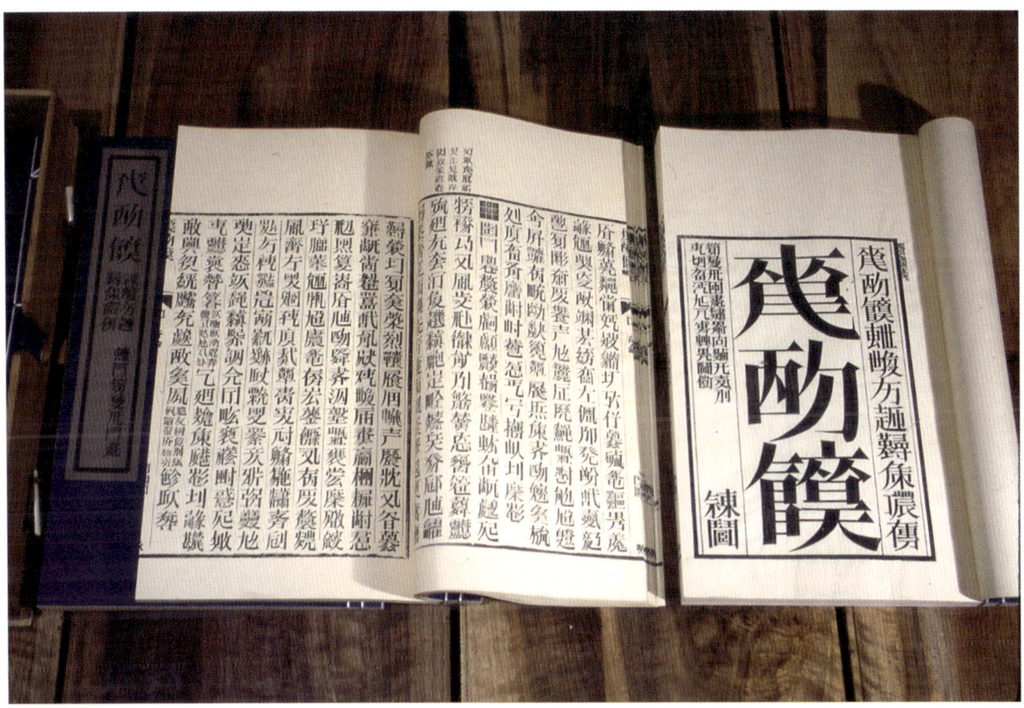

31. Xu Bing 徐冰, *Tianshu* 天书 *(Book from the Heaven)*, 1987–91, works on paper.

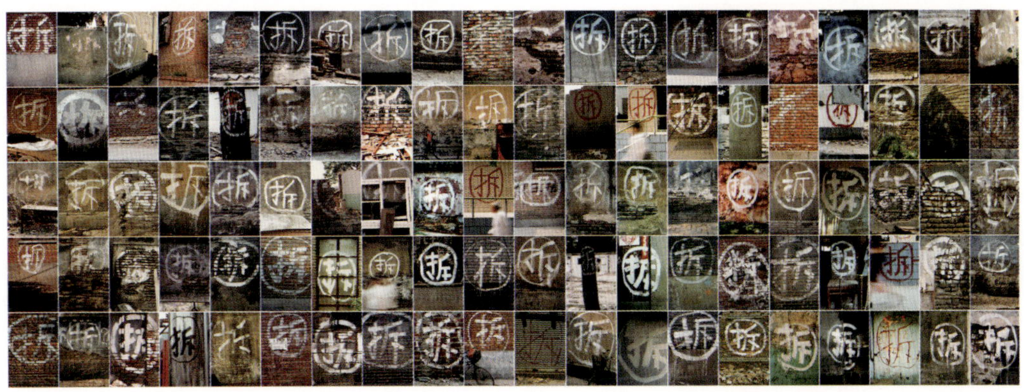

32. Wang Jinsong 王劲松, *Bai Chai Tu* 百拆图 *(A Hundred Chai)*, 1999, photograph.

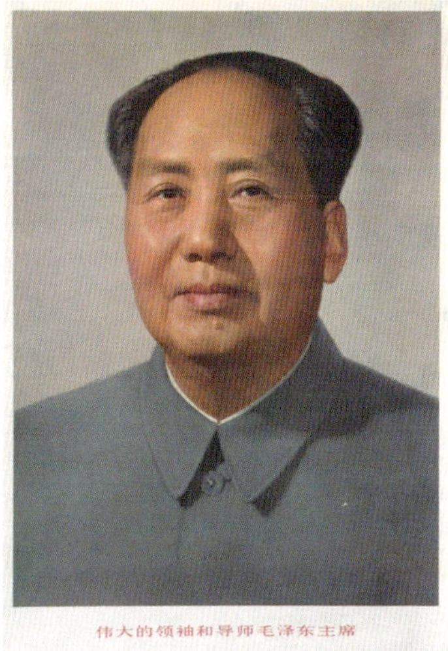

33. *Weida Lingxiu He Daoshi Mao Zedong Zhuxi* 伟大领袖和导师毛泽东主席 *(The Great Leader and Teacher Chairman Mao)*, print, 1967, collection of the author.

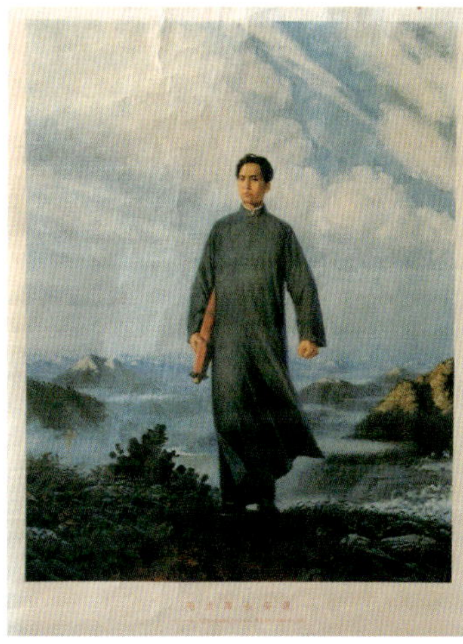

34. Liu Chunhua 刘春华, *Mao Zhuxi Qu Anyuan* 毛主席去安源 *(Chairman Mao Goes to Anyuan)*, 1969, poster reproduction of oil painting, collection of the author.

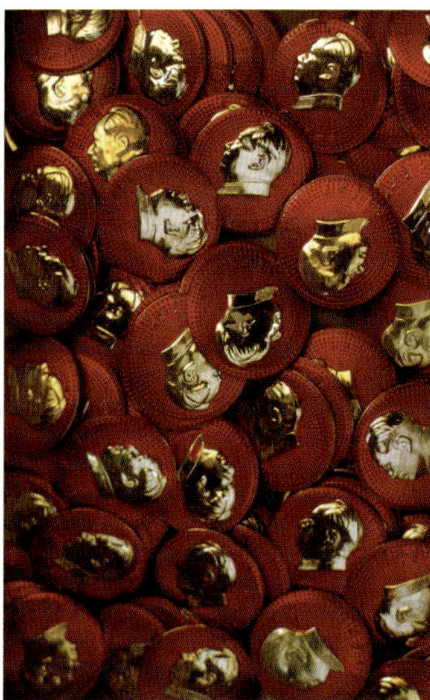

35. Mao badges, 1967–1969, collection of the author.

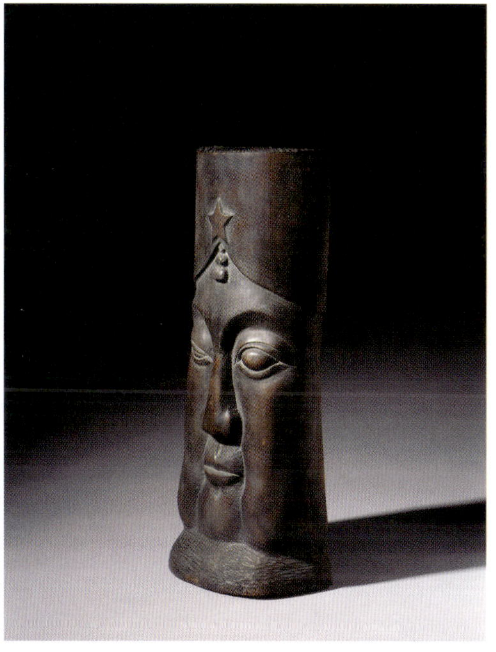

36. Wang Keping 王克平, *Ouxiang* 偶像 *(Idol)*, 1978, birch, stained, height ca. 40 cm.

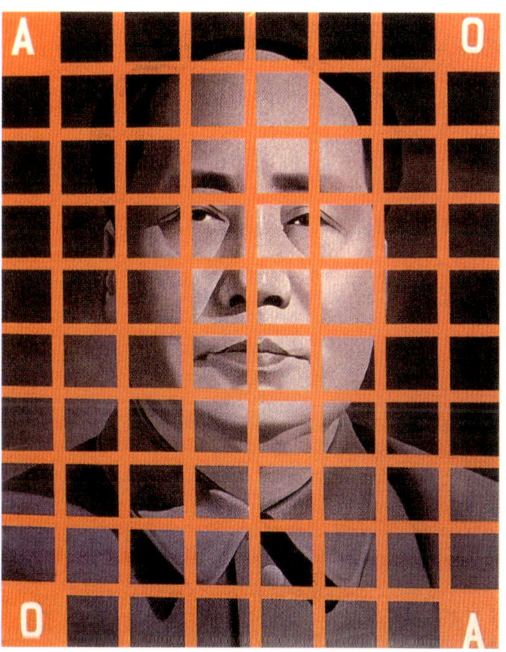

37. Wang Guangyi 王广义, *Mao Zedong* 毛泽东, 1988, oil on canvas, 150 × 120 cm.

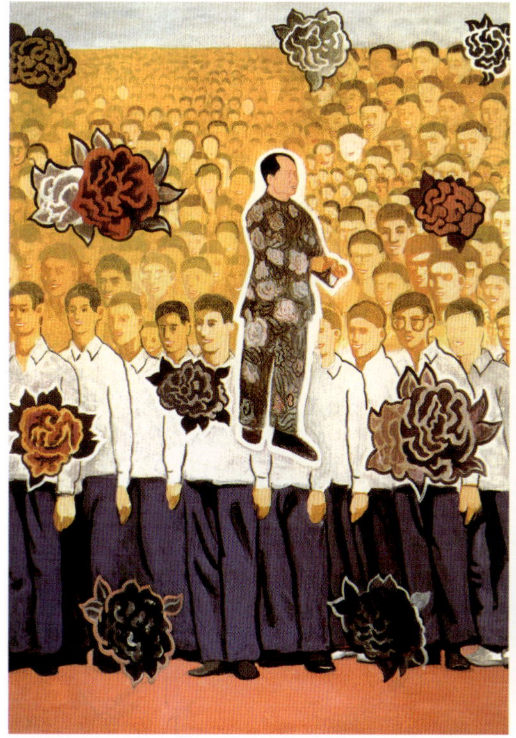

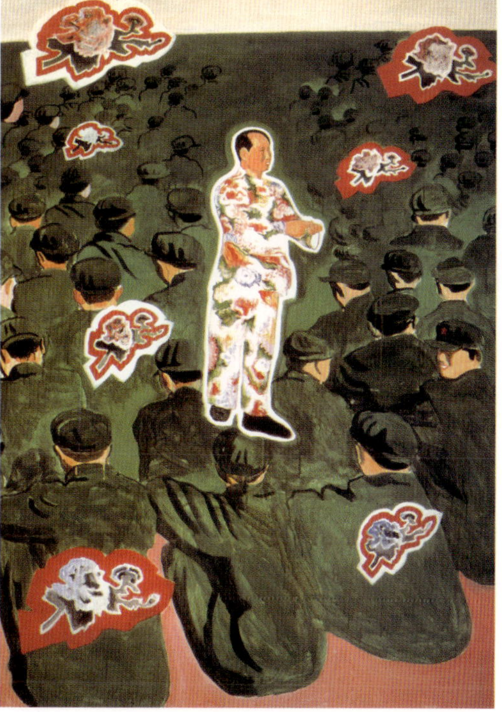

38. Yu Youhan 余有涵, *Mao He Tade Renmin* 毛和他的人民 *(Mao and His People)*, 1995, oil on canvas, 182 × 127 cm each, 2 piece.

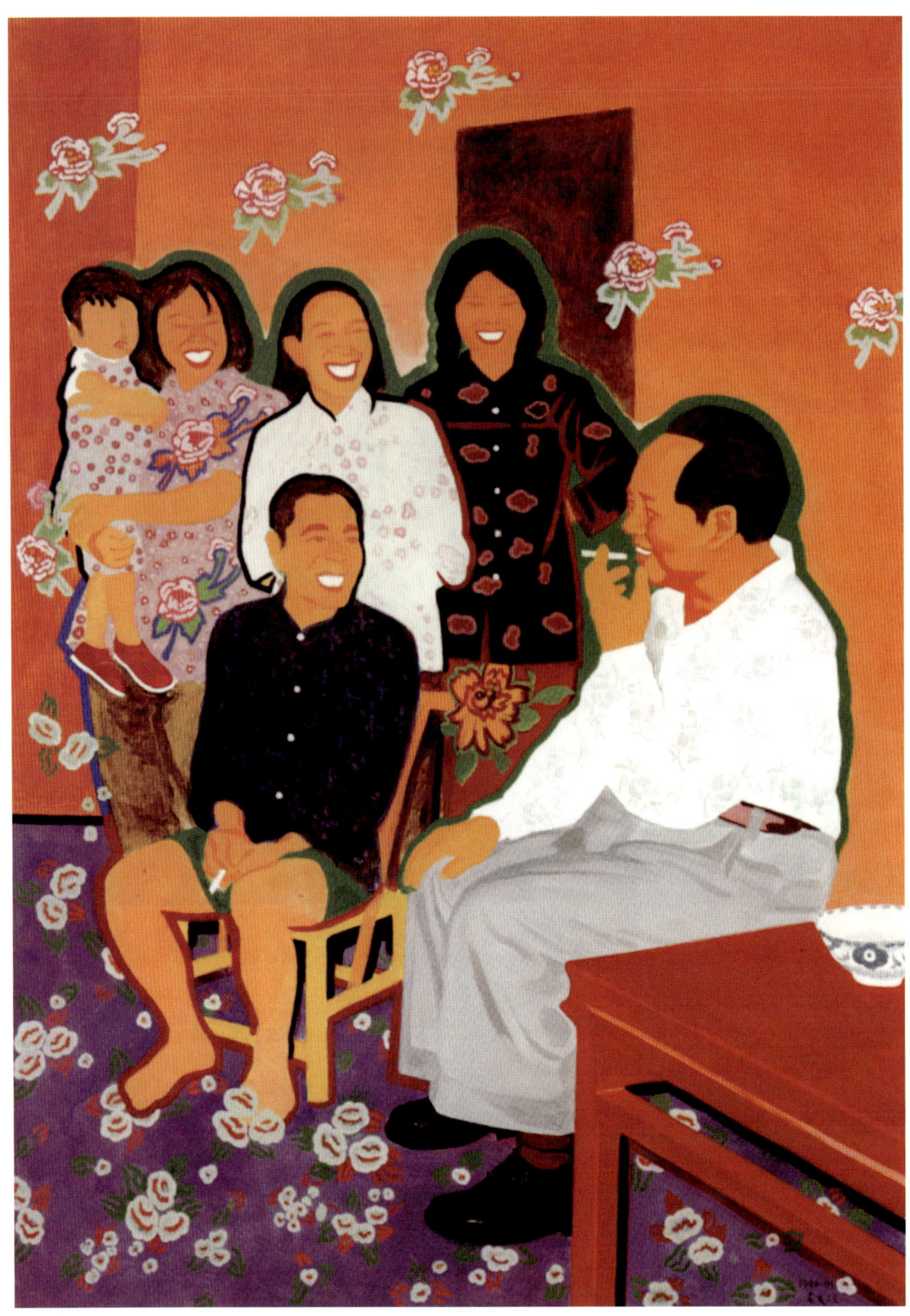

39. Yu Youhan 余友涵, *Yu Hunan Nongmin Tanhua* 与湖南农民谈话 *(Talking with Hunan Peasants)*, 1991, oil on canvas, 167 × 118 cm.

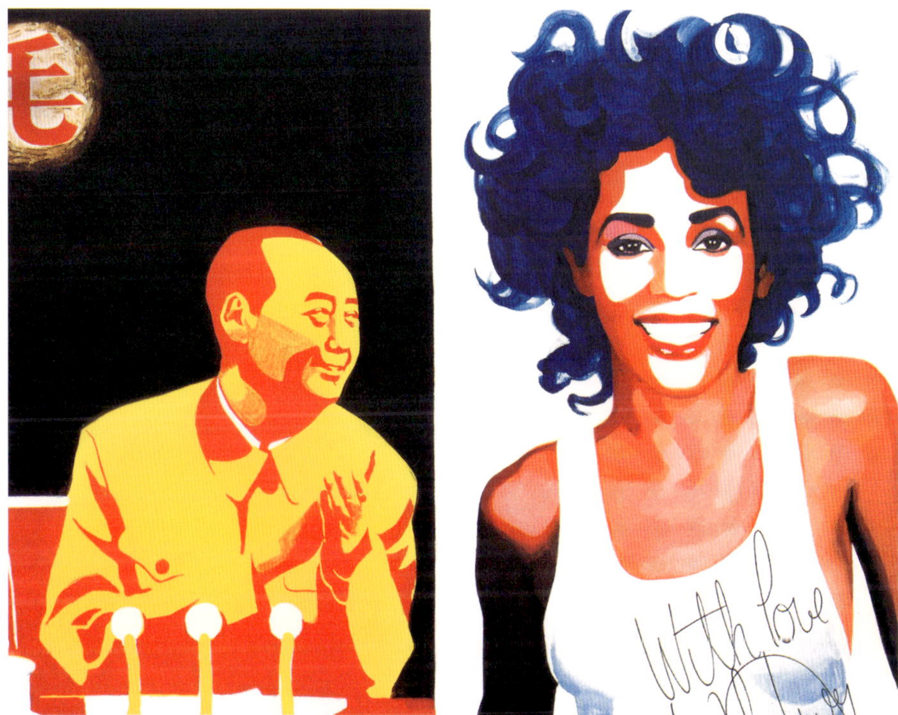

40. Yu Youhan 余友涵, *Mao Yu Whitney* 毛与惠特尼 *(Mao and Whitney)*, 1989, acrylic on canvas, 136 × 106 cm.

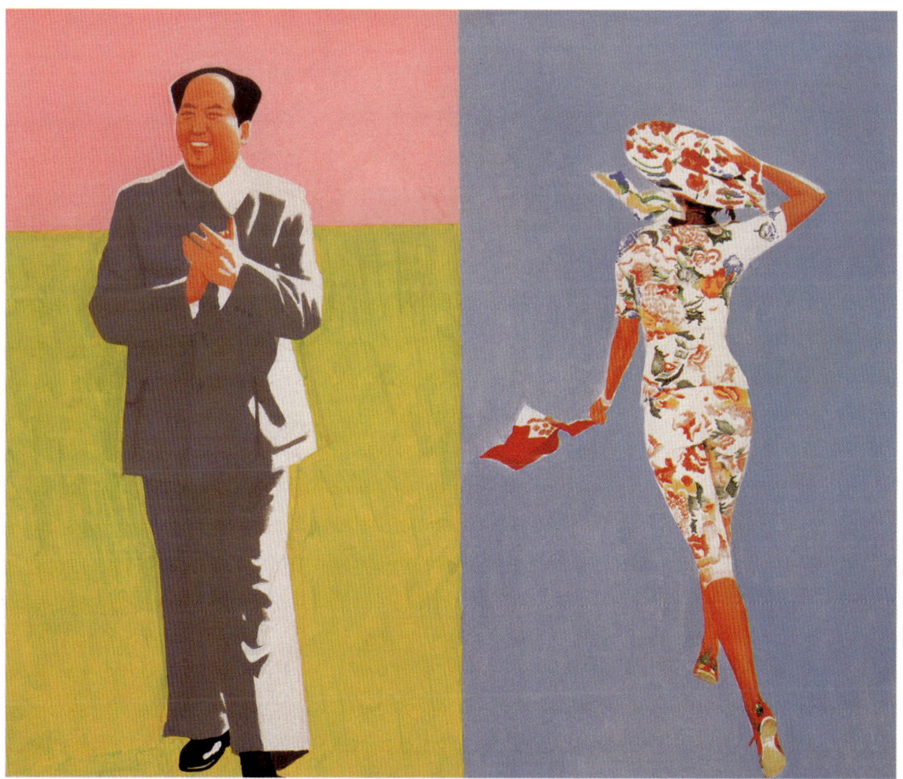

41. Yu Youhan 余友涵, *Mao Yu Hua Zhi Nü* 毛与花之女 *(Mao and a Flowery Girl)*, 1992, acrylic on canvas, 76 × 59 cm.

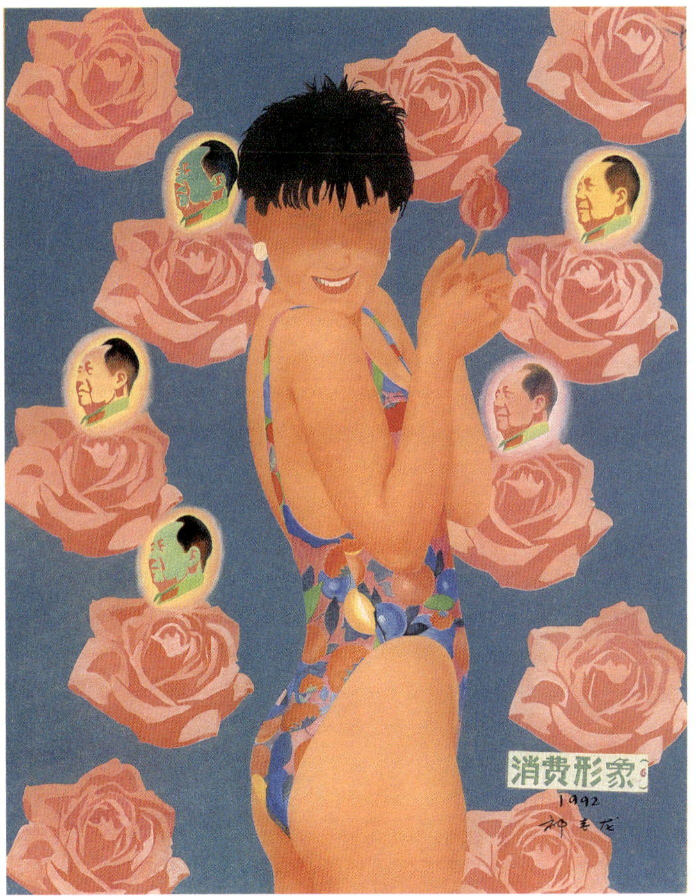

42. Qi Zhilong 祁志龙, *Xiaofei Xingxiang* 消费形象 *(Consumer Icons) No. 6*, 1992, oil on canvas, 100 × 80 cm, private collection.

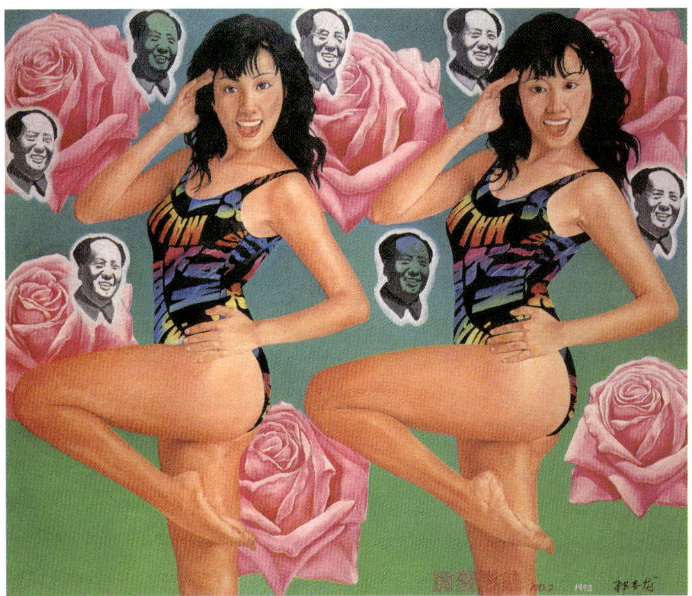

43. Qi Zhilong 祁志龙, *Xiaofei Xingxiang* 消费形象 *(Consumer Icons) No. 7*, 1992, oil on canvas, 145 × 170 cm.

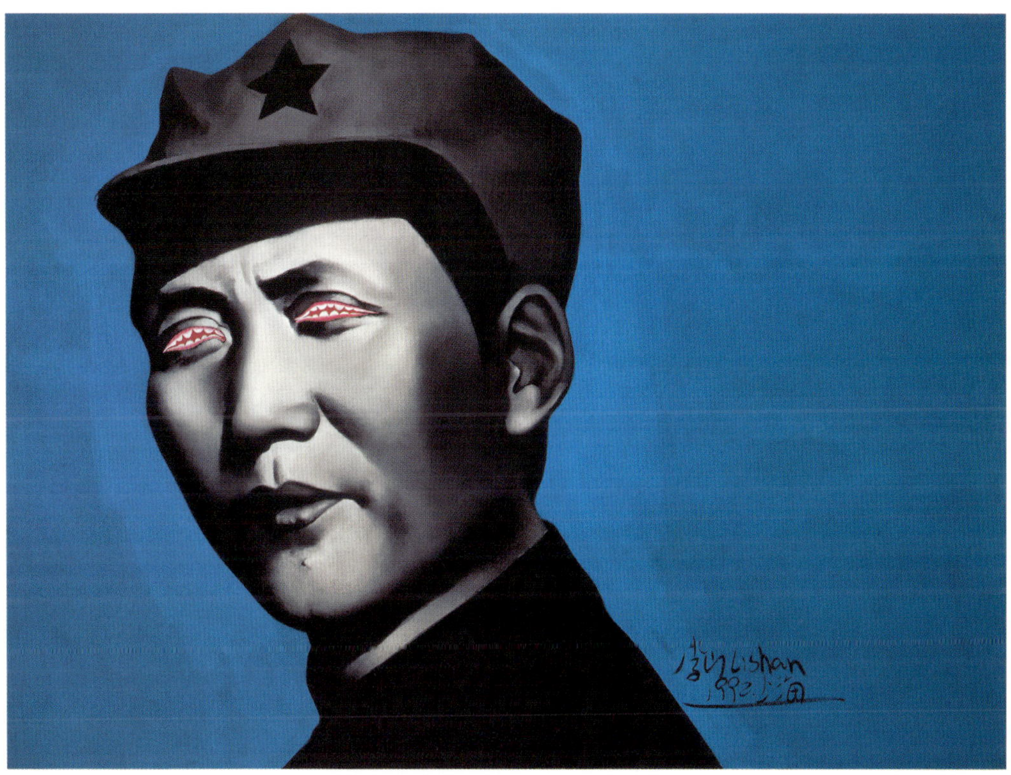

44. Li Shan 李山, *Yanzhi* 胭脂 *(Rouge) No. 24*, 1992, acrylic on canvas, 100 × 140 cm.

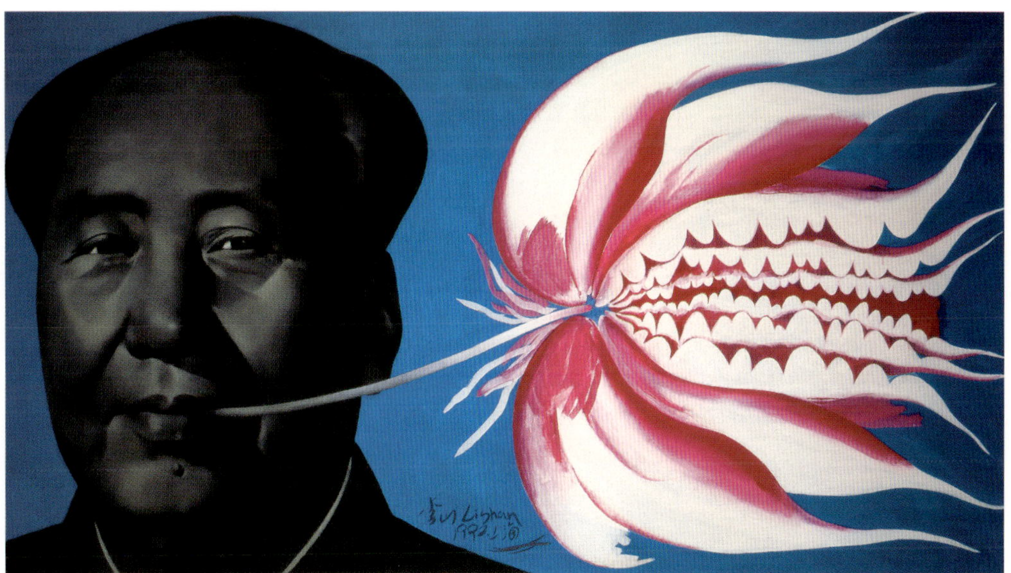

45. Li Shan 李山, *Yanzhi* 胭脂 *(Rouge) No. 22*, 1992, acrylic on canvas, 140 × 258 cm.

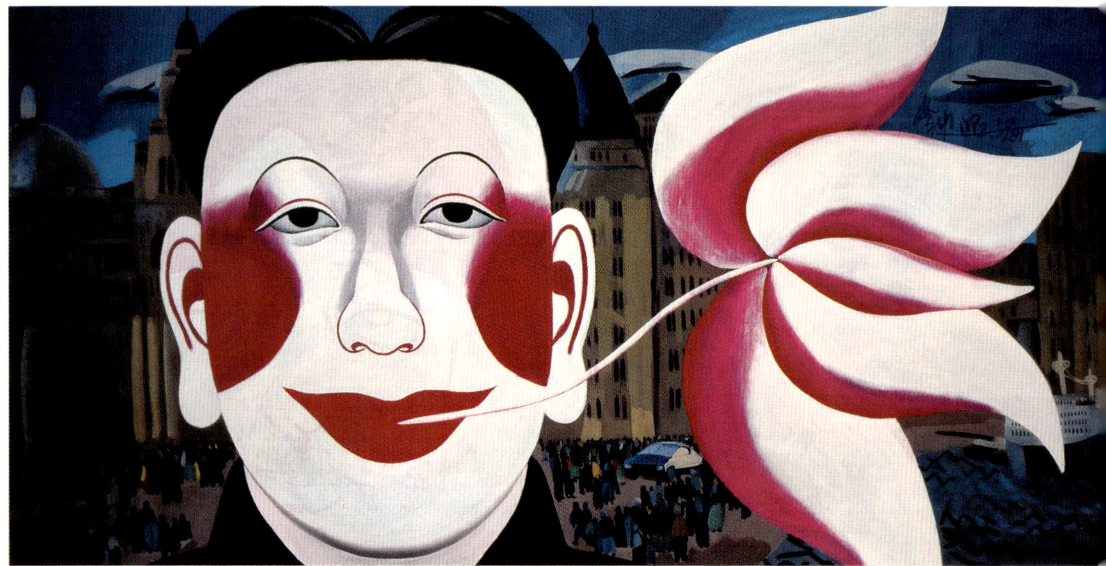

46. Li Shan 李山, *Yanzhi* 胭脂 *(Rouge) No. 21*, 1992, acrylic on canvas, 140 × 300 cm.

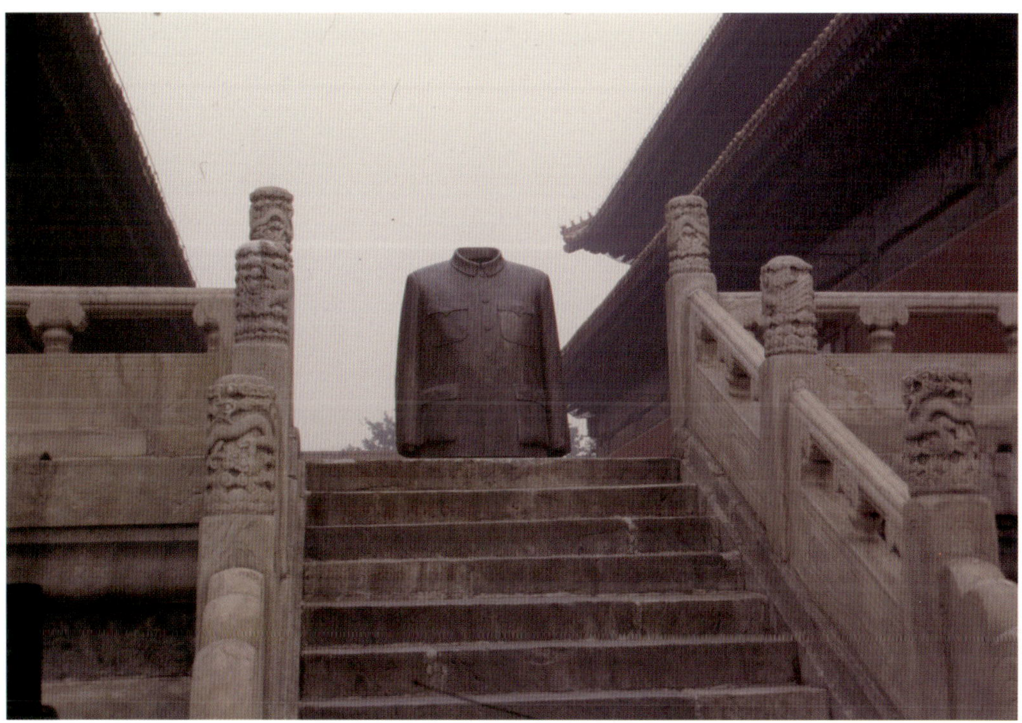

47. Sui Jianguo 隋建国, *Yibo* 衣钵 *(Legacy Mantle)*, 1997, glass fibre and metal, 140 cm high, installation view at Palace Museum, Beijing.

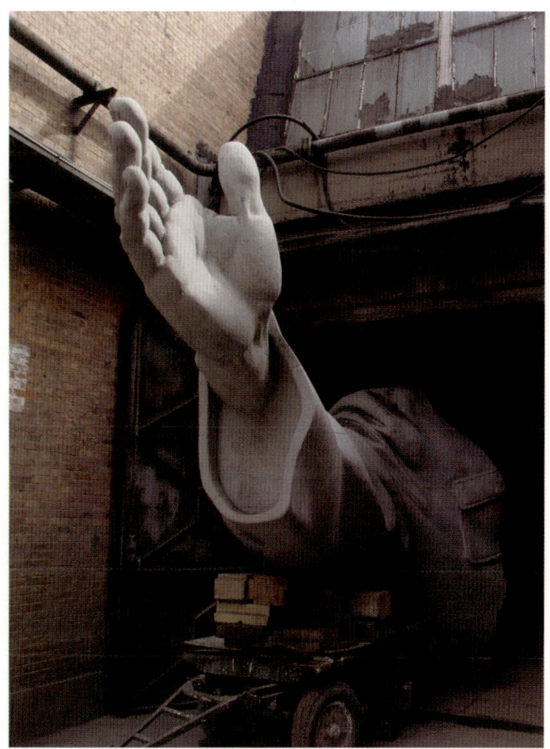

48. Sui Jianguo 隋建国, *Youshou* 右手 *(The Right Hand)*, 2003, glass fibre and cement, 700 cm long.

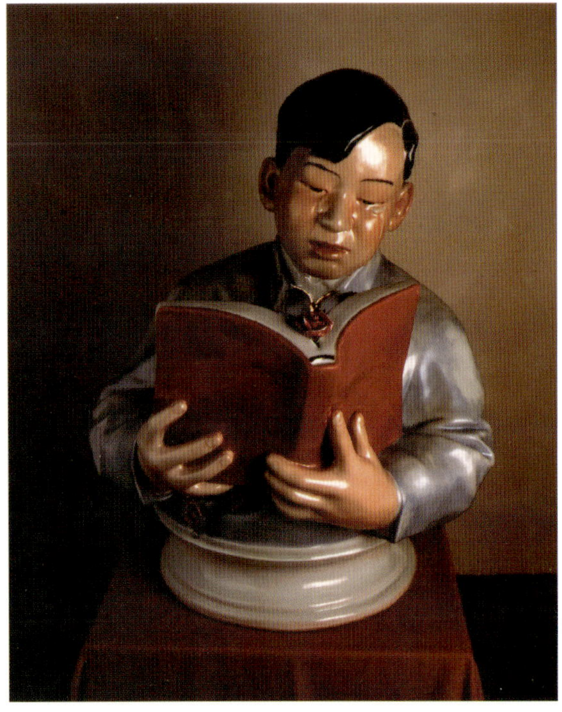

49. Xu Yihui 徐一辉, *Child and Book*, 1998–99, coloured ceramic, 61 × 50 × 50 cm.

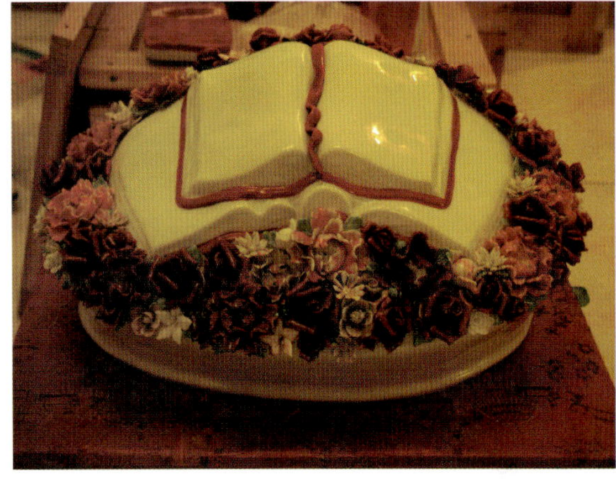

50. Xu Yihui 徐一辉, *Three Red Books*, 1998–99, coloured ceramic, 41 × 32 × 21 cm.

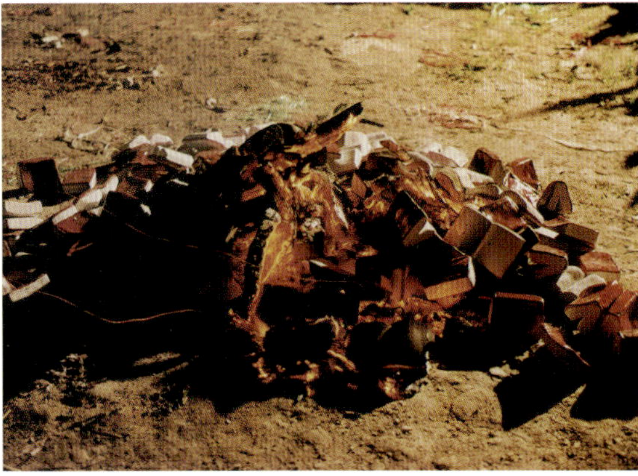

51. Xu Yihui 徐一辉, *Burning the Books*, performance in 2000, coloured ceramic, 240 pieces.

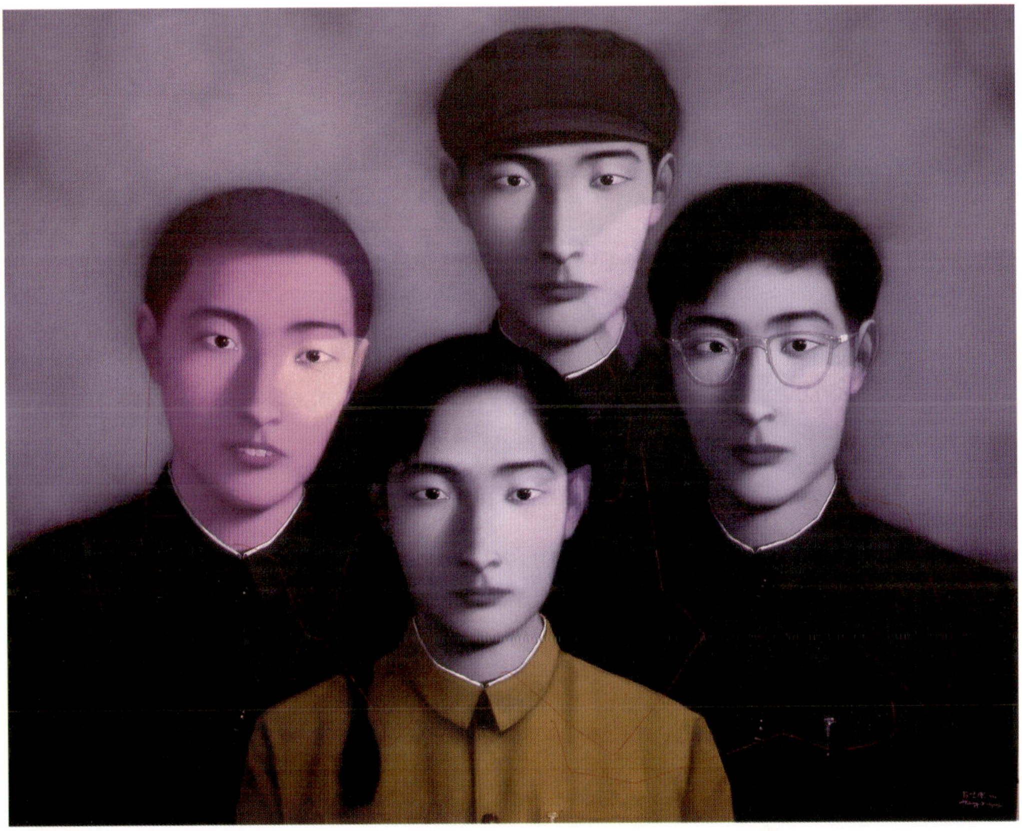

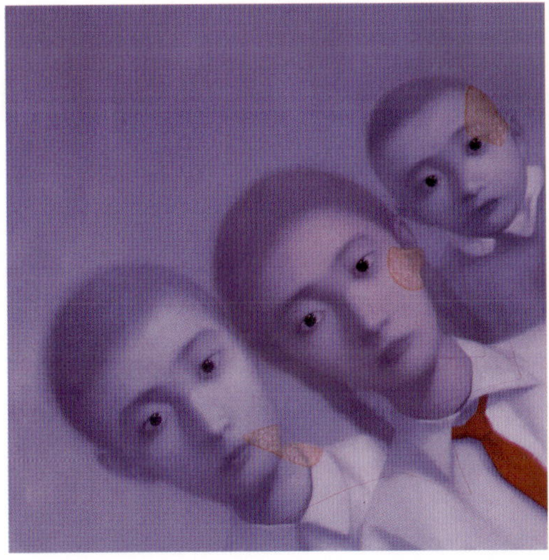

52. Zhang Xiaogang 张晓刚, *Da Jiating* 大家庭 *(Big Family): No. 1*, 1996, oil on canvas, 180 × 230 cm.

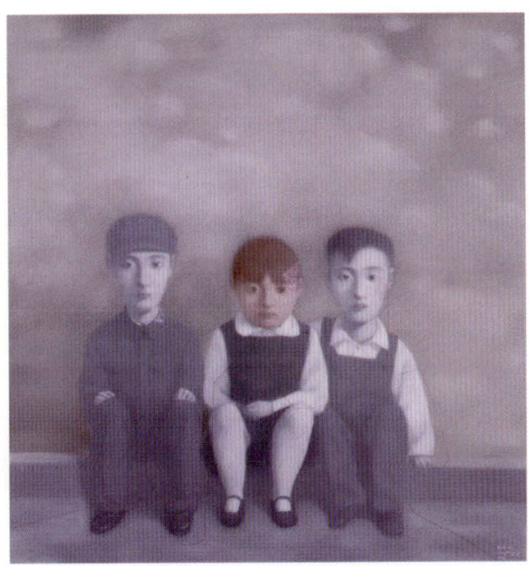

53. Zhang Xiaogang 张晓刚, *Da Jiating* 大家庭 *(Big Family): Honglingjin* 红领巾 *(Red Scarf)*, 1998, oil on canvas, 150 × 150 cm.

54. Zhang Xiaogang 张晓刚, *Da Jiating* 大家庭 *(Big Family): Tongnian* 童年 *(Childhood)*, 1998, oil on canvas, 150 × 150 cm.

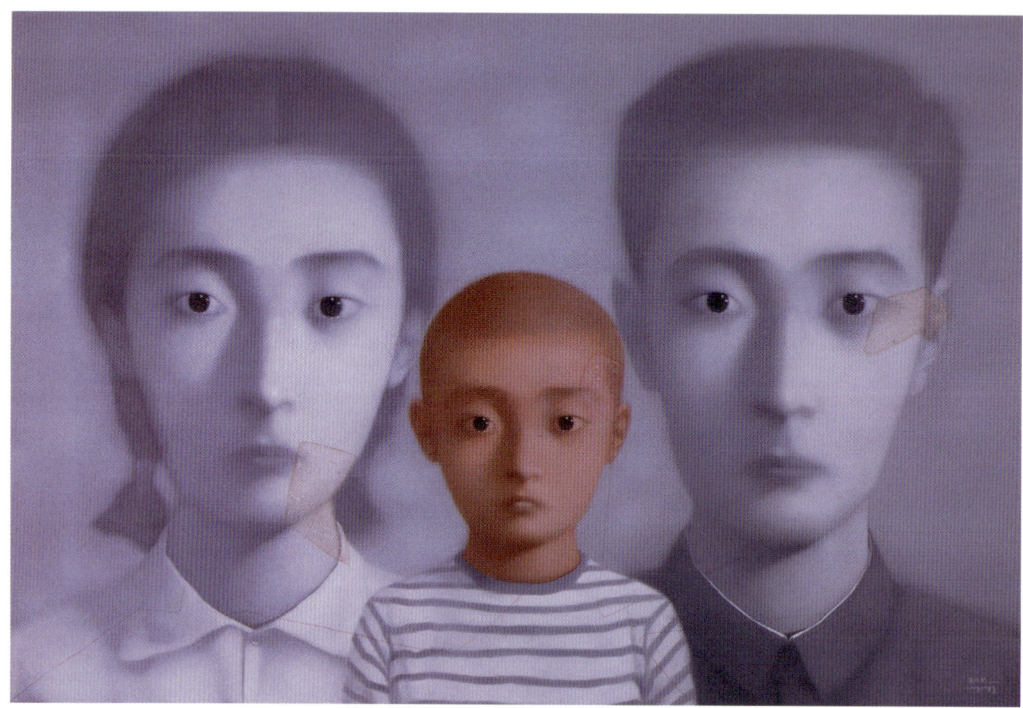

55. Zhang Xiaogang 张晓刚, *Da Jiating* 大家庭 *(Big Family): No. 10*, 2001, oil on canvas, 200 × 300 cm.

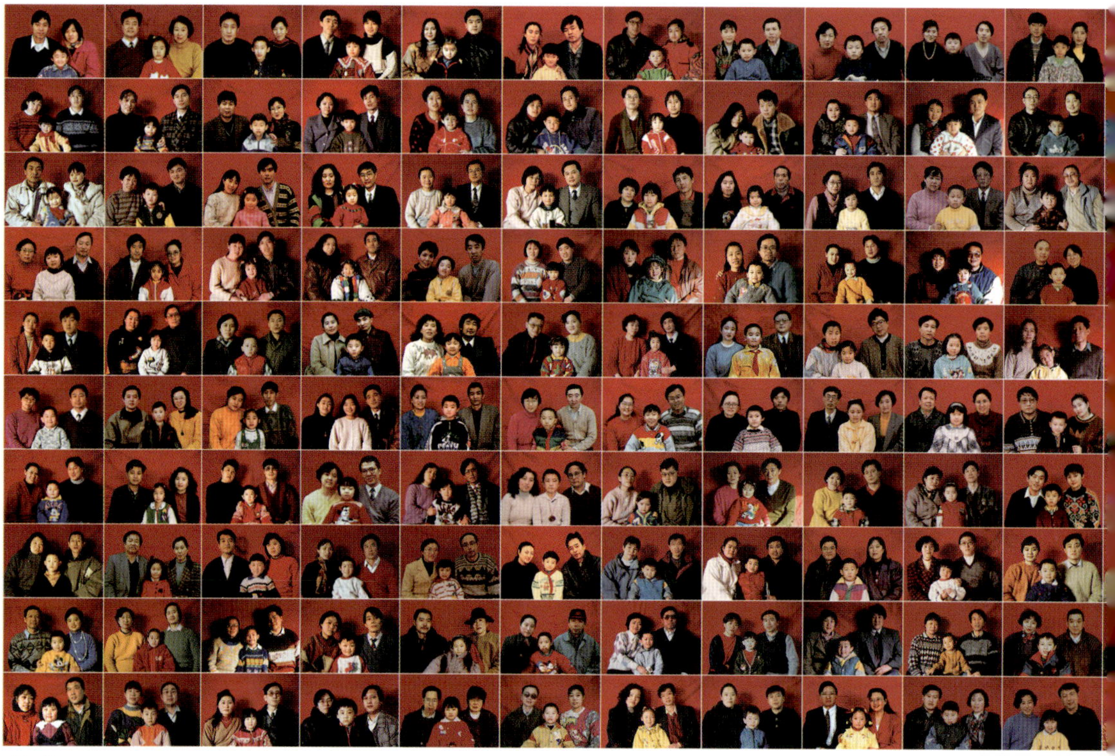

56. Wang Jinsong 王劲松, *Biaozhun Jiating* 标准家庭 *(Standard Family)*, 1996, photograph.

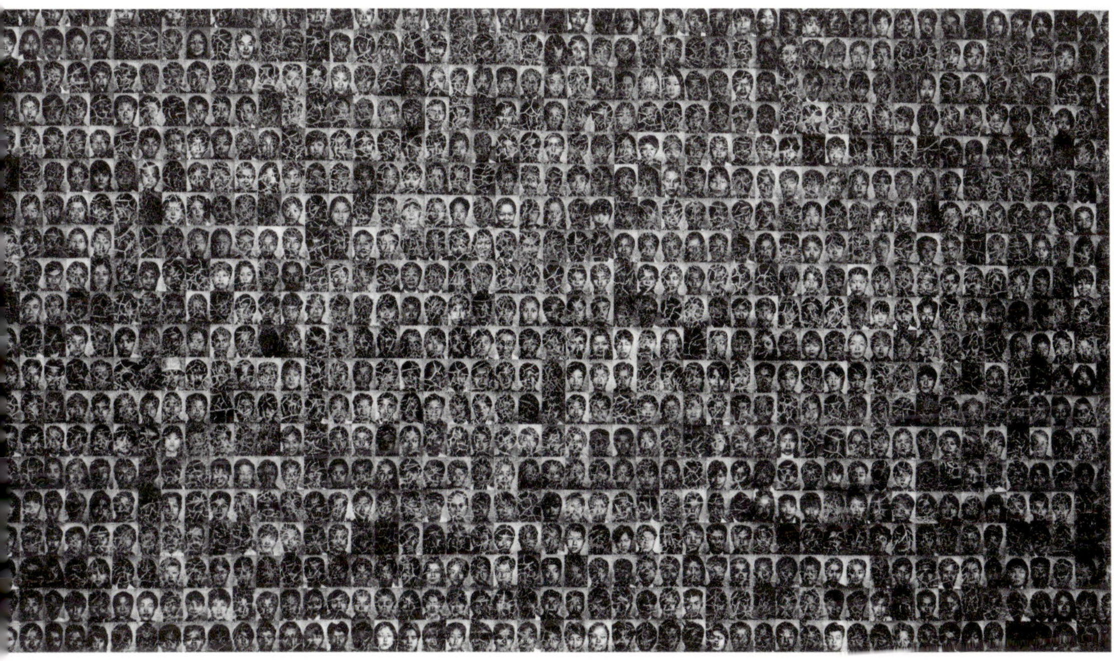

57. Bai Yiluo 白宜洛, *Renmin* 人民 *(People)*, 2001, photograph installation, 300 × 500 cm, detail.

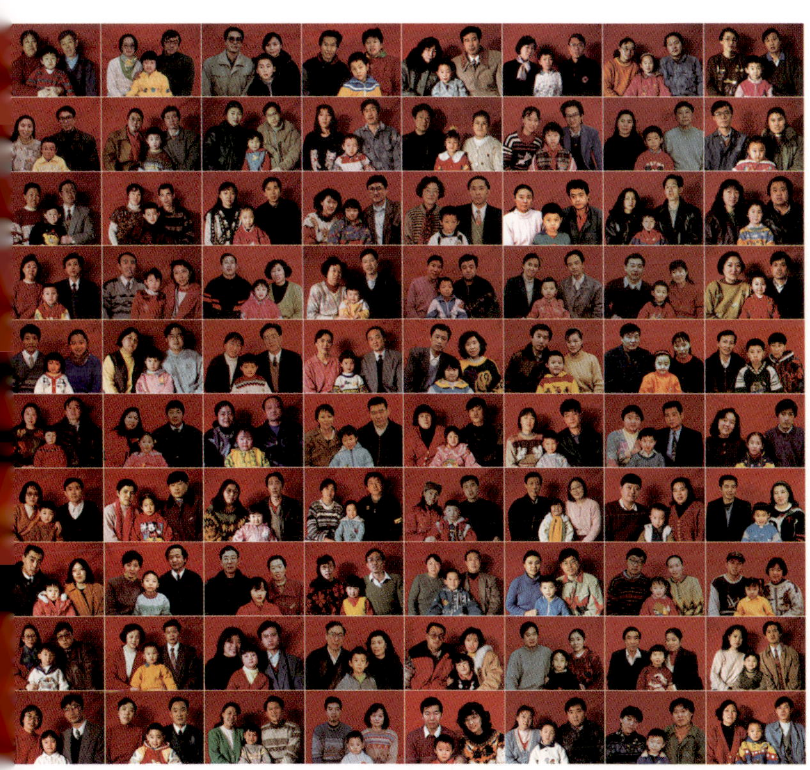

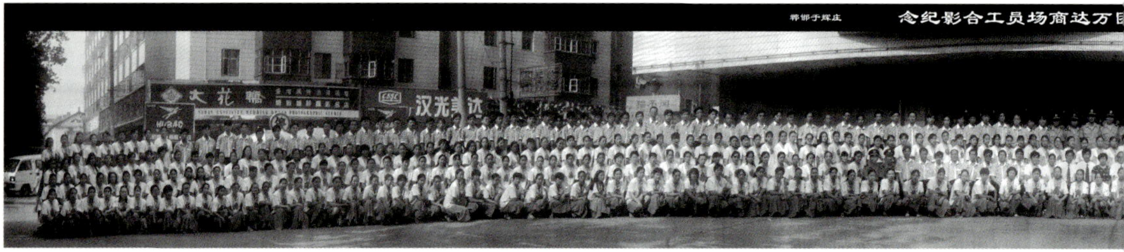

58. Zhuang Hui 庄辉, *Jiti Zhao* 集体照 *(Group Photo): Hebei Sheng Handan Shi Yangguang Jituan Wanda Shangchang Yuangong Heying* 河北省邯郸市阳光集团万达商场员工合影 *(Group Photo of Full Staff of Wangda Department Store of Yangguang Group), Handan, Hebei Province*, 13 July 1997, photograph.

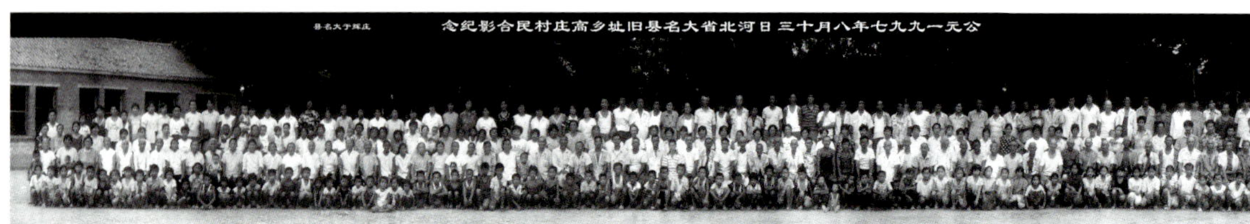

59. Zhuang Hui 庄辉, *Jiti Zhao* 集体照 *(Group Photo): Hebei Sheng Daming Xian Jiuzhi Xiang Gaozhuang Cunmin Heying* 河北省大名县旧址乡高庄村民合影 *(Group Photo of Gao Village, Jiuzhi District, Daming County, Hebei Province)*, 13 August 1997, photograph.

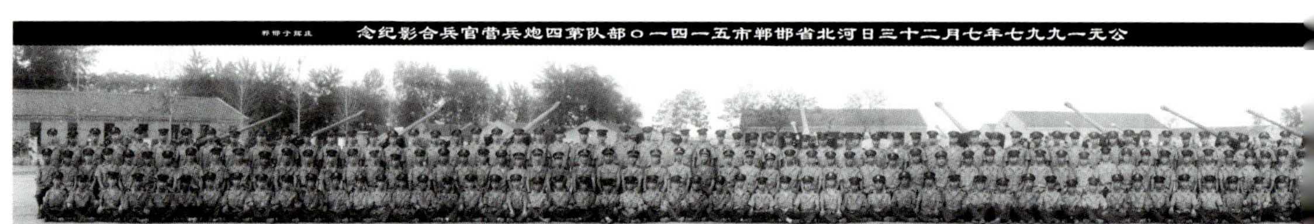

60. Zhuang Hui 庄辉, *Jiti Zhao* 集体照 *(Group Photo): Hebei Sheng Handan Shi Wu Yi Si Yi Ling Budui Disi Paobingying Guanbing Heying* 河北省邯郸市五一四一零部队第四炮兵营官兵合影 *(Group Photo of Military Camp Officers of 51410 Army, 4th Artillery Division, Handan, Hebei Province)*, 23 July 1997, photograph.

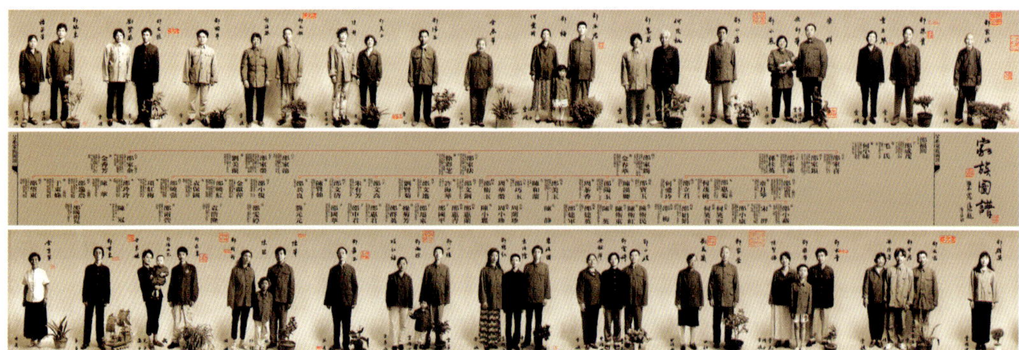

61. Shao Yinong 邵逸农 and Mu Chen 慕辰, *Jiapu* 家谱 *(Family Register)*, 2000, photograph.

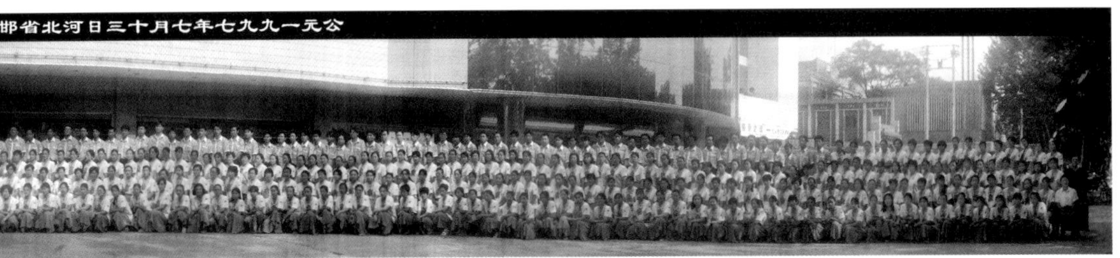

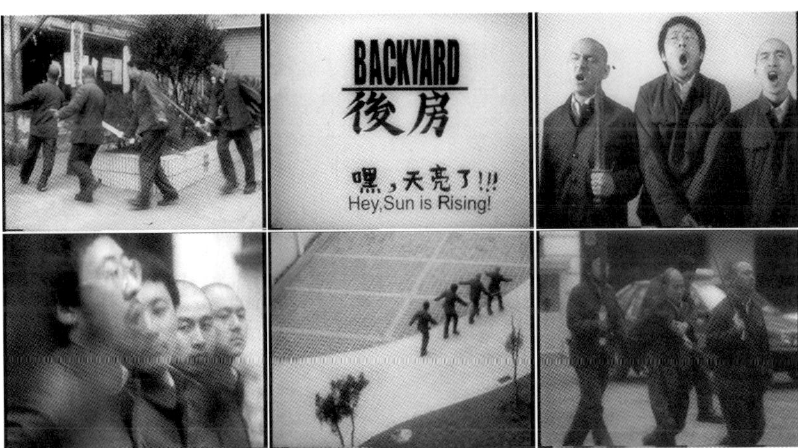

62. Yang Fudong 杨福东, *Houfang – Hei, Tianliangle* 后房—嘿，天亮了！*(Backyard – Hey, Sun is rising!)*, 2001, still images of 13 minutes 35 mm black & white film.

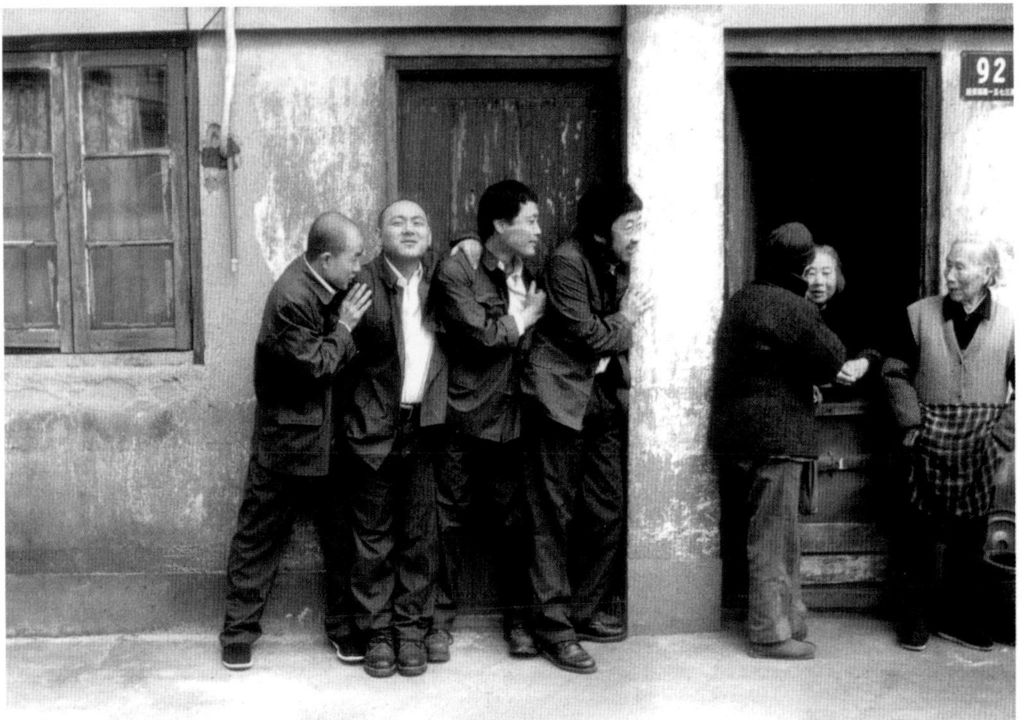

63. Yang Fudong 杨福东, *Houfang – Hei, Tianliangle* 后房—嘿，天亮了！*(Backyard – Hey, Sun is rising!)*, still image of film.

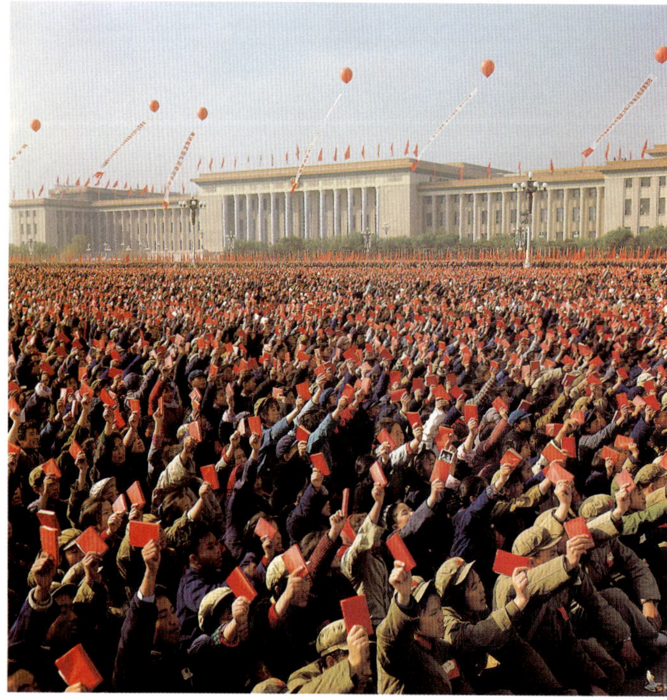

64. *The hearts of the revolutionary people are turned to the great leader Chairman Mao, Renmin Huabao* 人民画报 *(People's Pictorial)*, Vol. 2, 1967.

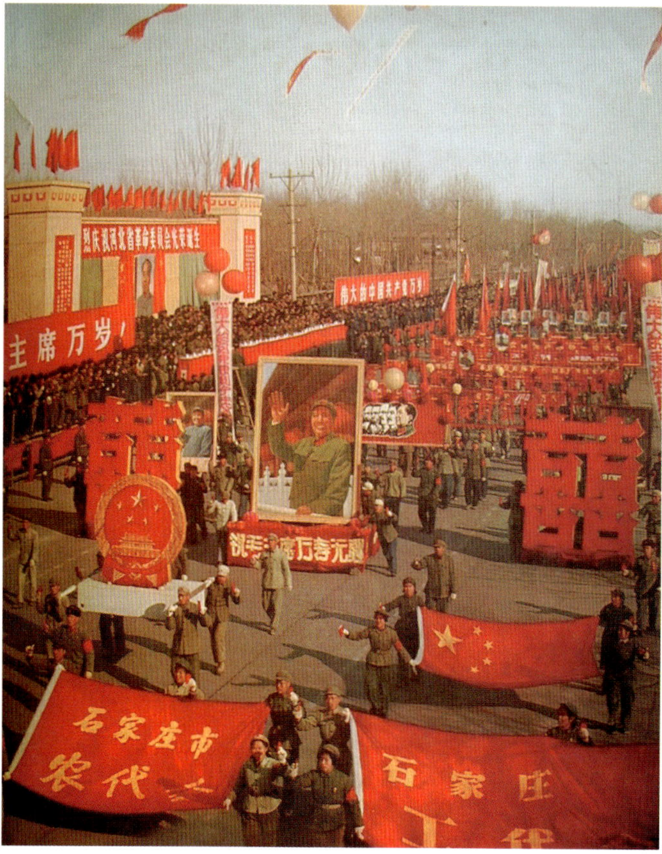

65. Photograph, *Renmin Huabao* 人民画报 *(People's Pictorial)*, Vol. 238, April 1968.

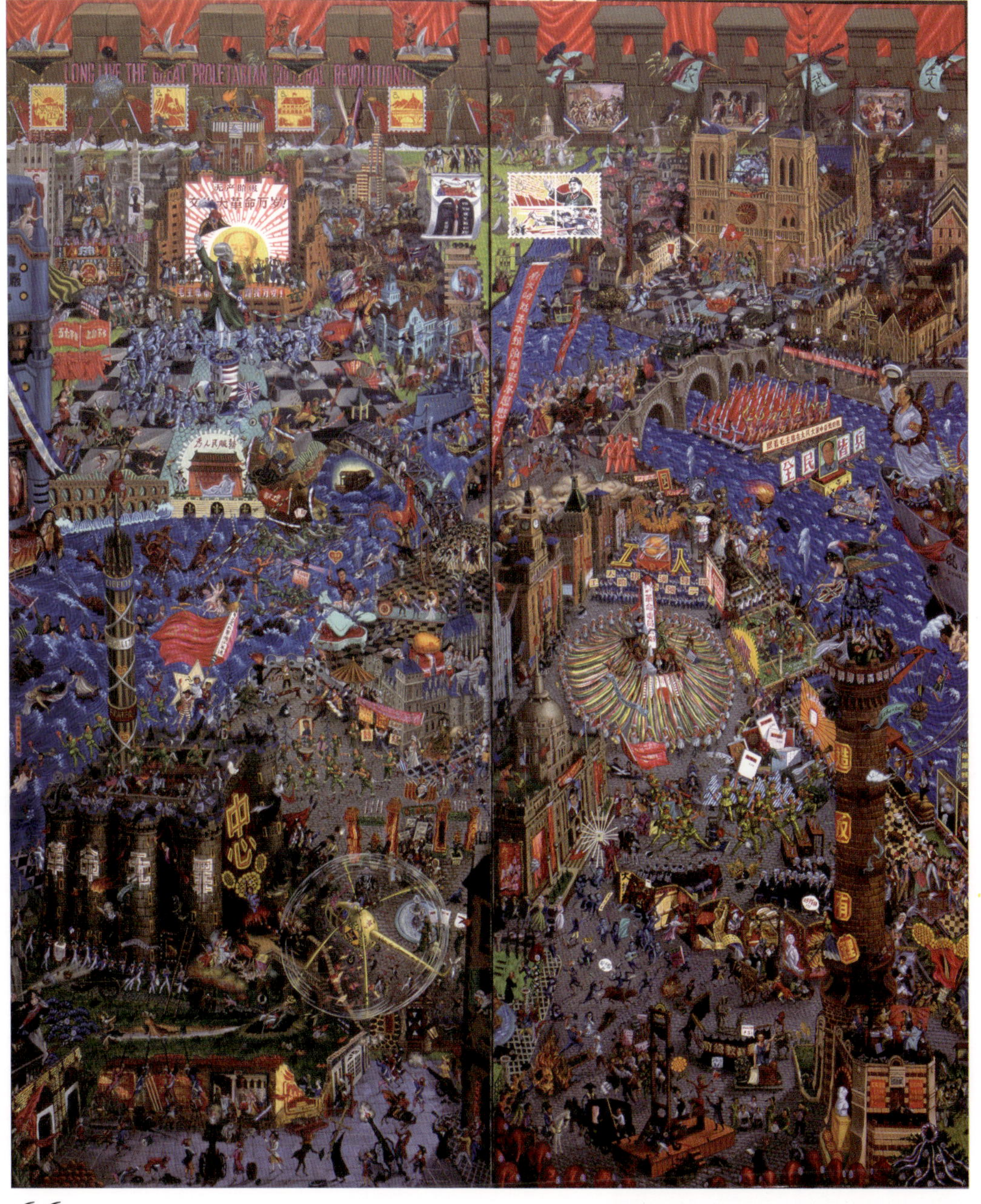

66. Liu Dahong 刘大鸿, *Shuangcheng Ji* 双城记 (*A Tale of Two Cities*), 1999, oil on canvas, 200 × 240 cm.

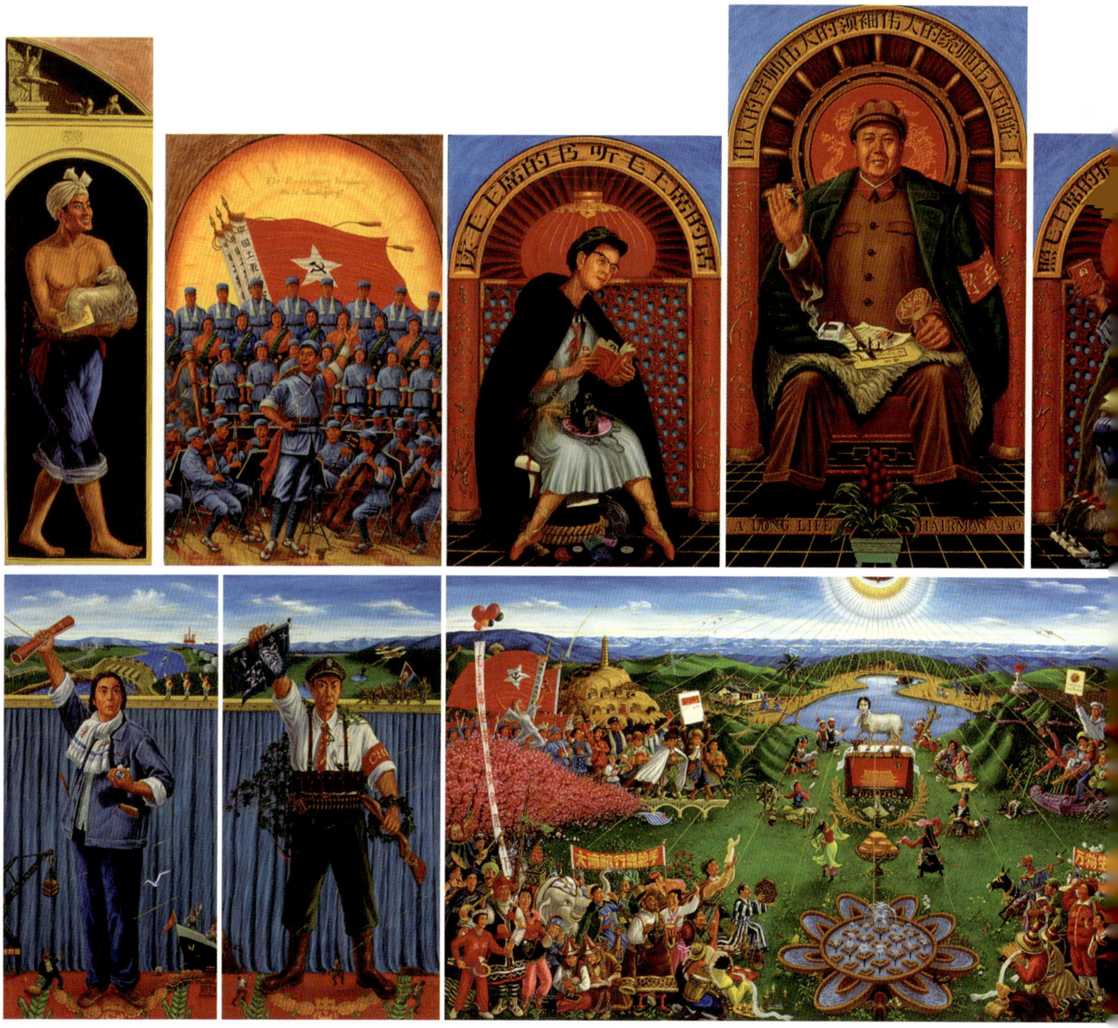

67. Liu Dahong 刘大鸿, *Jitan* 祭坛 *(Sacrificial Altar)*, 1999–2000, oil on canvas, detail.

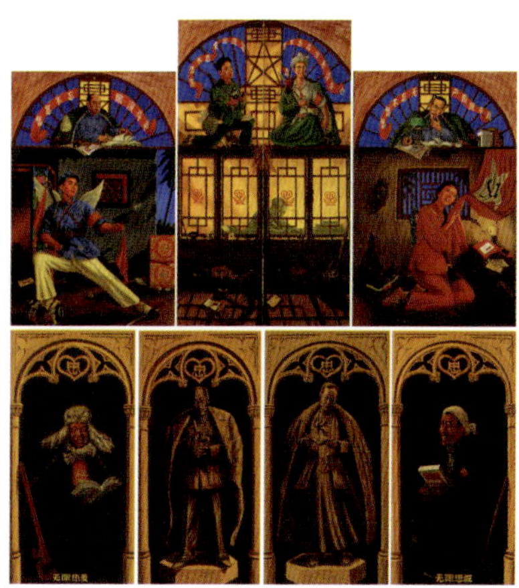

68. Liu Dahong 刘大鸿, *Jitan* 祭坛 *(Sacrificial Altar)*, detail.

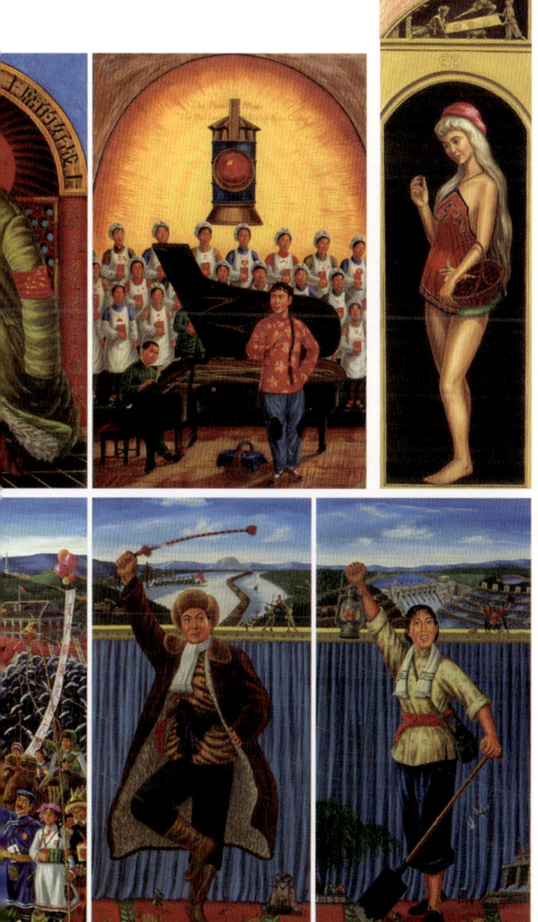

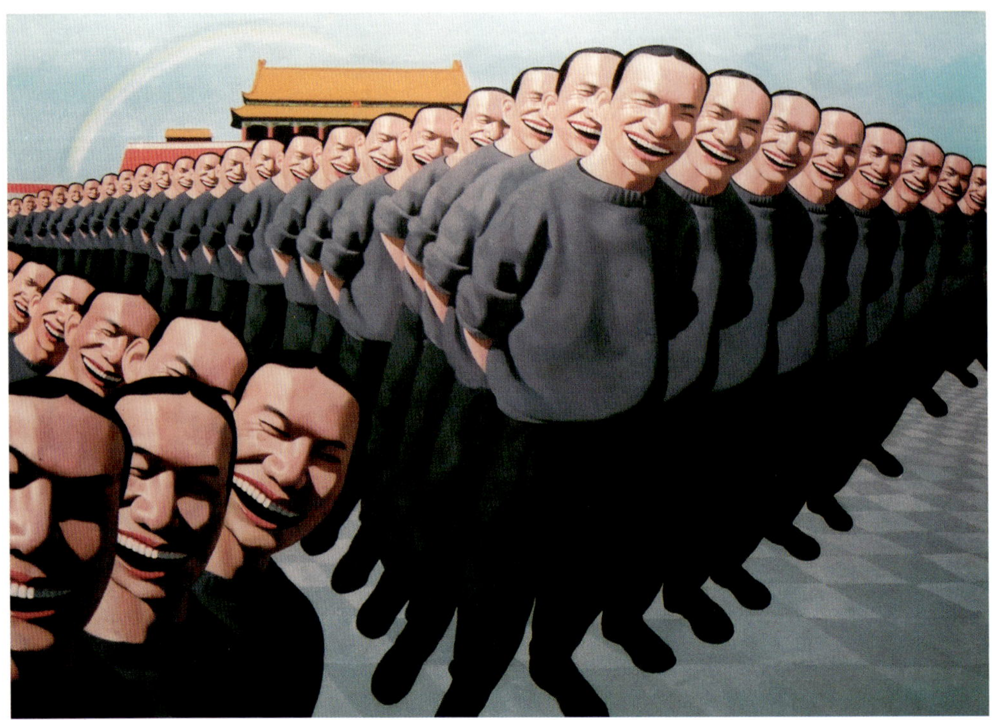

69. Yue Minjun 岳敏君, *Dakuangxi* 大狂喜 *(Great Joy)*, 1992–1993, oil on canvas, 185 × 250 cm.

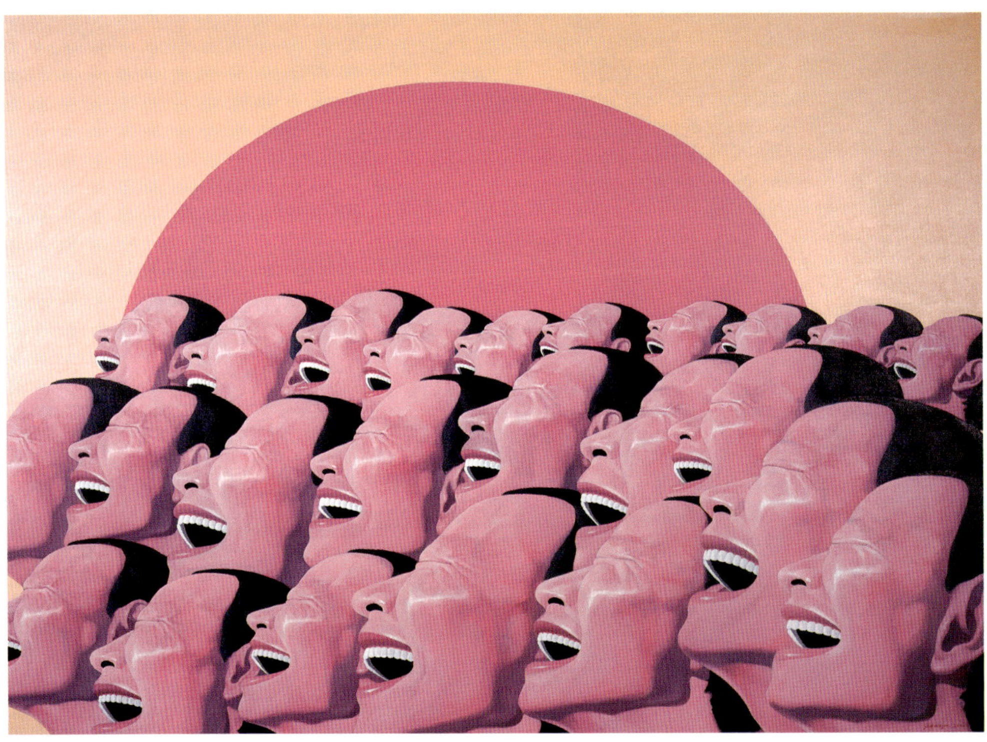

70. Yue Minjun 岳敏君, *Maihai Haoqing* 满怀豪情 *(Lofty Sentiment)*, 1999, oil on canvas, 300 × 220 cm.

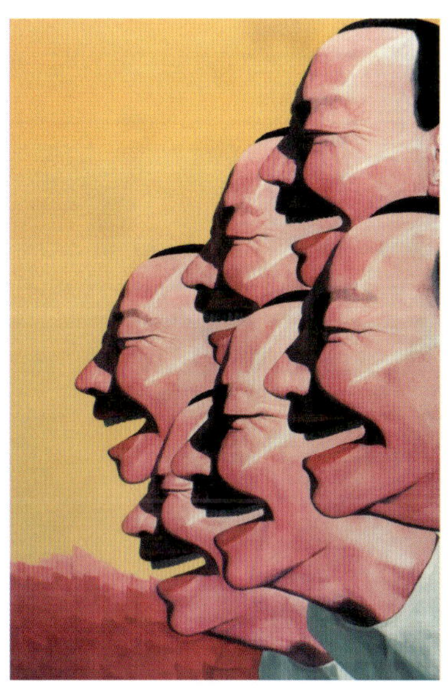

71. Yue Minjun 岳敏君, *Taiyang* 太阳 *(the Sun)*, 2000, acrylic on canvas, 200 × 280 cm.

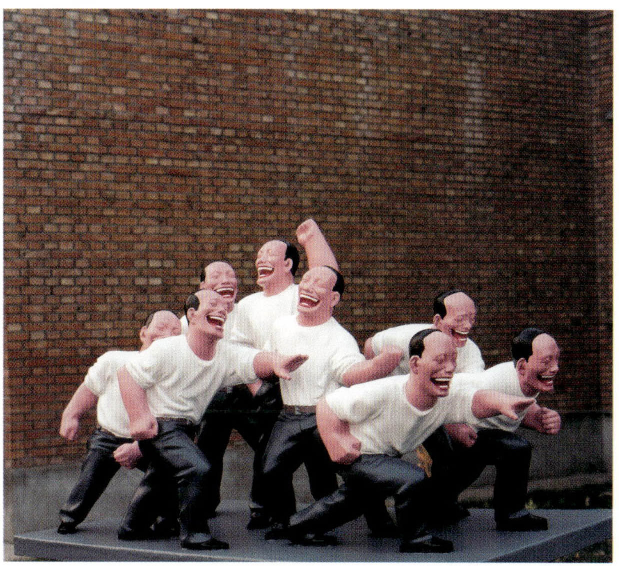

72. Yue Minjun 岳敏君, *Langman Zhuyi Xianshi Zhuyi Yanjiu* 浪漫主义和现实主义研究之六*(Romanticism and Realism Study – 6)*, 2003, acrylic on fibreglass reinforced plastics, 88 × 163 × 90 cm

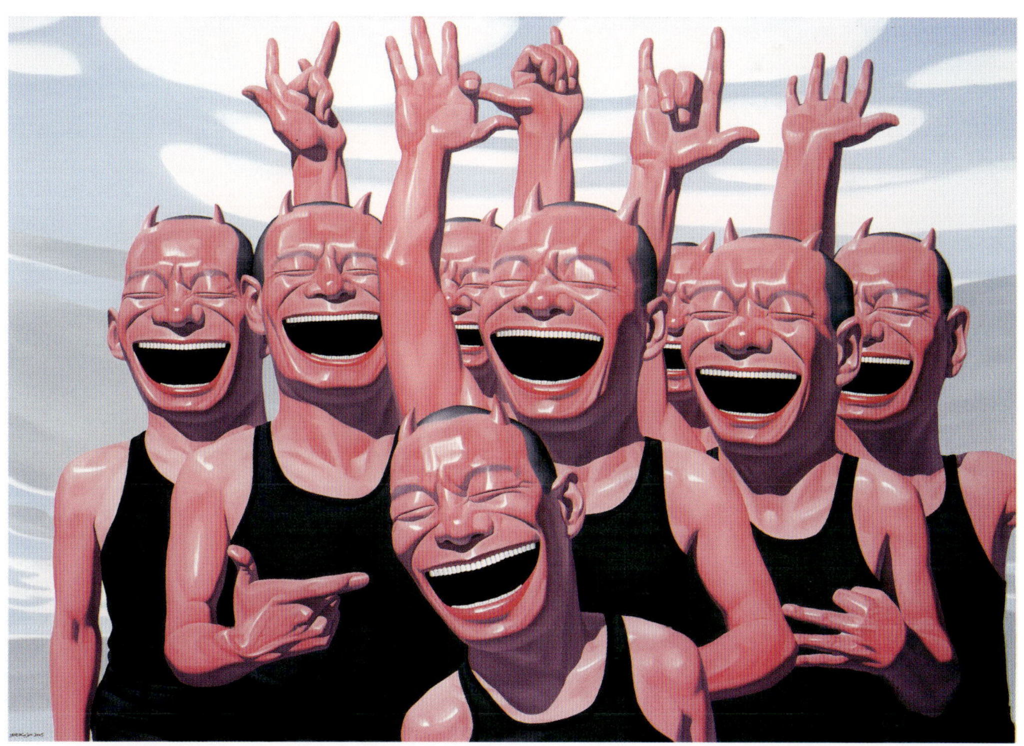

73. Yue Minjun 岳敏君, *Renshou Zhijian* 人兽之间 *(Between Men and Beasts)*, 2005, oil on canvas, 400 × 280 cm.

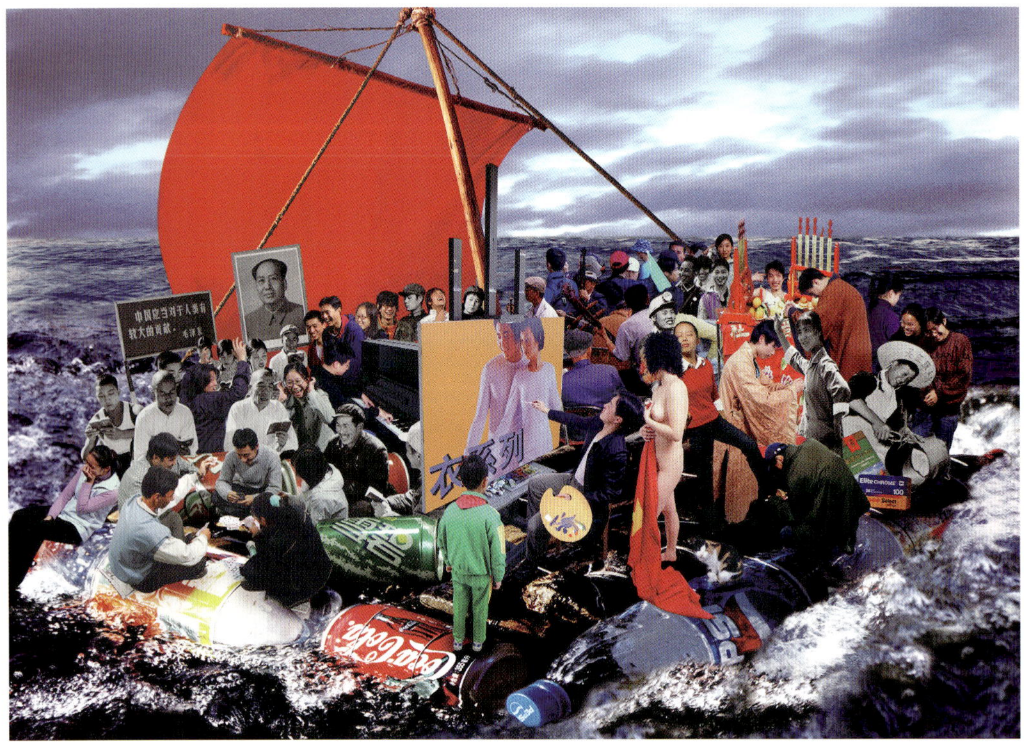

74. Hu Jieming 胡介鸣, *Meiduosa Zhifa* 美多撒之伐 *(Raft of the Medusa)*, *No. 3*, 2002, photograph.

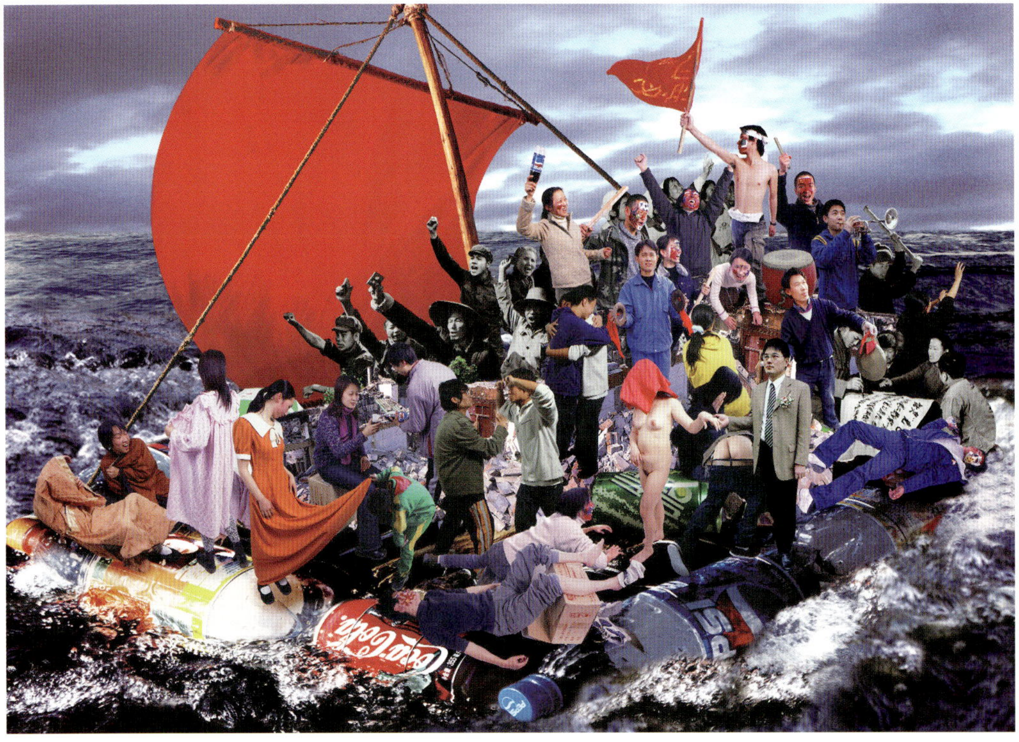

75. Hu Jieming 胡介鸣, *Meiduosa Zhifa* 美多撒之伐 *(Raft of the Medusa)*, *No. 4, 2002*, photograph.

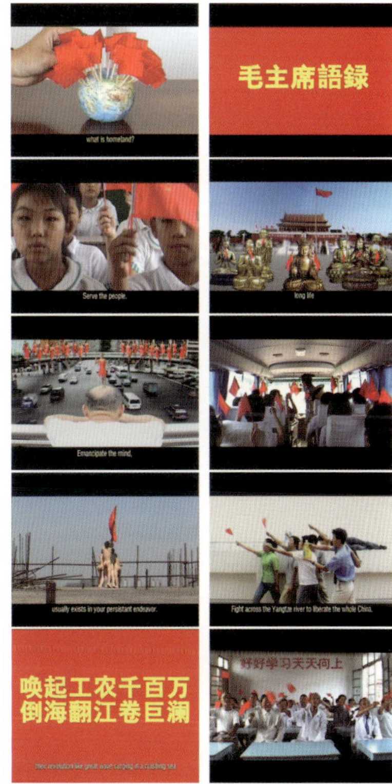

76. Zhou Hongxiang 周弘湘, *Hongqi Piao* 红旗飘 *(The Red Flag Flies)*, 2002, still images of video.

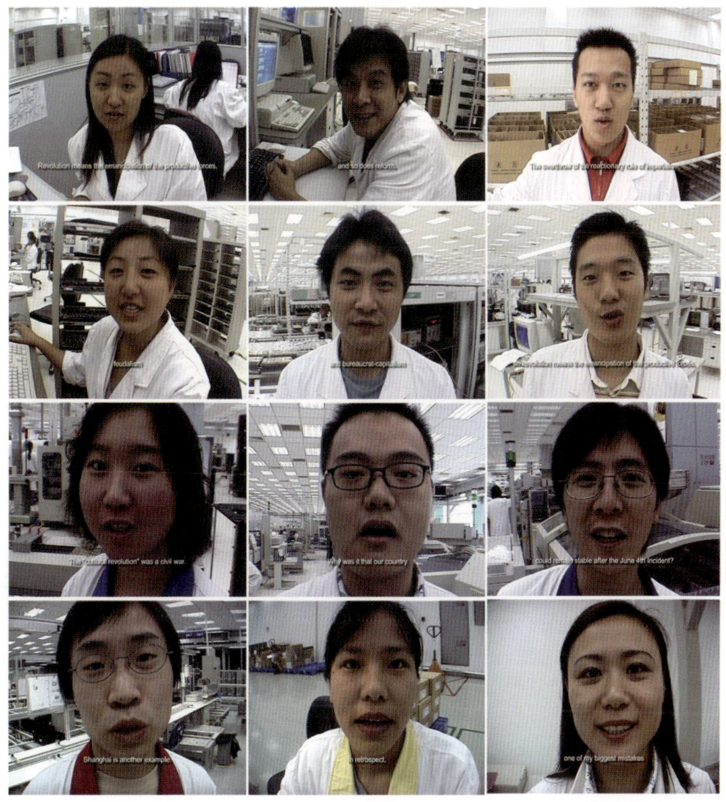

77. Yang Zhenzhong 杨振忠, *Chuntian de Gushi* 春天的故事 *(Spring Story)*, 2003, still images of video.

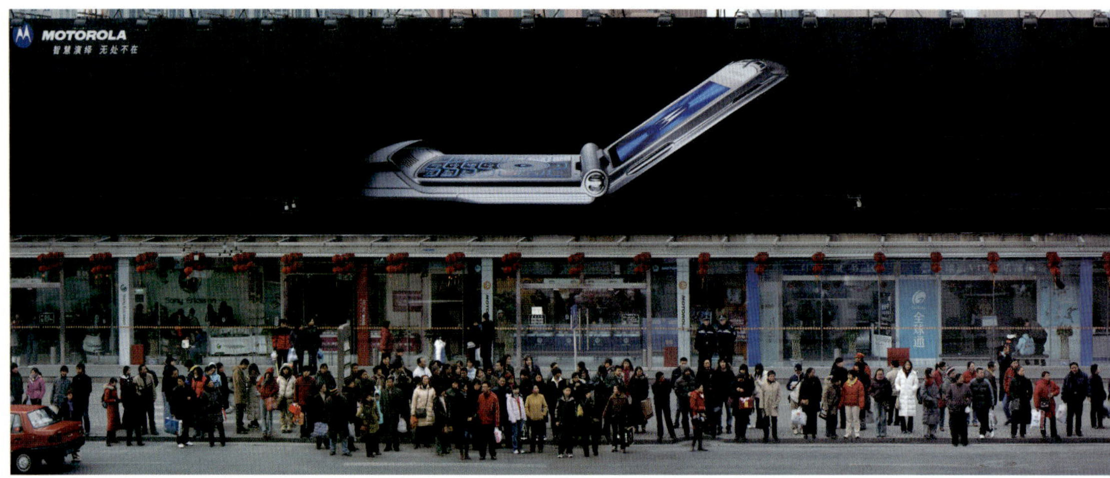

78. Miao Xiaochun 缪晓春, *Dai* 待 *(Await)*, 2002, photograph.

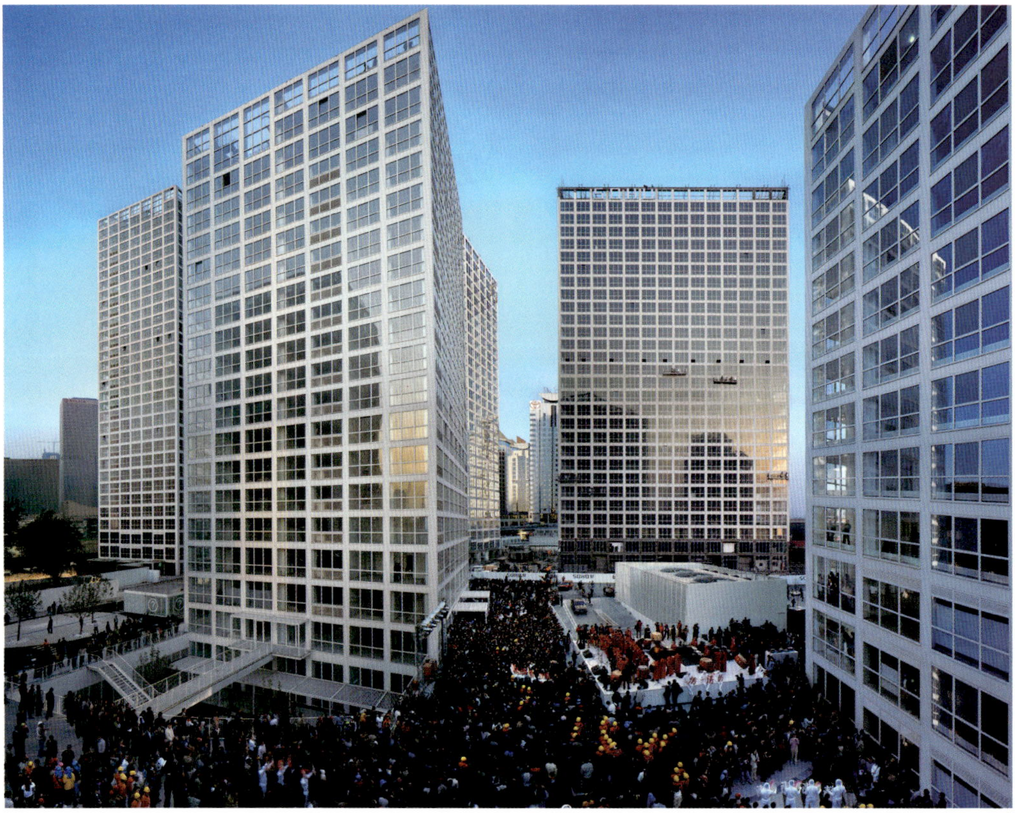

79. Miao Xiaochun 缪晓春, *Qing* 庆 *(Celebration)*, 2002, photograph.

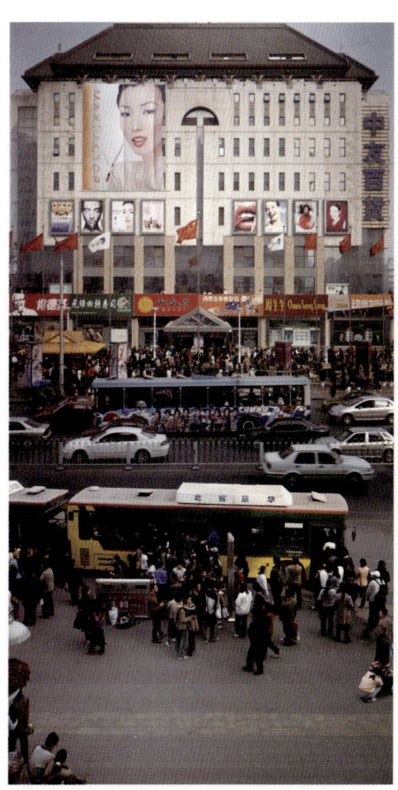

80. Miao Xiaochun 缪晓春, *Chao* 潮 *(Tide)*, 2006, photograph.

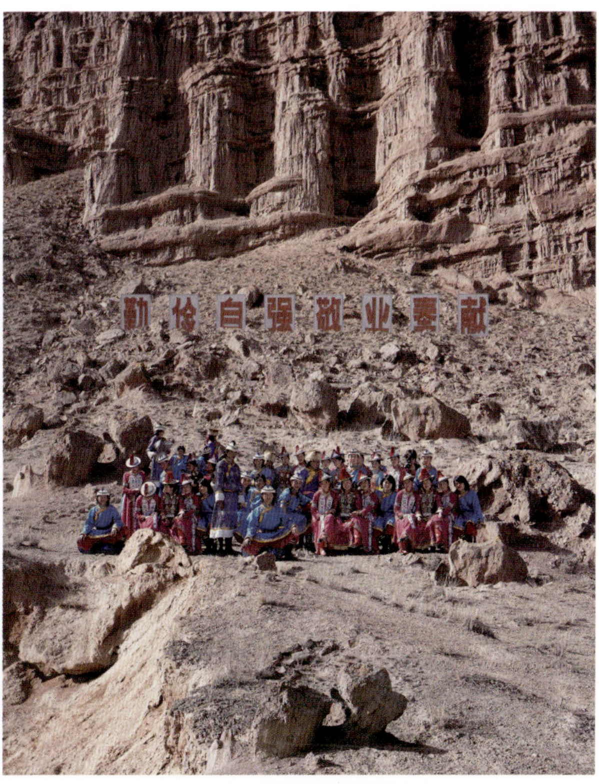

81. Wang Chuan 王川, *Shaoshu Jiti* 少数集体 *(Minority Collective)*, 2006, photograph.

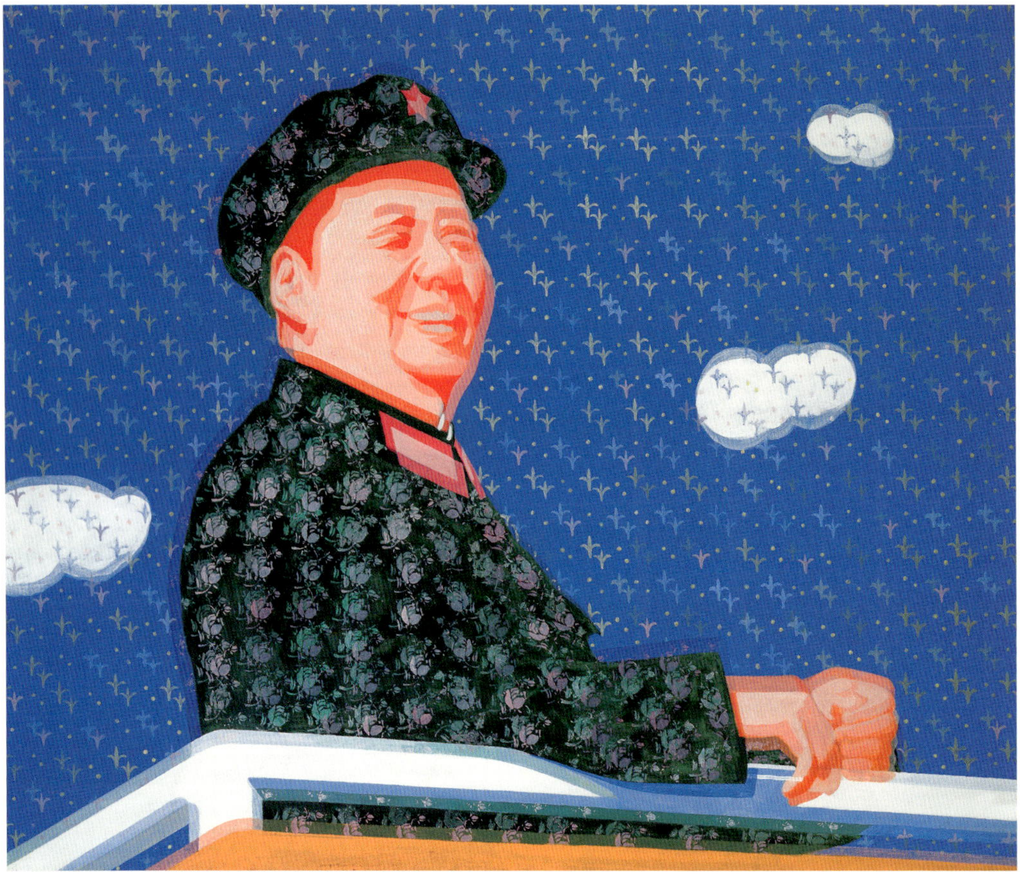

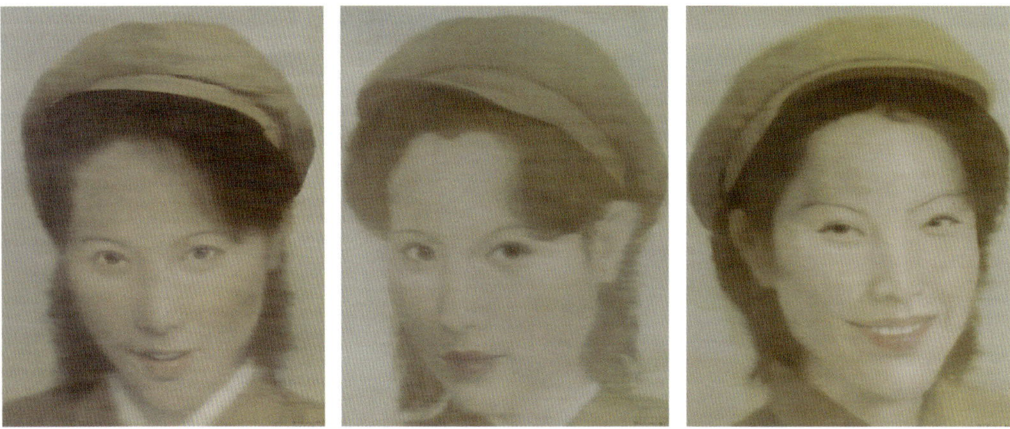

82. Yu Youhan 余友涵, *Zai Tiananmen Chenglou Shang* 在天安门城楼上 *(On the Tiananmen Tower)*, 1990, acrylic on canvas, 160 × 131 cm.

83. Qi Zhilong 祁志龙, *Biaoqing* 表情 *(Expression)*, 2002–03, oil on canvas, 162 × 130 cm each.

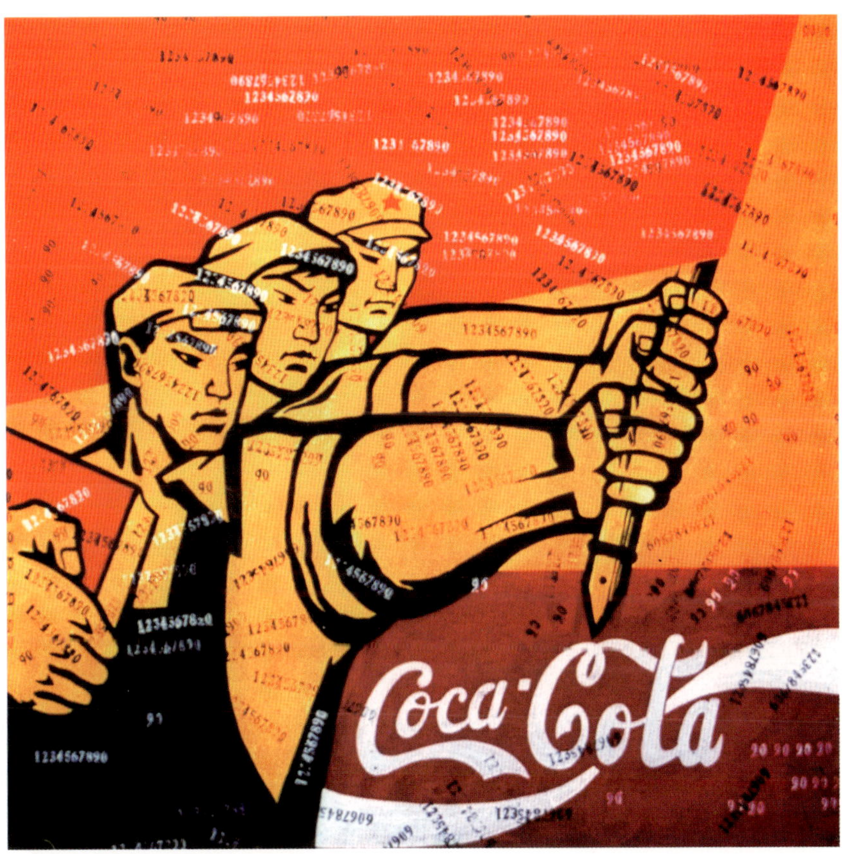

84. Wang Guangyi 王广义. *Dapipan: Kekou Kele* 大批判：可口可乐 *(Great Criticism: Coca-Cola)*, 1993, oil on canvas, 200 × 200 cm.

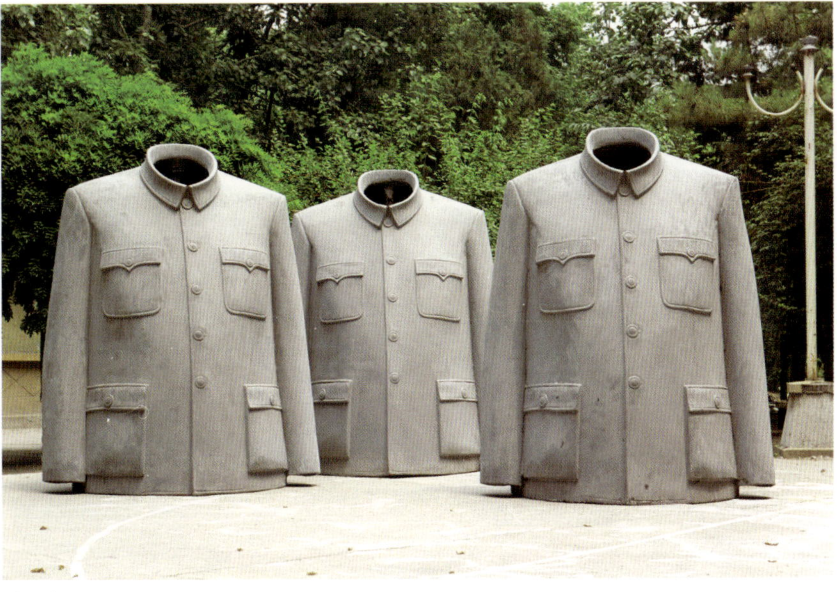

85. Sui Jianguo 隋建国, *Yibo* 衣钵 *(Legacy Mantle)*, 1997, coloured glass fibre, 240 cm high.

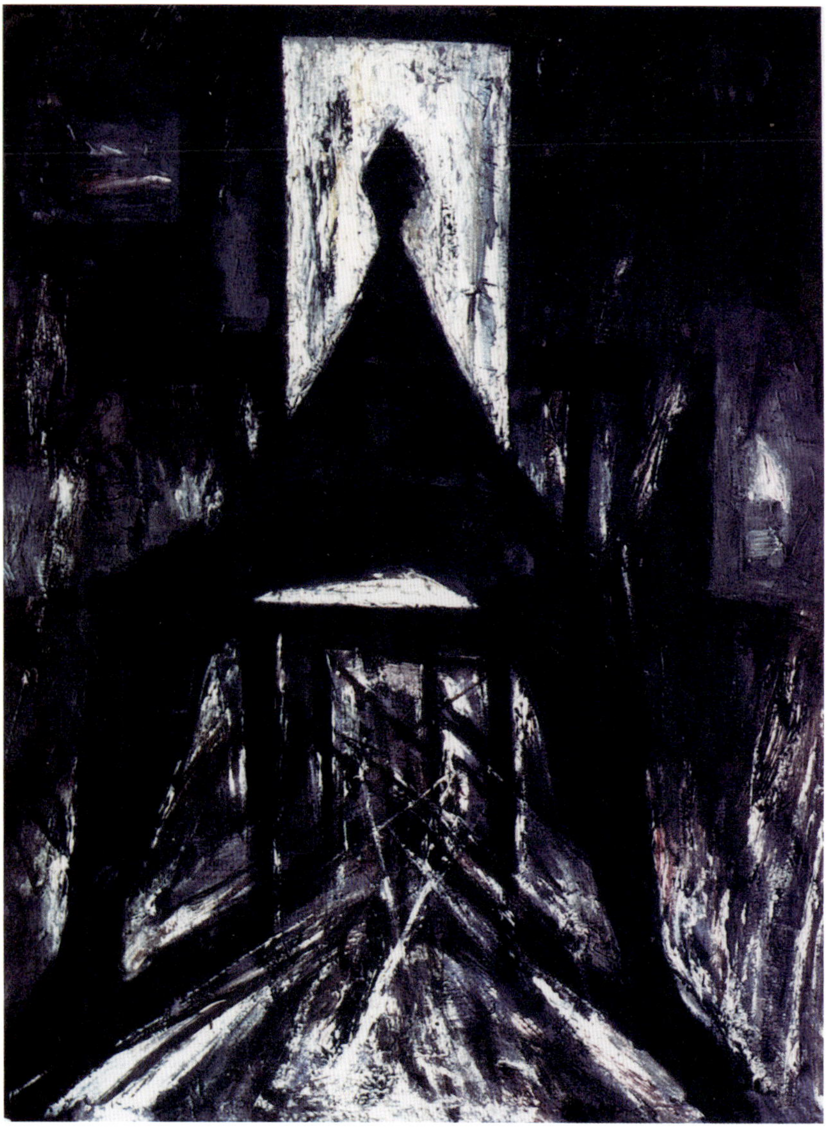

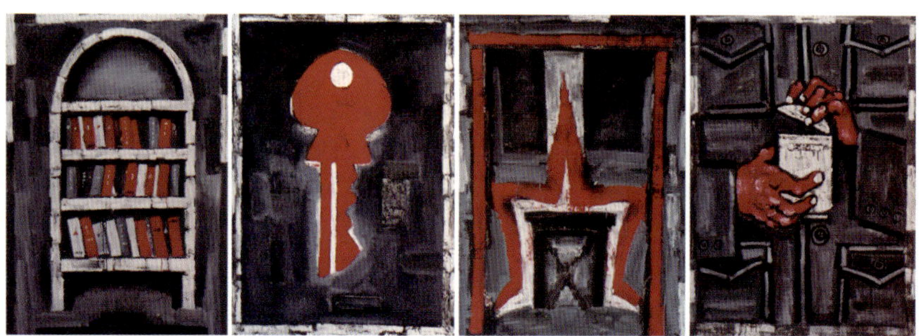

86. Mao Xuhui 毛旭辉, *Jiazhang* 家长 *(The Parent): Parent in the Chair*, 1989, oil on canvas, 101 × 81 cm.

87. Mao Xuhui 毛旭辉, *Jiazhang* 家长 *(The Parent): Quanli de Cihui* 权力的辞汇 *(Vocabulary of Power)*, 1993, oil on canvas, 8 pieces, 180 × 130 cm each.

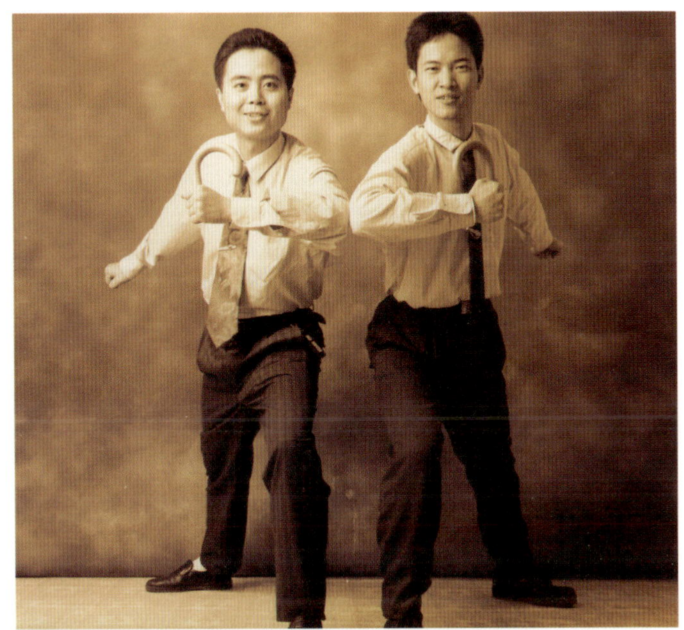

88. Qiu Zhijie 邱志杰, *Hao 好 (Fine): No. 2*, 1998, photograph.

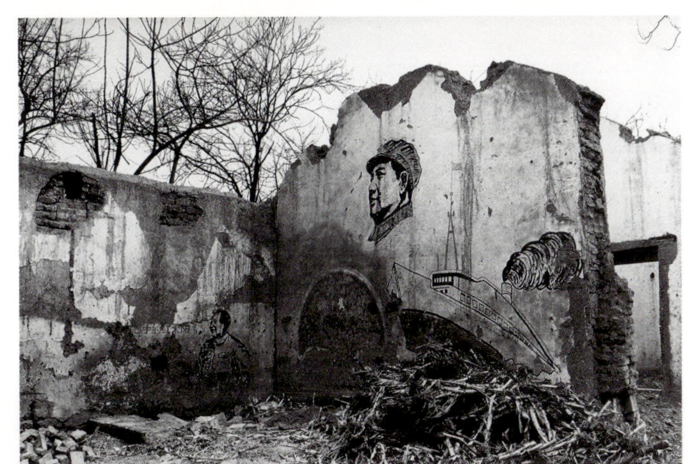

89. Wang Tong 王彤, *Wenge Yijing 文革遗景 (Vestiges of the Cultural Revolution): Mengjin County, Henan*, 1995, photograph.

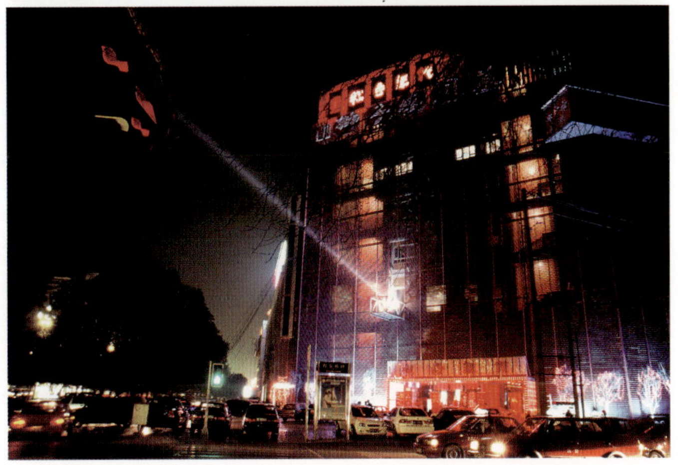

90. Liu Jiakun 刘家琨, *Hongse Niandai 红色年代 (The Red Era)*, 2000–01, architecture, Chengdu, Sichuan Province, China.

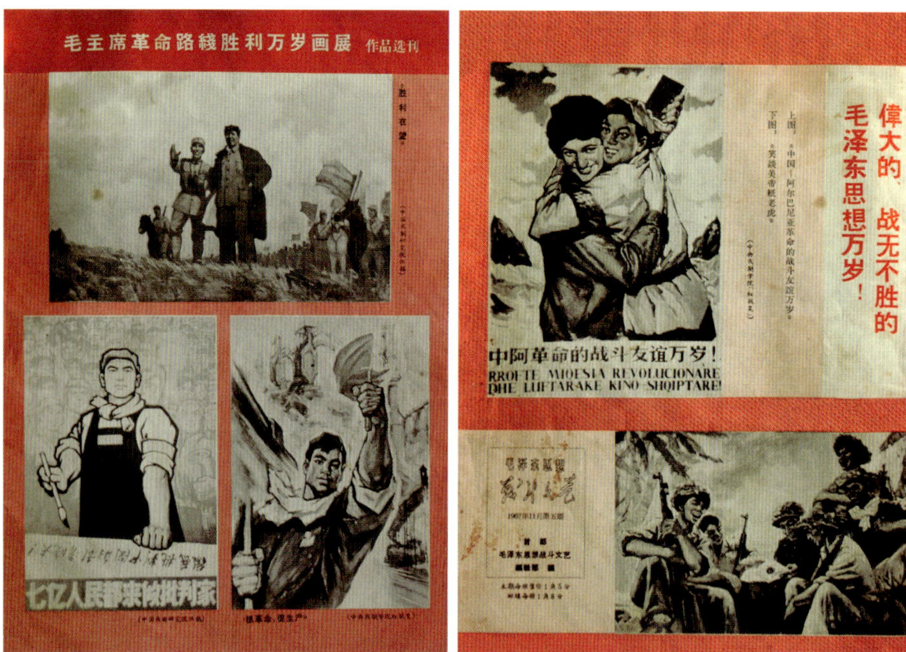

91. *Mao Zedong Sixiang Zhandou Wenyi* 毛泽东思想战斗文艺 (*Revolutionary Art and Literature of Mao Zedong Thought*), November 1967. All visual materials in this paper are personal collections of the author.

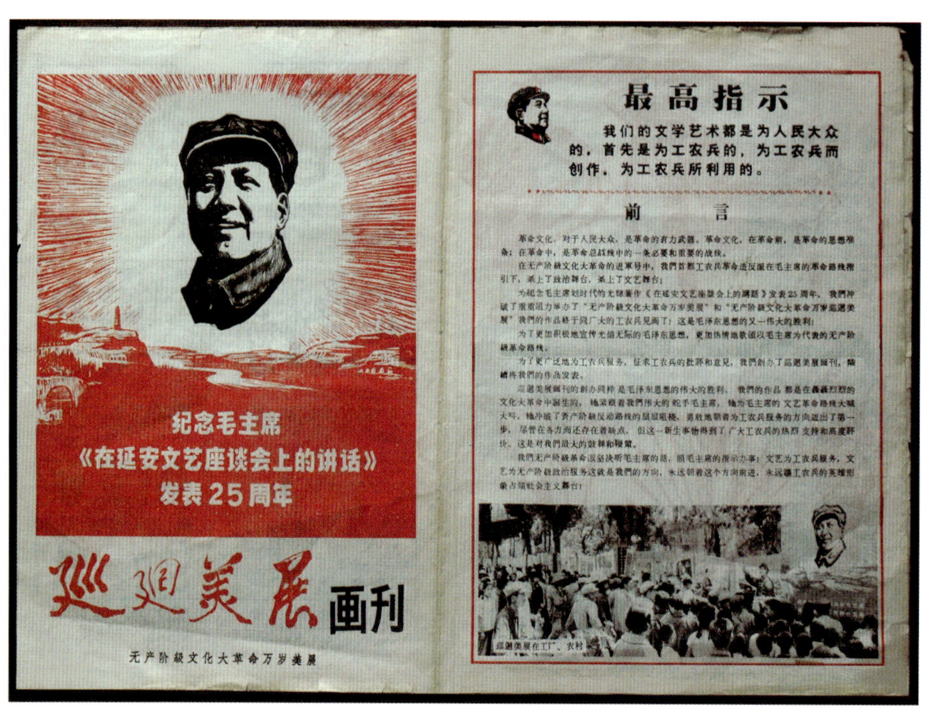

92. *Xunhui Meizhan Huakan* 巡回美展画刊 (*Touring Art Exhibition Pictorial*), 1967.

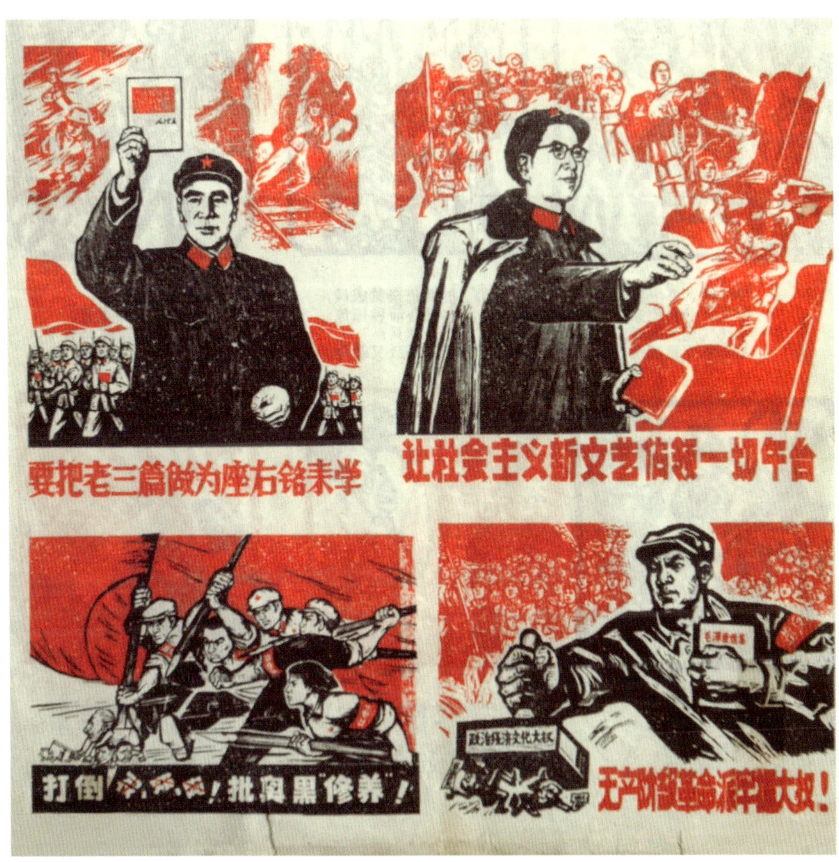

93. *Hongse Meishu* 红色美术 *(Red Art)*, June 1967.

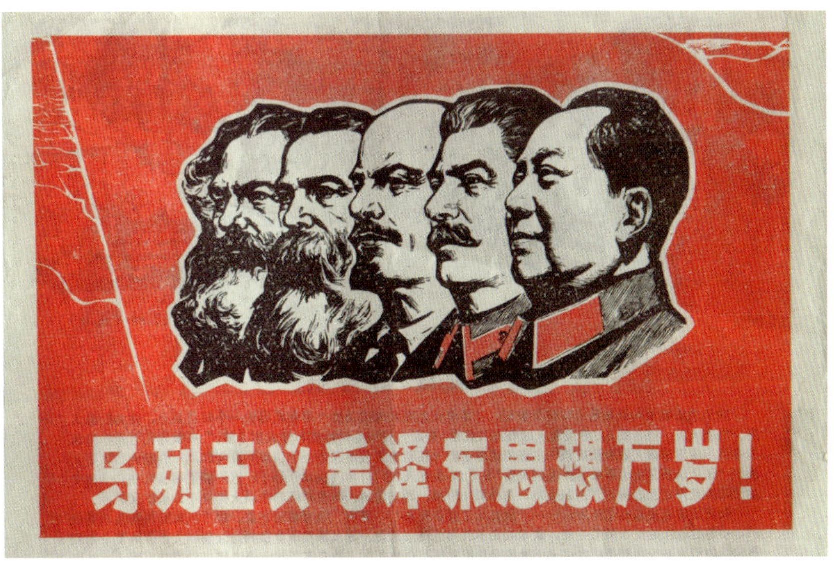

94. *Hongse Meishu* 红色美术 *(Red Art)*, June 1967.

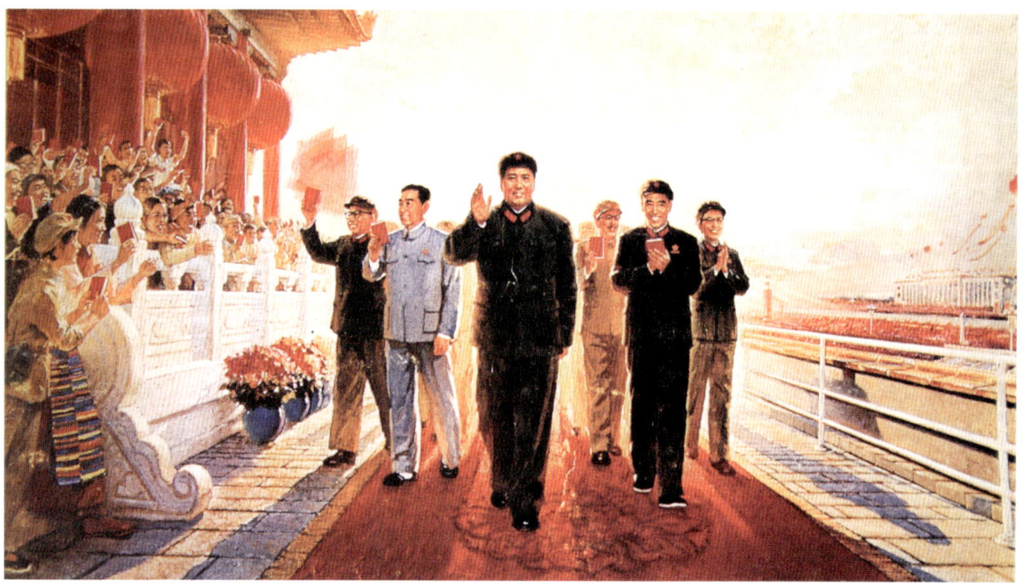

95. Anonymous, *Dongfang Hong* 东方红 *(East Is Red)*, 1967, oil on canvas.

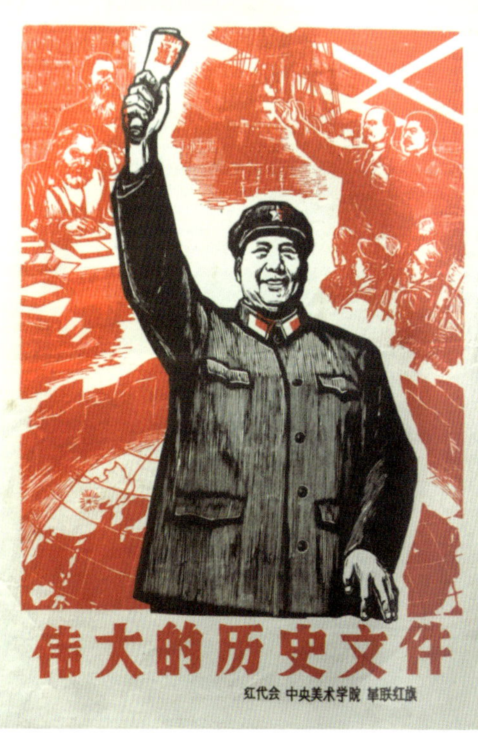

96. *Xin Meishu* 新美术 *(New Art)*, November 1967.

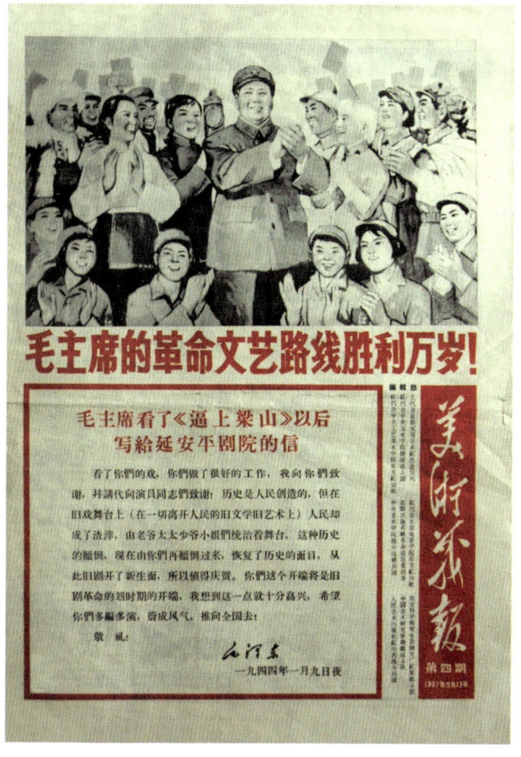

97. *Meishu Zhanbao* 美术战报 *(Art War Bulletin)*, May 1967.

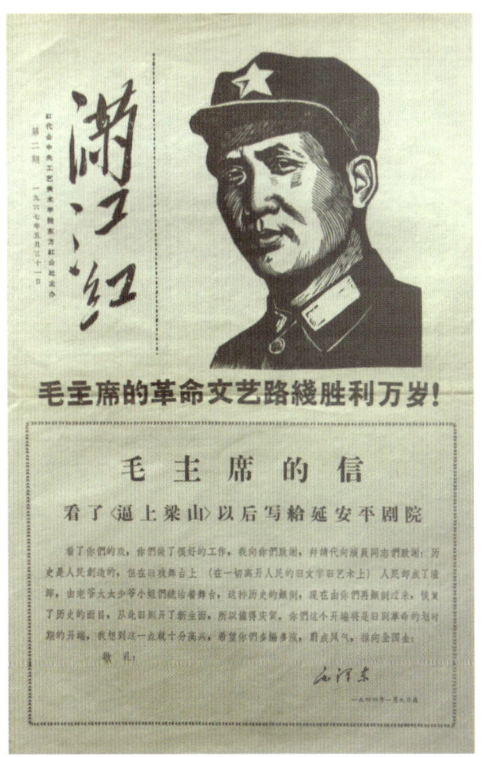

98. *Manjianghong* 满江红 *(Crimson Flooding into the River)*, May 1967.

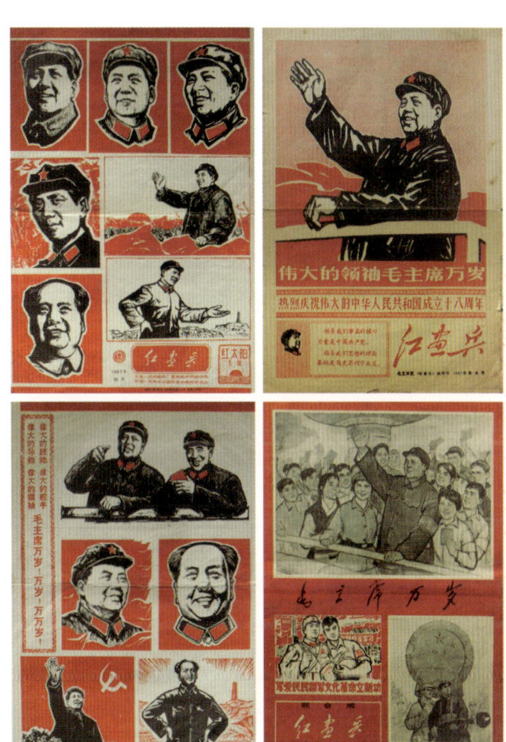

99. *Honghuabing* 红画兵 *(Red Artist Soldiers)*, 1967.

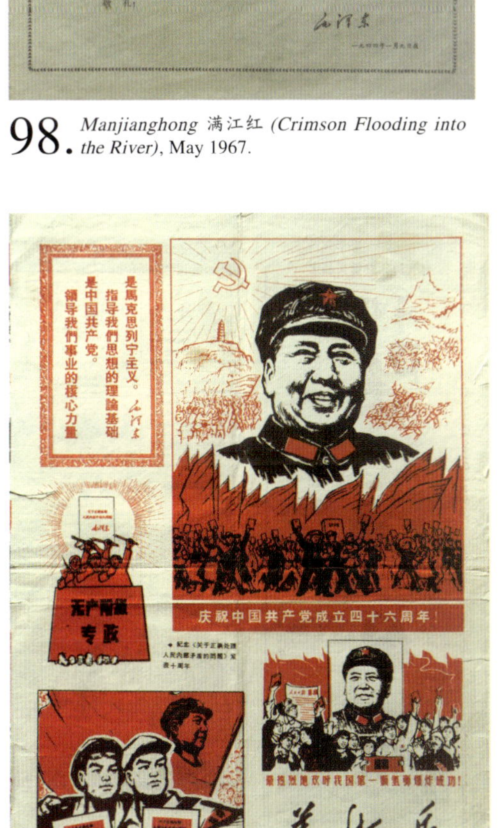

100. *Meishubing* 美术兵 *(Art Soldiers)*, July 1967.

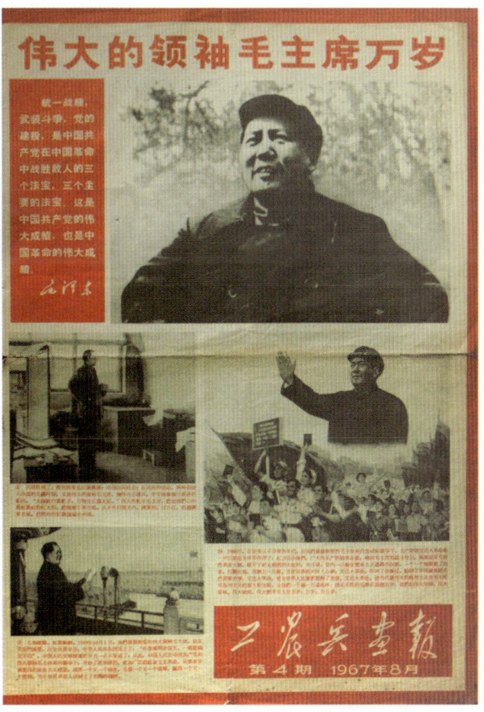

101. *Gongnongbing Huabao* 工农兵画报 *(Worker-Peasant-Solider Pictorial)*, August 1967.

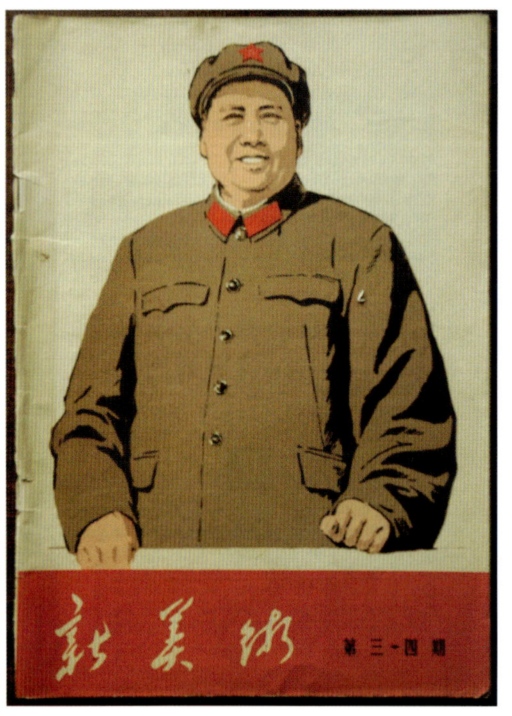

102. *Xin Meishu* 新美术 *(New Art)*, February 1968.

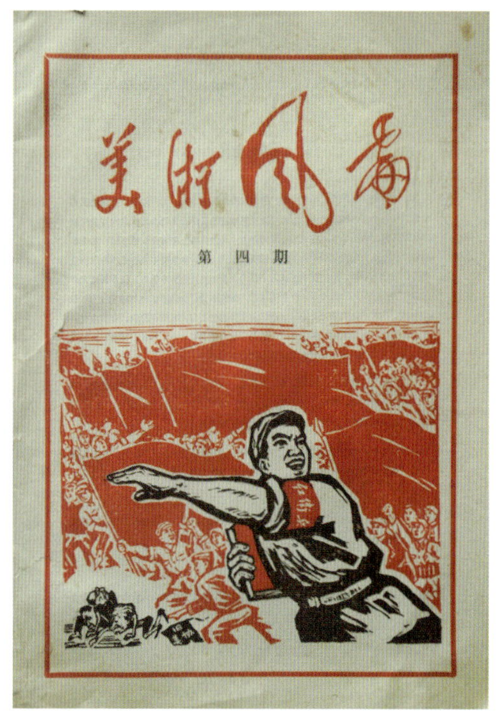

104. *Meishu Fenglei* 美术风雷 *(Art Tempest)*, September 1967.

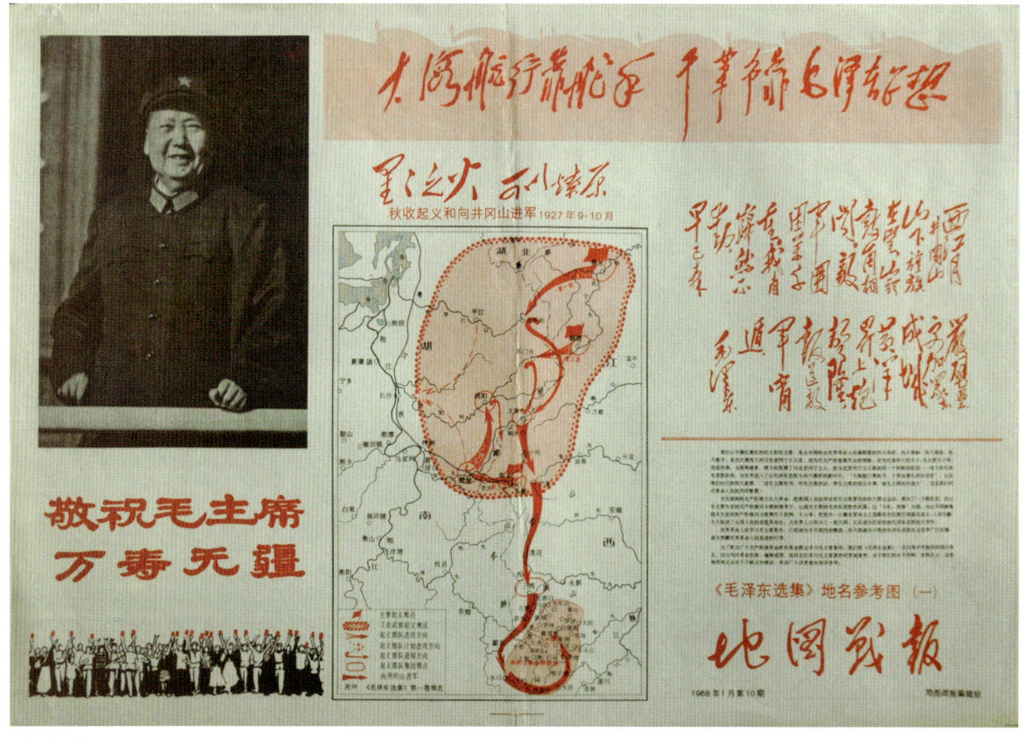

103. *Ditu zhanbao* 地图战报 *(Maps War Bulletin)*, January 1968.

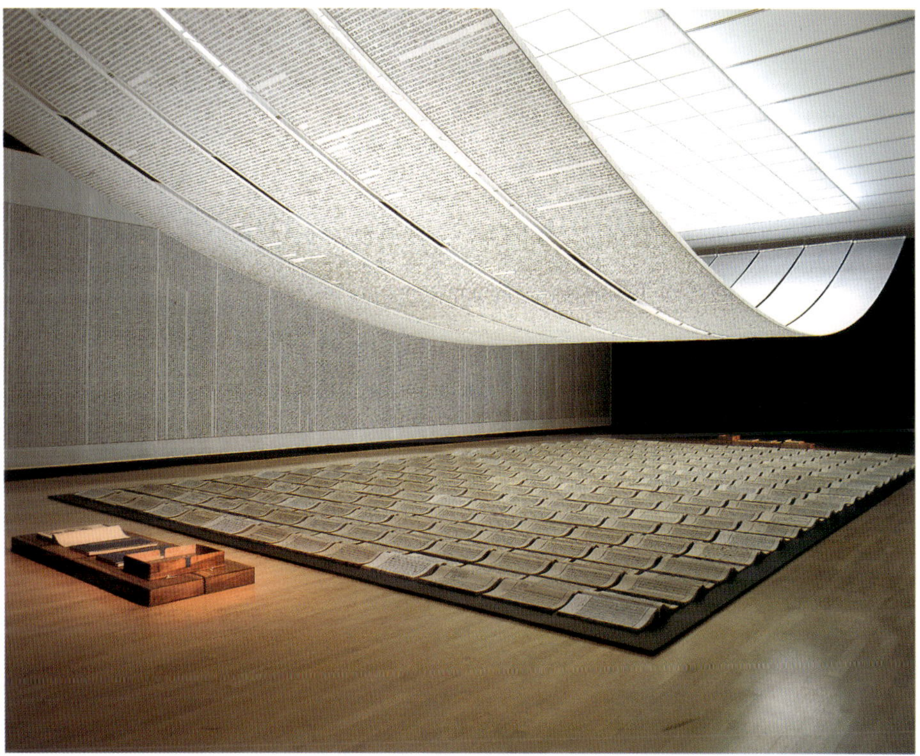

105. Xu Bing 徐冰, *Tianshu* 天书 *(Book from the Heaven)*, 1991–92, installation view.

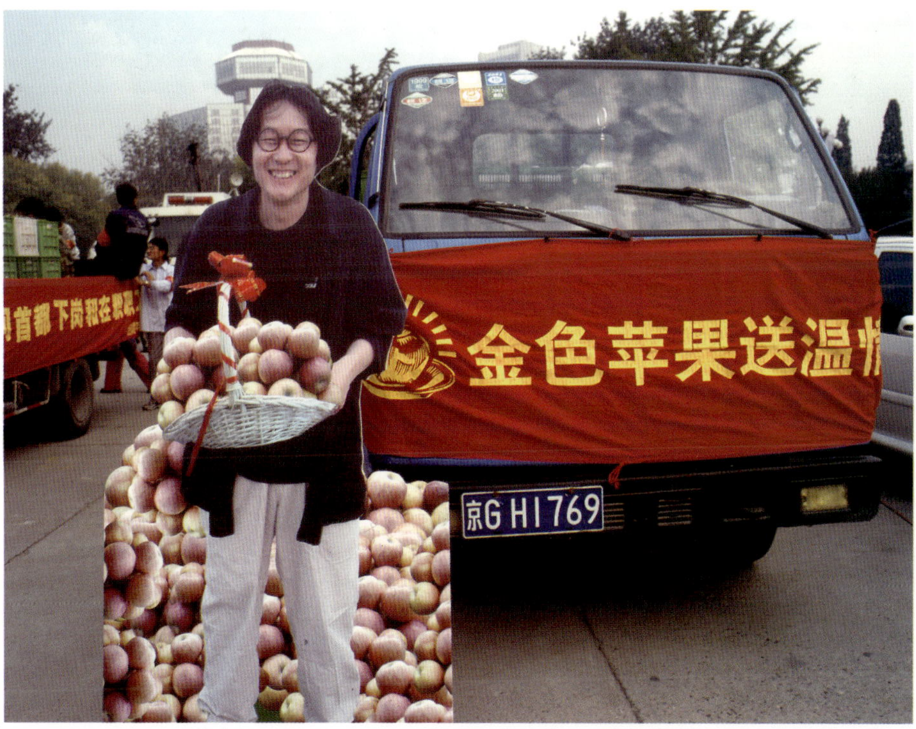

106. Xu Bing 徐冰, *Jinse Pingguo Song Wenqing* 金色苹果送温情 *(Warmly Presenting the Golden Apples)*, performance, 2002, Beijing.

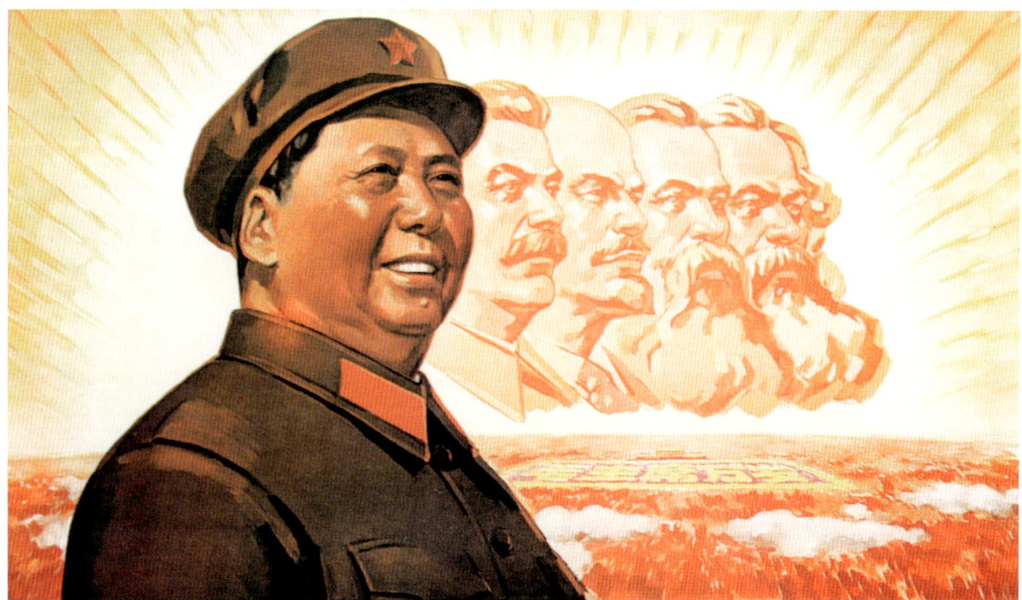

107. Wang Zhaoda 王肇达, *Mao Zedong Sixiang Shi Dangdai Makesi Liening Zhuyi de Dingfeng* 毛泽东思想是当代马克思列宁主义的顶峰 *(Mao Zedong Thoughts are the Pinnacle of Contemporary Marxism and Leninism)*, 1968, colour on paper.

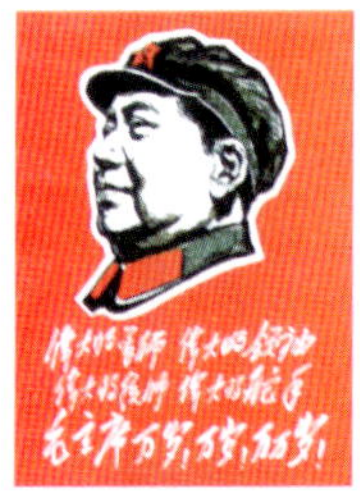

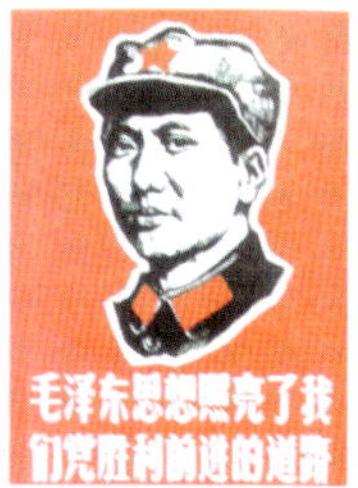

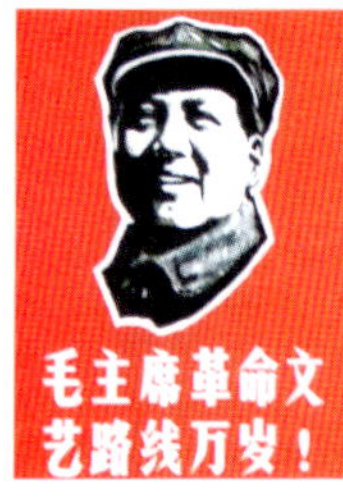

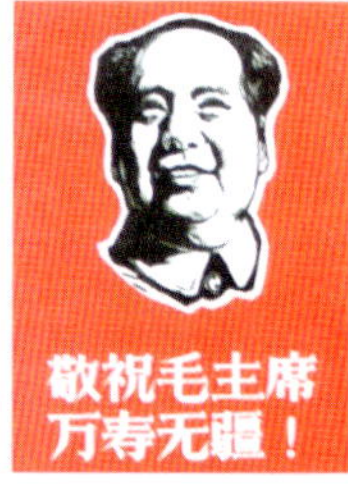

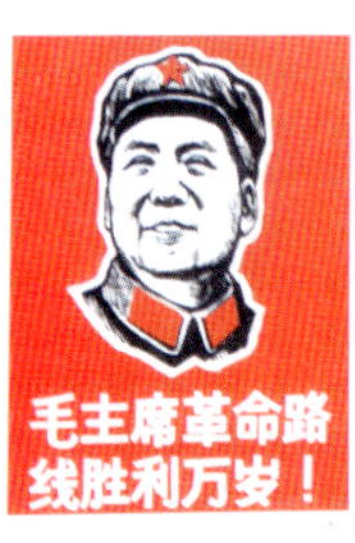

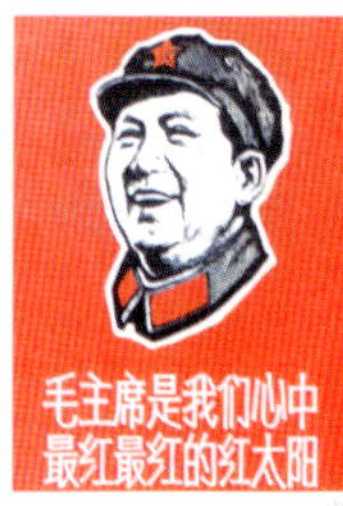

108. Shen Yaoyi 沈尧伊, *Mao Zhuxi Wansui — Mao Zhuxi Banhua Xiaoxiang Huibian* 毛主席万岁 – 毛主席版画肖像汇编 *(Long Live Chairman Mao — Chairman Mao Portrait Prints Collection)*, 1967, poster reproduction.

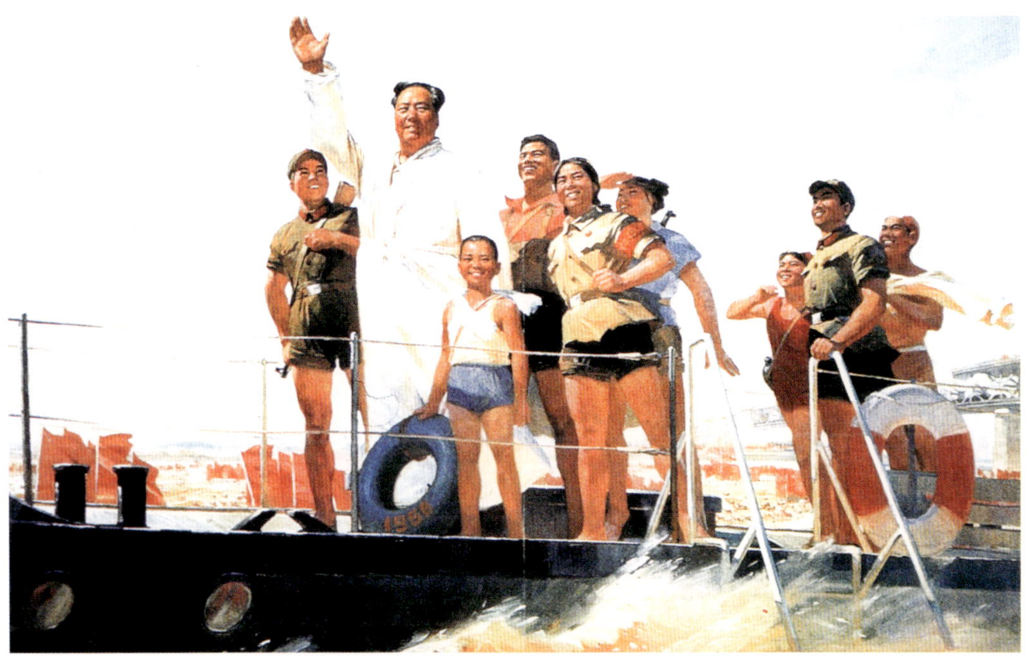

109. Tang Xiaohe 唐小禾, *Zai Dafeng Dalang Zhong Qianjin* 在大风大浪中前进 *(Forging ahead in Wind and Waves)*, 1966, oil on canvas.

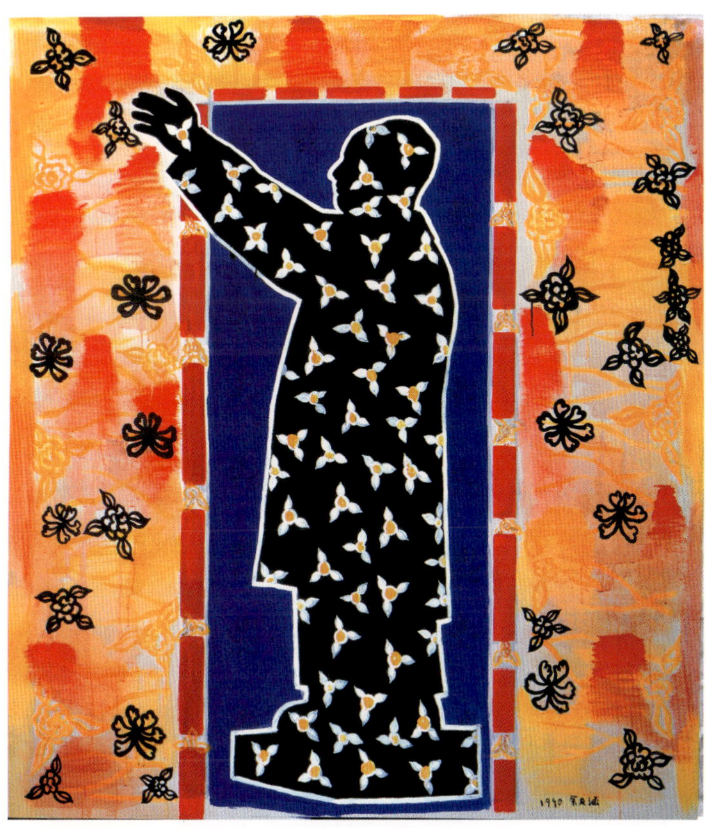

110. Yu Youhan 余友涵, *Zhaoshou* 招手 *(Big Wave)*, 1990, oil on canvas.

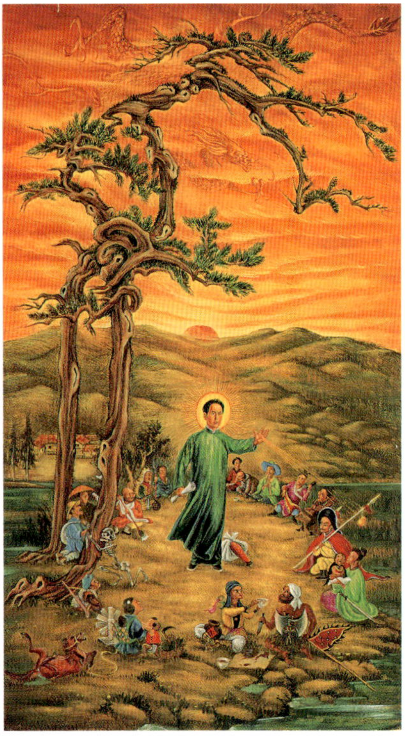

111. Liu Dahong 刘大鸿, *Siji zhi Chun* 四季之春 *(Four Seasons Spring)*, 1991, oil on canvas.

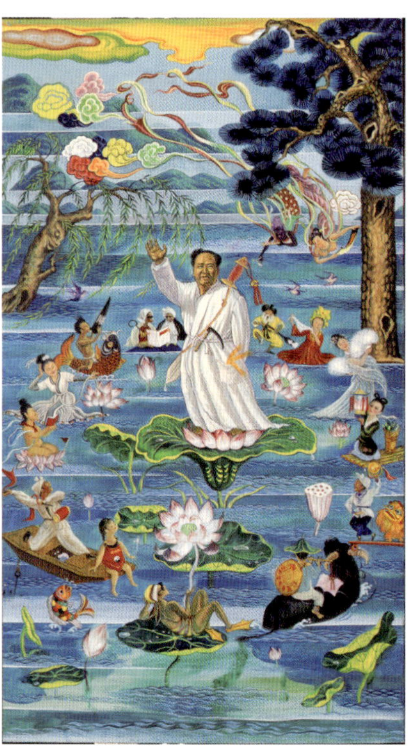

112. Liu Dahong 刘大鸿, *Siji zhi Xia* 四季之夏 *(Four Seasons Summer)*, 1991, oil on canvas.

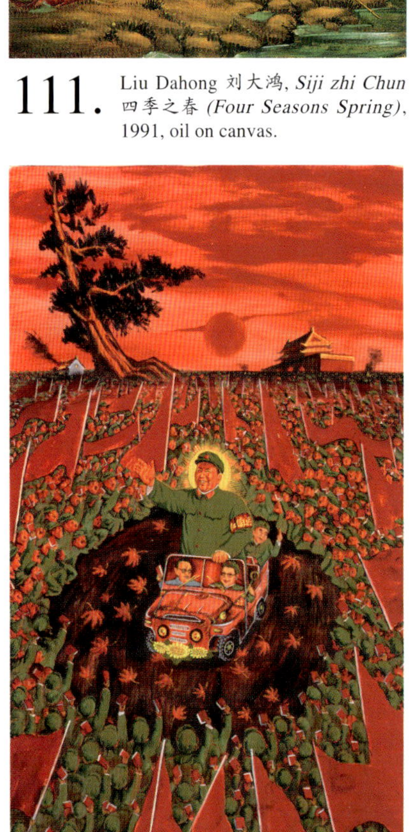

113. Liu Dahong 刘大鸿, *Siji zhi Qiu* 四季之秋 *(Four Seasons Autumn)*, 1991, oil on canvas.

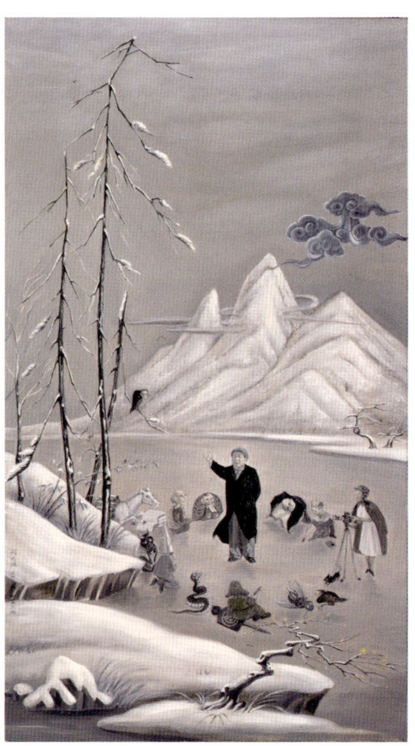

114. Liu Dahong 刘大鸿, *Siji zhi Dong* 四季之冬 *(Four Seasons Winter)*, 1991, oil on canvas.

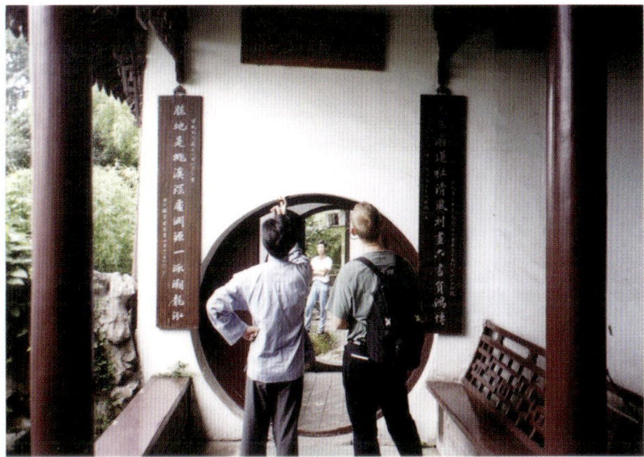

115. Covered passage in a garden, photograph by the Chang Tsong-zung.

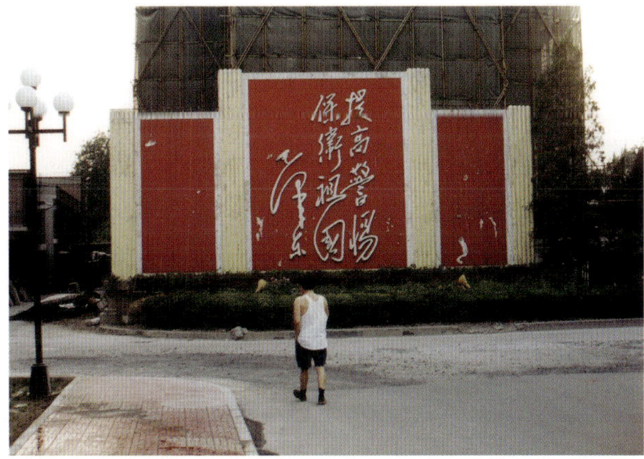

116. Billboard with Mao Zedong's text and calligraphy, photograph by Chang Tsong-zung.

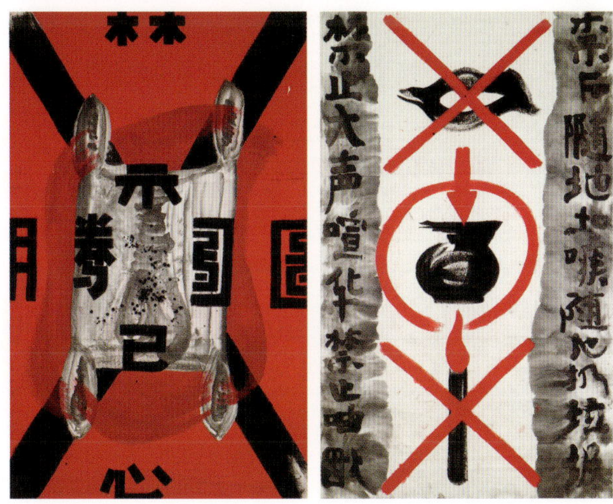

117. Gu Wenda 谷文达, *Totem and Taboo*, 1986, ink and colour on paper, 3 pieces.

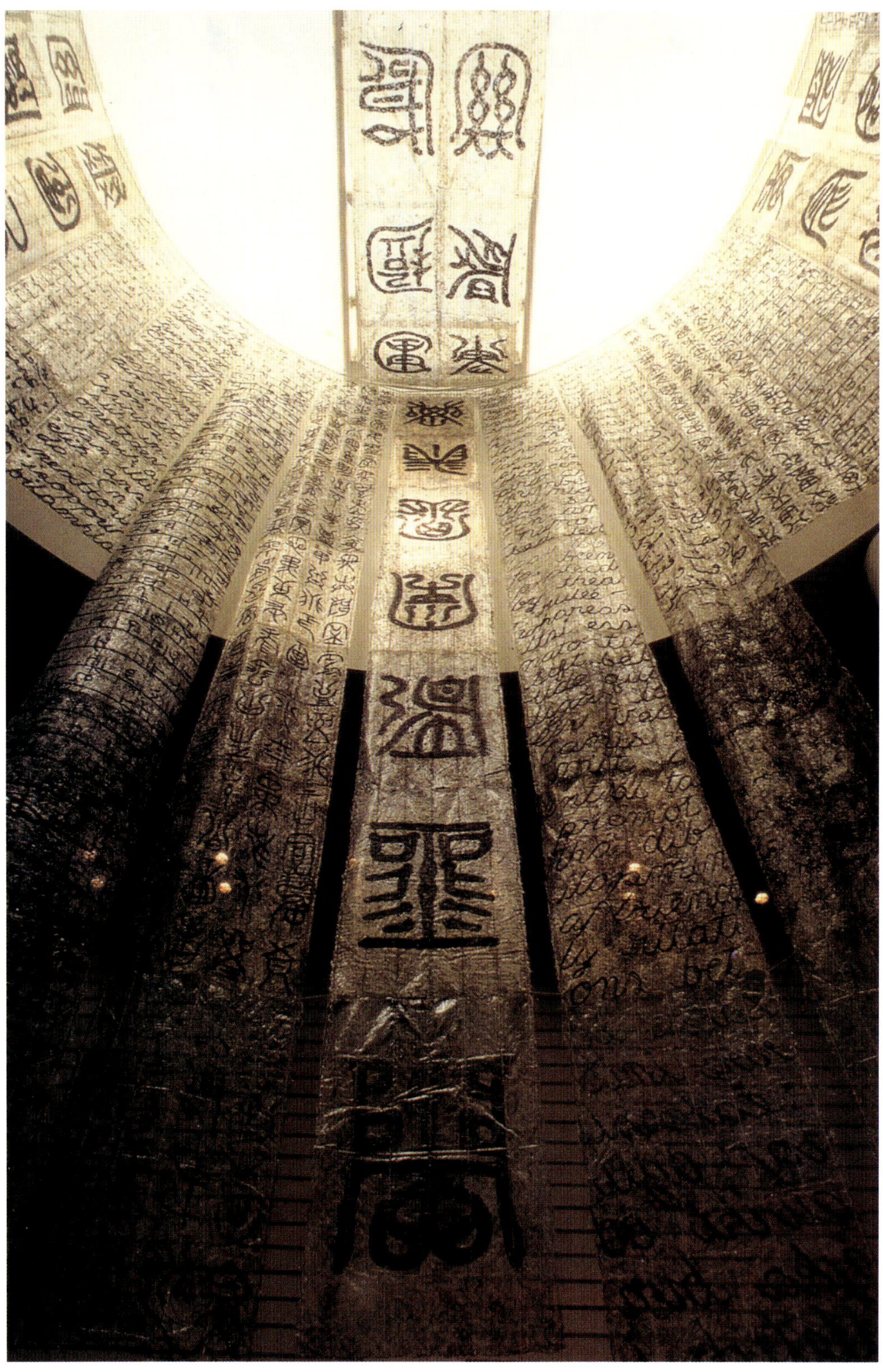

118. Gu Wenda 谷文达, *United Nations — Babel of Millennium*, 1999, human hair, installation view at San Francisco Museum of Modern Art.

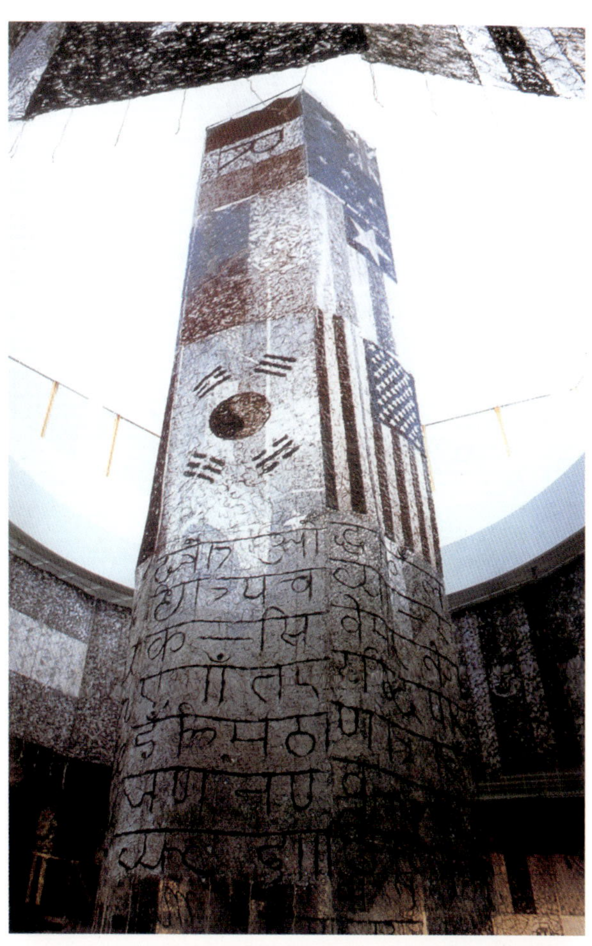

119. Gu Wenda 谷文达, *United Nations — Man and Space*, 2000, human hair, installation view at the Third Kwangju Biennial.

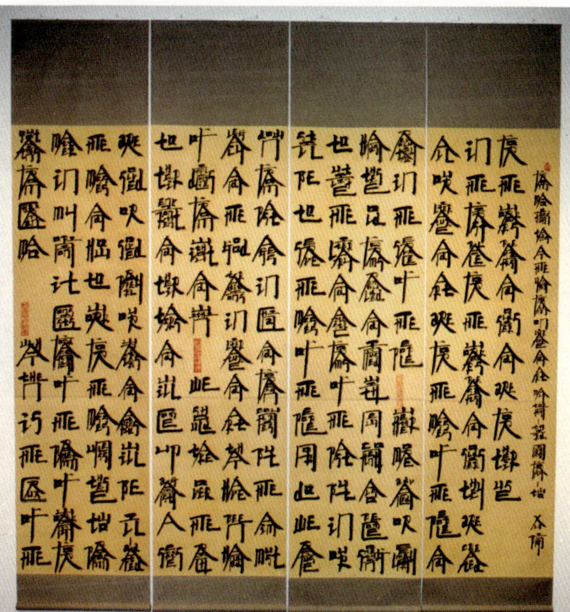

120. Xu Bing 徐冰, *Square Word Calligraphy: Quotation from Chairman Mao*, 1996, ink on paper.

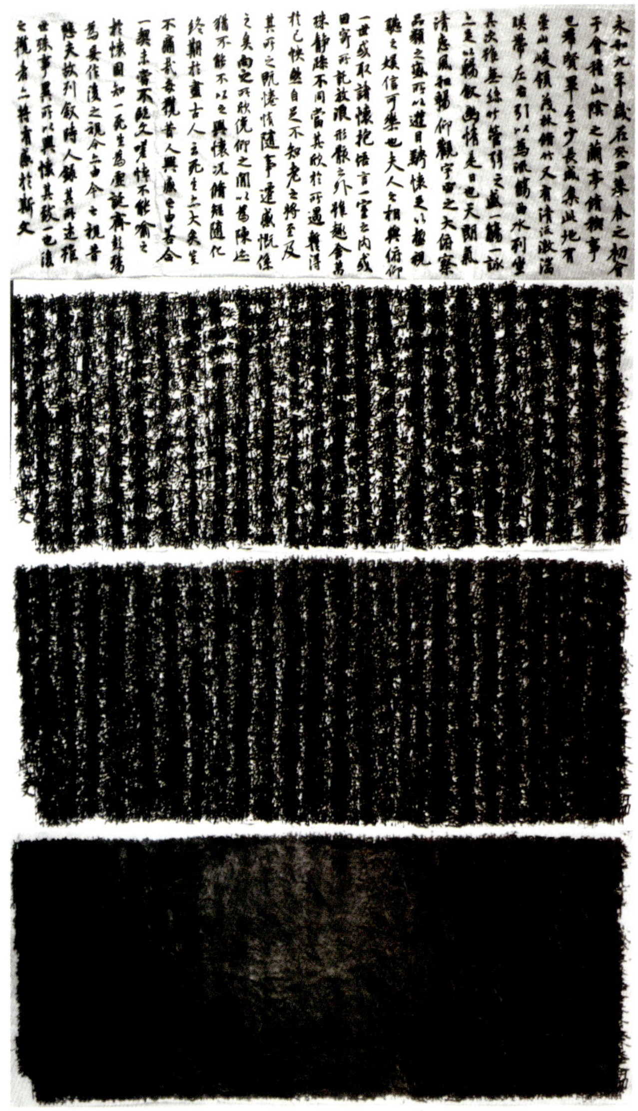

121. Qiu Zhijie 邱志杰, *Lingmo Lantingxu Yiqianbian* 临摹兰亭序一千遍 *(Copying the Preface of Orchid Pavilion One Thousand Times)*, 1995–1996.

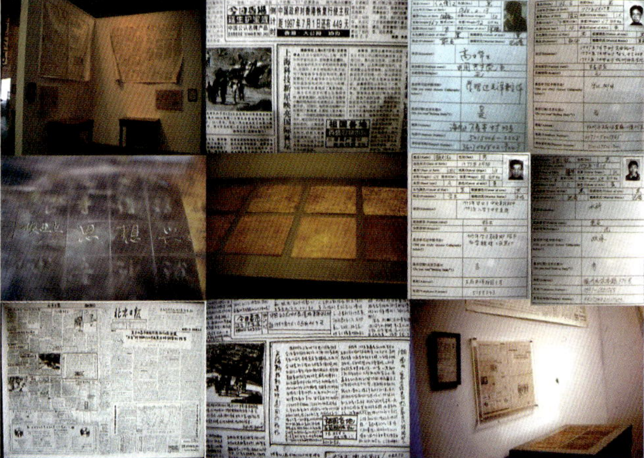

122. Qiu Zhijie 邱志杰, *April 8th*, 1996, installation.

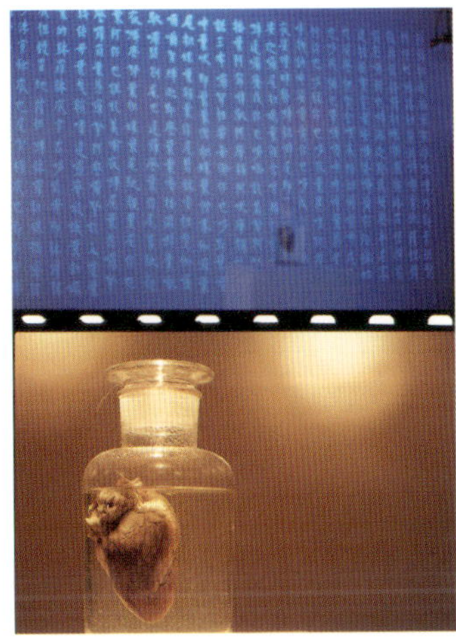

123. Qiu Zhijie 邱志杰, *Xinjing 心经 (Heart Sutra)*, 1999, installation.

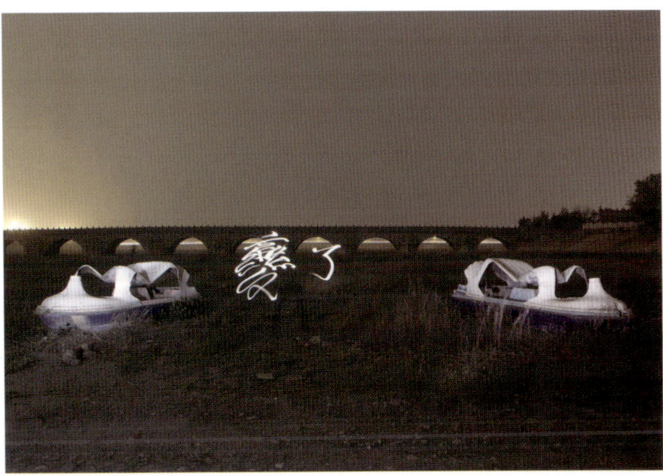

124. Qiu Zhijie 邱志杰, *Light Calligraphy: It's Changed Beijing Lugou Bridge*, 2005, photograph.

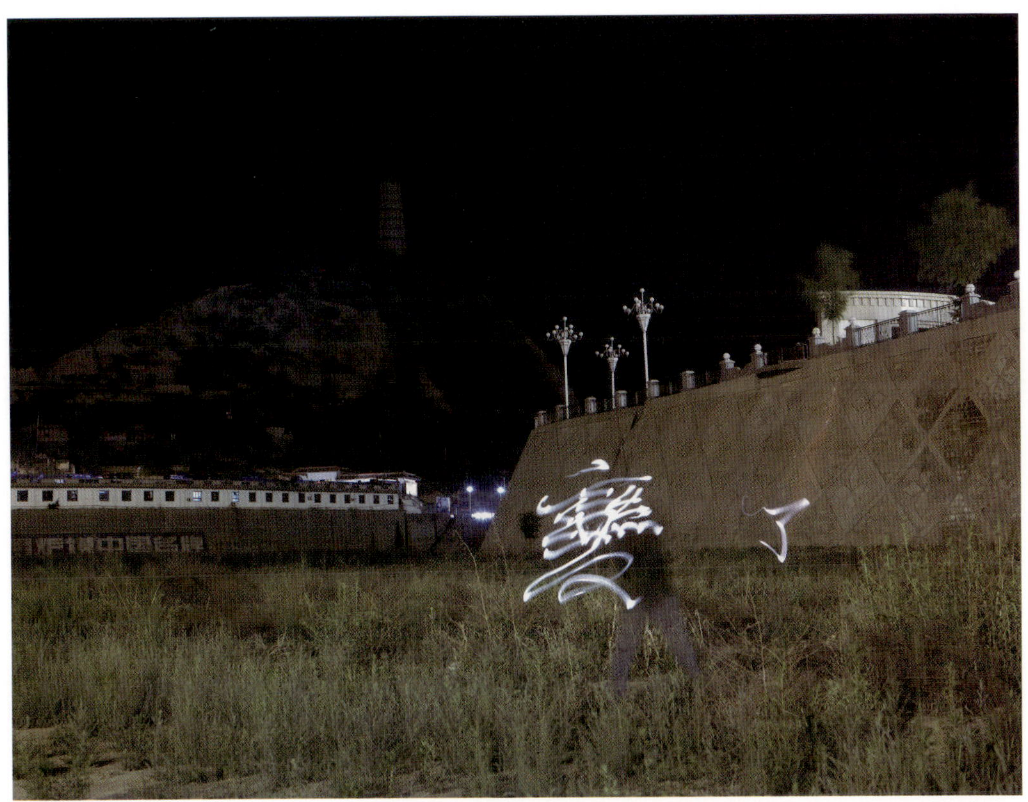

125. Qiu Zhijie 邱志杰, *Light Calligraphy: It's Changed Yan'an*, 2005, photograph.

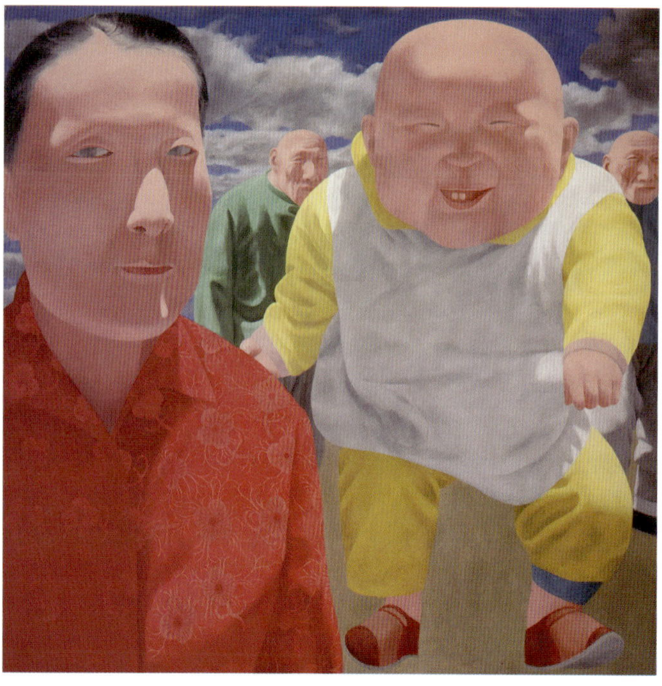

126. Fang Lijun 方力钧, *Series 2: No. 7*, 1992, oil on canvas.

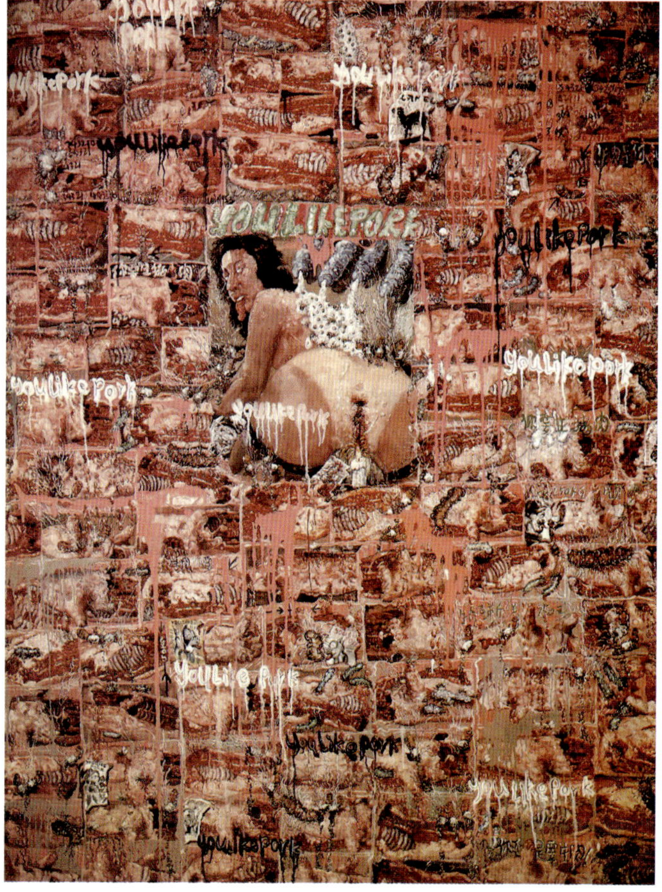

127. Liu Wei 刘炜, *You Like Pork*, 1995, oil on canvas.

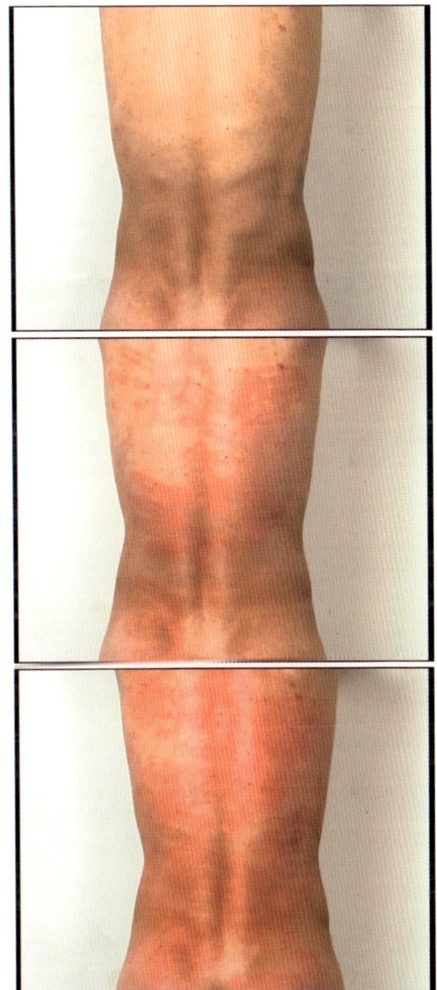

128. Xu Zhen 徐震, *Caihong* 彩虹 *(Rainbow)*, 1999, video, 4 minutes.

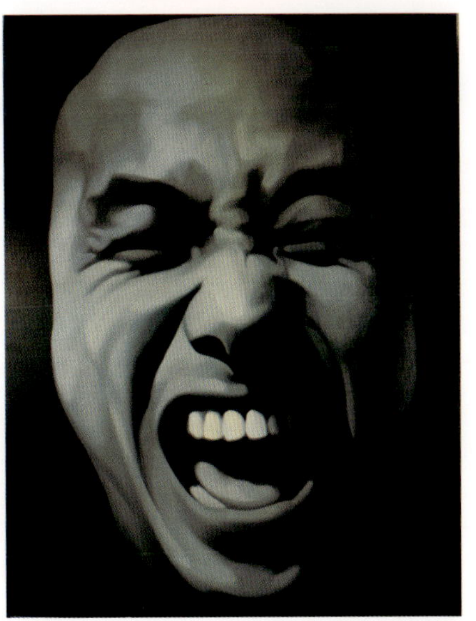

129. Geng Jianyi 耿建翌, *A Second State*, 1987, oil on canvas.

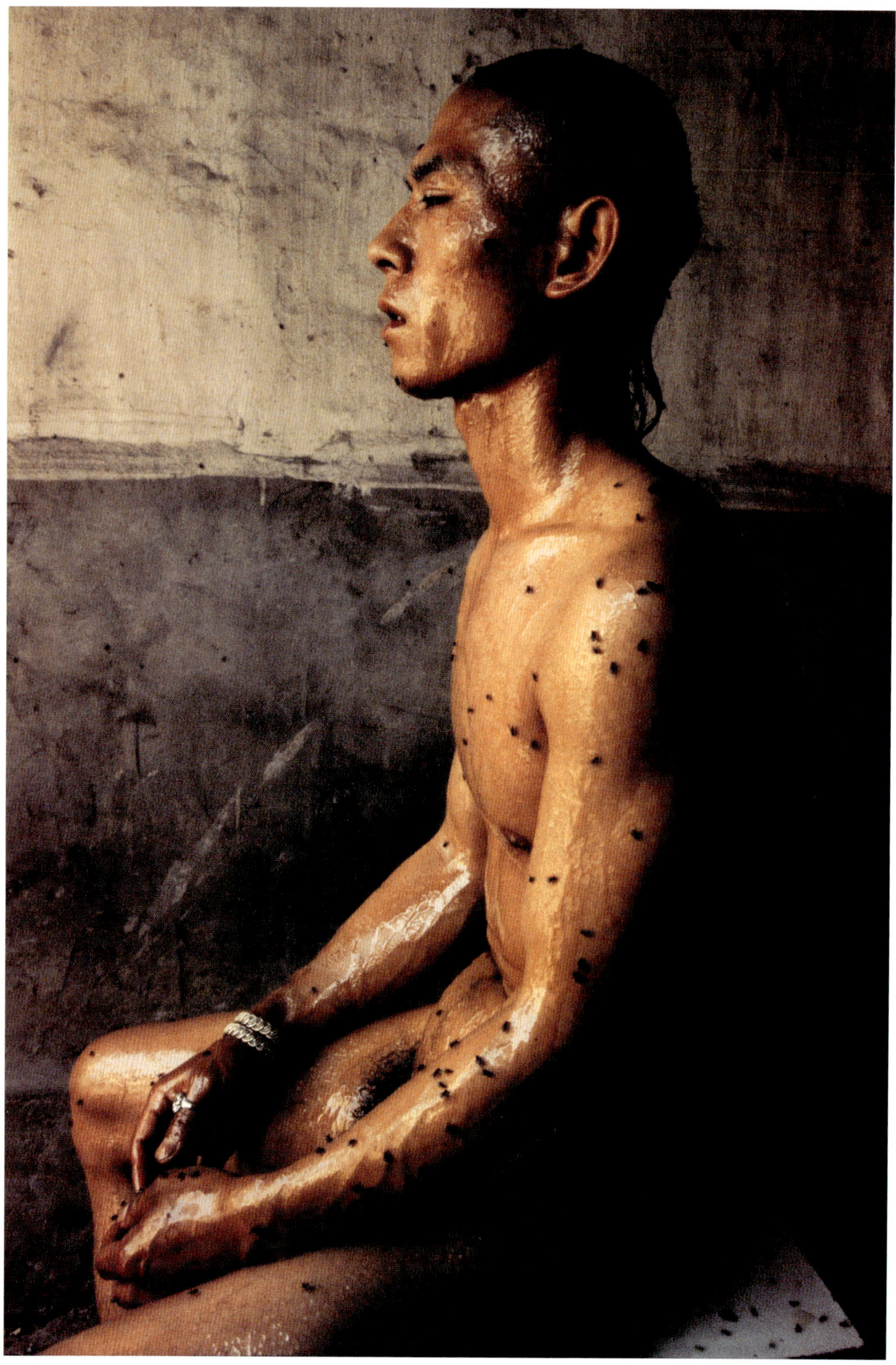

130. Zhang Huan 张洹, *12 Square Metres*, 1994, performance, Beijing.

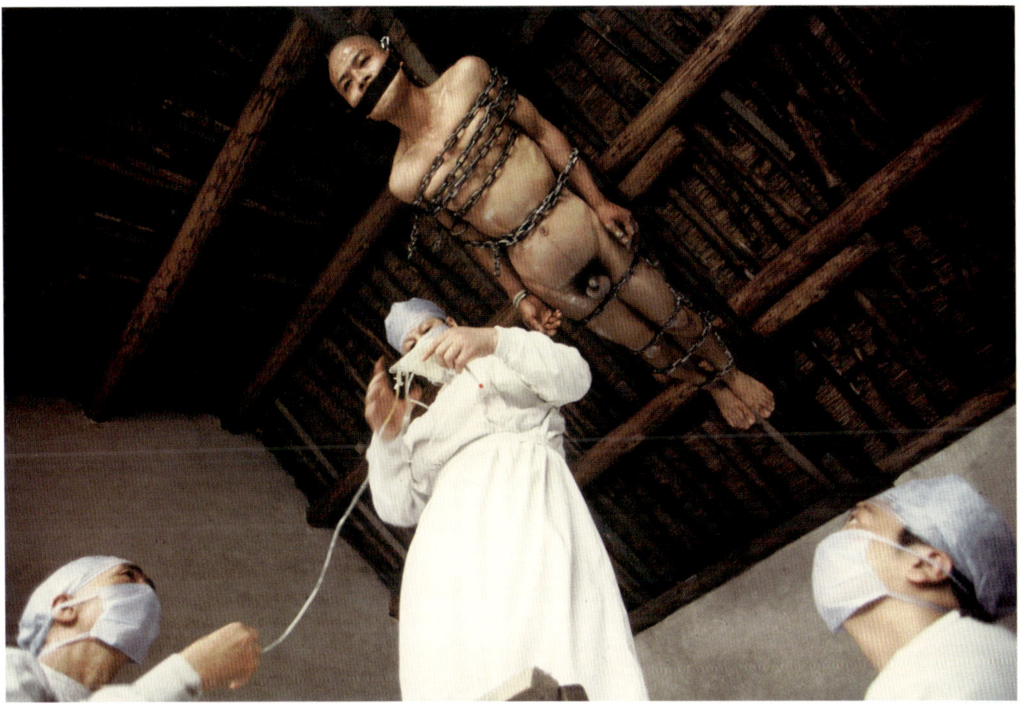

131. Zhang Huan 张洹, *65 kg*, 1994, performance, Beijing.

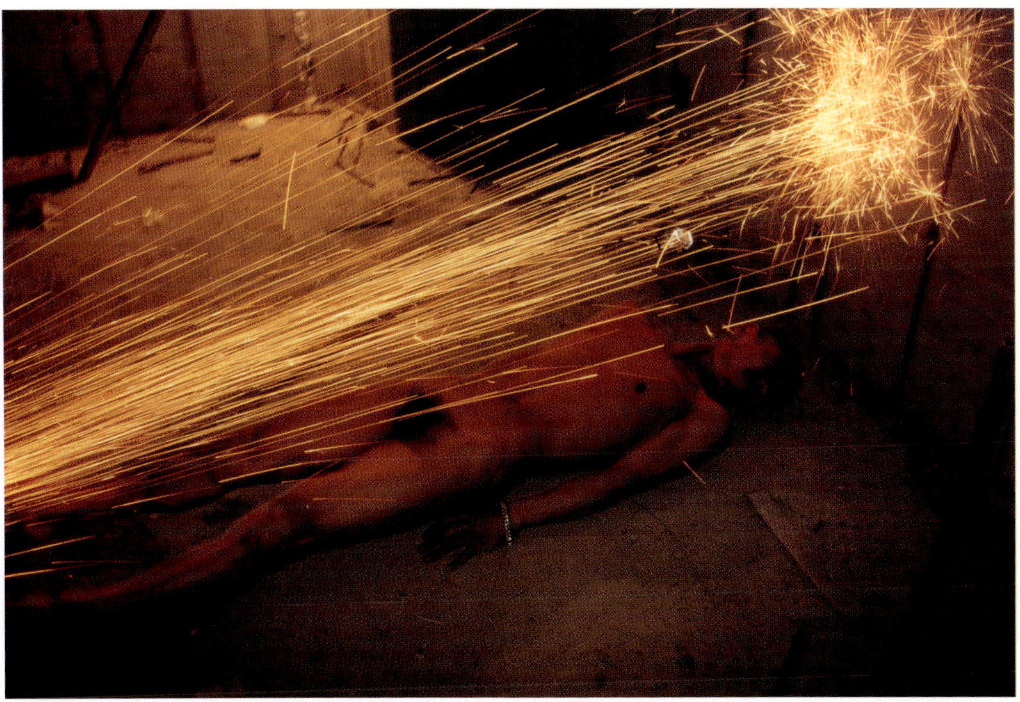

132. Zhang Huan 张洹, *25 mm Threading Steel*, 1995, performance, Beijing.

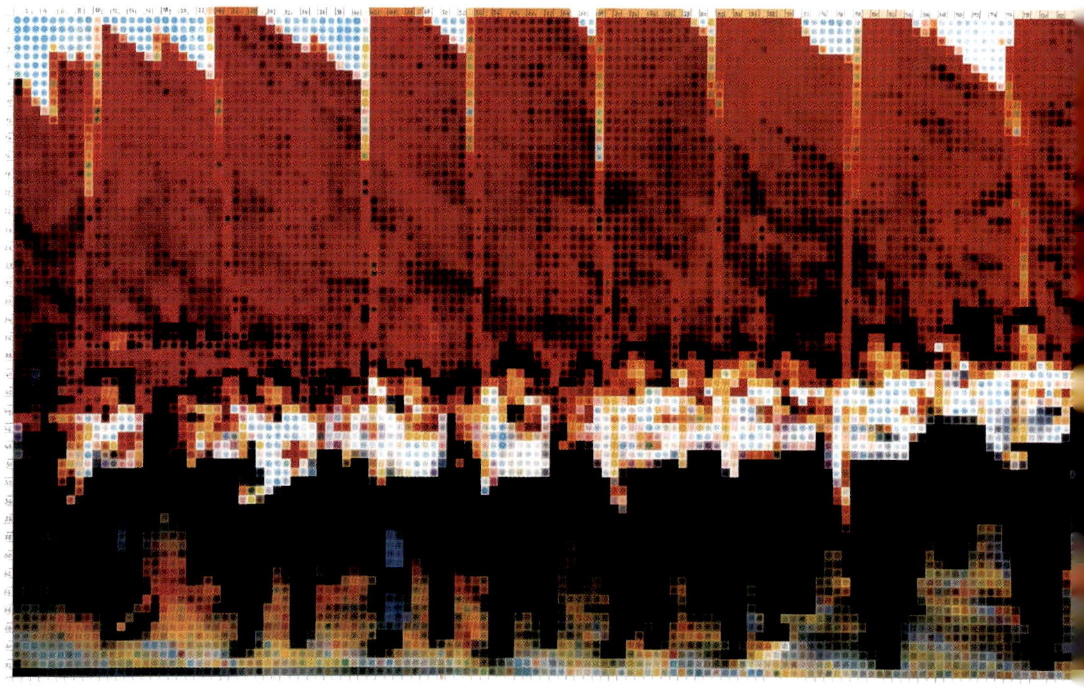

133. Shao Yinong 邵逸农 and Mu Chen 慕辰, *Jiyi Zuobiao: Hong Haiyang* 记忆座标：红海洋 *(Axis of Memory: Red Sea)*, 2003, hand-coloured photograph.

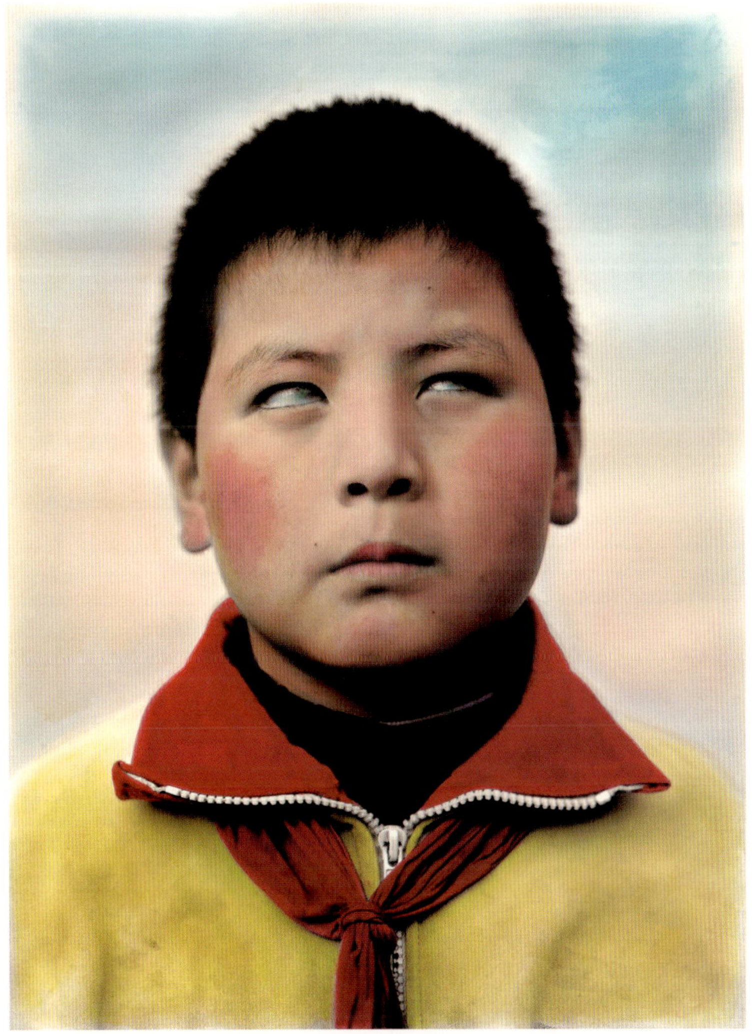

134. Shao Yinong 邵逸农 and Mu Chen 慕辰, *Hongse Tonghua* 红色童话 *(Fairy Tales in Red Era)*, No. 1, 2004, hand-coloured photogragh.

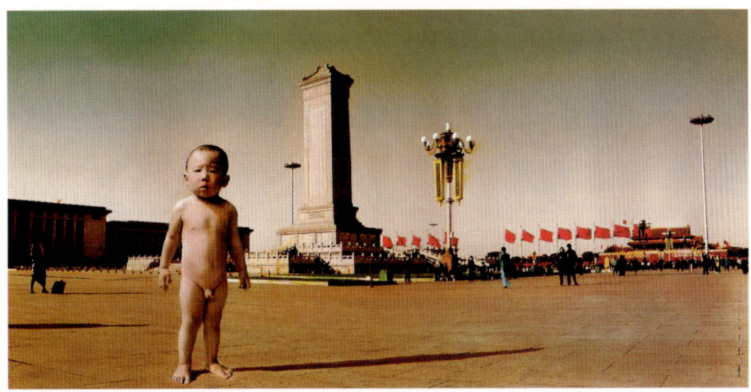

135. Shao Yinong 邵逸农 and Mu Chen 慕辰, *Tongnian Liuying: Jinian Bei* 童年留影：纪念碑 *(Childhood: the Monument to People's heroes)*, 2001, hand-coloured C-type print.